—— $\mathcal{L}$aura ——
Z

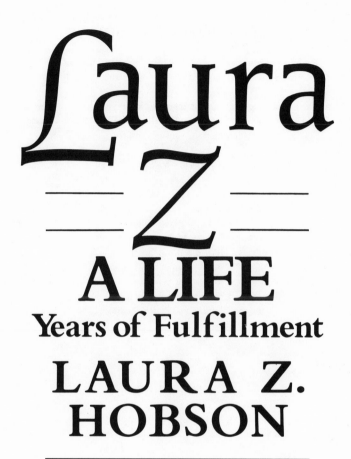

Laura Z

A LIFE
Years of Fulfillment

LAURA Z. HOBSON

Introduction by Norman Cousins
Afterword by Christopher Z. Hobson

DONALD I. FINE, INC.  *NEW YORK*

Library of Congress Catalogue Card Number: 83-45342
ISBN: 0-917657-19-5
Manufactured in the United States of America
10 9 8 7 6 5 4 3 2 1

TO
DONALD I. FINE,
WHO PERSUADED ME TO TRY IT

INTRODUCTION
BY
Norman Cousins

AFTER I PUT DOWN Laura Hobson's second and concluding volume of her autobiography, *Years of Fulfillment,* I recalled Eleanor Roosevelt's characterization of F.D.R.'s mother. "Now, there was a *grande dame,"* she said. Mrs. Roosevelt didn't use the term invidiously. She was describing a woman who knew how to take command, who left no doubts about her meaning, whose relationships with the people around her were uncluttered by ambiguity or uncertainty, and who drove forward in a straight line toward her objectives in a way that won respect and even awe from all who knew her.

Laura Hobson to my mind fits that picture. Absence of purpose or will power was the least descriptive thing anyone might say about her. Both purpose and will power were the sources of her enthusiasm and energy, which spilled over to her relationships with friends. In the opening pages of this autobiography she tells of writing the first two paragraphs of this book and then telephoning her editor and publisher, Don Fine, to read the opening lines. Quintessential Hobson. I thought back over at least half a dozen times, while Laura was writing *The Trespassers* and *Gentleman's Agreement.* "Cuzz," she would say over the phone, "I want to read something to you. It's from the book." It could be two paragraphs or two pages. Her voice was electric with the creation. She didn't rush the delivery. "I think I've got it," she said. "What do you think?" Swept along by her enthusiasm, I would reach for the proper supporting adjectives. Occasionally she would reread the same section in part or whole. I knew that I was not the first telephone receiver. Dick Simon and Lee Wright of Simon and Schuster, her then publishers, were usually the primary and prime beneficiaries of her creative outpourings.

It could hardly be said of her that she experienced her "recollections in tranquillity," to use Wordsworth's famous phrase. When she says that she didn't want to hold anything back in her autobiography, she was referring not just to the content but to the style of her life. In this promise to the reader she is spectacularly successful. Her frankness at times can be devastating, especially when she names those with whom she had liaisons, an enterprise generally not associated with tranquil effects on those involved. Frankness was her style and it was never slowed up by indirection or circumlocutions. Paradoxically, there was no meanness in the references, only a basic understanding of human frailties.

Few writers I know were more painstaking in expression. One sees a reflection of this trait when she refers to conversations or letters and fixes her gaze on certain words or phrases that convey specific meaning to her far beyond the general meaning assigned to them. Whether in her books or letters or conversations, she liked to analyze words, scrutinizing the nuances behind the nuances. Few things were more characteristic of her than her question: "What did he [or she] mean by that?" But I don't think anyone ever wondered what Laura meant about anything.

Laura's precision in writing was a vital element in her craftsmanship. She never attained the stature or recognition accorded the Porters or Whartons or Glasgows or other Twentieth Century writers whom she admired; but she gives no ground to anyone in her precise use of language or the importance she attached to sequence. Her words and the ideas they describe fit together like beads on a string. She may not have followed Emily Dickinson's advice—"tell it slant"—but above all she knew how to move print from the page to the mind of the reader.

This particular trait was, in part, the heritage of her training and experience as promotion writer for Time, where the copy was expected to reflect the product itself—sharp, precise, arresting, original. Critics of her books looked for exquisite subtleties; what they found was the straight-on work of a writer whose notion of literary craftsmanship was total clarity and the sustained attention of the reader. That she succeeded in this purpose finds its evidence in the remarkable success of her best-known novel, *Gentleman's Agreement*; it must also be recognized that the book's theme was a strong factor in the public's response. She used human interest and everyday situations rather than sociological analysis or preachments as her techniques.

Another quality in her writing, especially when viewed in retrospect, gives force to her books: she is strong in the kind of detail that all too often drops out of period pieces. Every age has its minor themes and secondary players. One thinks about time stretches in terms of catch phrases—"Jazz Age" or "Lost Generation," etc. But there are other accents that characterize a period; and it is in these respects that Laura Hobson demonstrates particular strength. The things people turn to in their newspapers and magazines; the events that make small paragraphs or that are used as filler material in the papers; the people who don't make page one but who nonetheless provide the interesting and sometimes the significant minutiae of the times. Laura Hobson had a good eye for all these sometimes small but telling signs. As we reread her novels and read her autobiography we delight in these sharply seen sidelights.

A large part of my life has been spent in publishing and communications in general. I like to think I haven't forgotten too many of the details—until I read her books, especially her personalized accounts—and then I realize how much had been dimmed by transitional and subsequent developments. I had forgotten, for example, about such publishing ventures as the newspaper *PM* in New York, which for a time was Topic-A among people in the communications industry. Also: the relative novelty of psychoanalysis and the way those under treatment would quickly find their way to one another in living-room groupings; or the princely sum represented by a $20,000 annual salary, or the awe with which writers would point to $30,000 paid for the screen rights to novels. It is useful to be reminded that there was once a time, not so long ago, when you could buy a Hershey bar or a Baby Ruth for five cents, and when politicians would seek favor by promising to retain a five-cent subway fare. The period in which Laura did her writing was marked by the fierce sweep of Nazism over Europe and its tremors, but there were also substantial changes in habits of thought, carrying along all sorts of lesser but nonetheless interesting currents and cross-currents.

It was, for example, a time when comparatively few people owned television sets; in Laura's autobiography you recapture the experience of being invited out to dinner at a house with a television set. It was a time, too, when a young man from Minneapolis by the name of Hubert Humphrey was coming to public notice and was making friends with influential persons in the publishing world like Laura Hobson. (It was through Laura that I first met HHH.)

Humphrey appealed to Laura as a vigorous, independent, fresh new voice in American politics—someone whose antitotalitarianism did not make an exception for the Soviet Union. Those on the right who didn't like Humphrey because of his liberalism made themselves look ludicrous when they called him "Red" or "Commie-lover."

Laura Hobson never gave her intellectual proxy to the Communist Party and therefore had no need to attack her friends in order to appear ideologically sanitary. In marked contrast were former members of the party who swung all the way over to the far right, where they had no difficulty in finding applause. Laura was especially irked by those who had supported the Soviet Union through all its early flip-flops, including the non-aggression pact with Nazi Germany in 1939 that freed Adolf Hitler to launch the war in Europe. These supporters had the arrogance, when they later broke with the party, to attack those who were consistently non-communist. Lillian Hellman didn't hesitate in her autobiography to excoriate those who, she said, were *prematurely* anti-communist. Laura naturally wondered where Lillian Hellman received her credentials as America's intellectual czar, presuming to pass judgment on writers who perceived the fallacies of communism before she did.

Laura never allowed her opposition to totalitarianism to deflect her from the conviction that the United States had no alternative except to reduce the volatile nuclear confrontation with the Soviet Union. She supported the efforts of Presidents Eisenhower, Kennedy, Johnson, and Nixon to improve relations with the Soviet Union as a matter of common survival. But she also recognized that the attempt to abolish weapons was only a necessary step towards the basic objective, which was the abolition of war itself. That was why, with writers like Oscar Hammerstein, Russel Crouse, Walter Cronkite and Rex Stout, she met regularly to gain public acceptance of the cause of world peace through world law.

Through all these movements, Laura held to a steady course. She could be persuasive without being polemical; eloquent without being strident; analytical without being academic. She was caught up in the issues of her times but she never sacrificed her independence of thought. For her, the ability to probe and find one's way to the truth of things was the ultimate test of freedom. No one could ever doubt that she passed this test.

Burton Roscoe, a critic who did most of his work in the Thirties, called his autobiography *Before I Forget*. We turn to Laura Hobson's books to recall the things we tend to forget and we relish the reminders. Laura Hobson knows how to select such themes and sub-themes in writing about her own life, and to present them in a way that nurtures the memory even as it serves the enjoyment of reading.

—Norman Cousins
Los Angeles, April, 1986

ONE

"*THIS, THEN, IS NOT* the end of my story, but only a pause in the telling of it."

That is the way I ended the first half of my autobiography, *Laura Z: A Life,* right after the account of the movie sale and publication day of *Gentleman's Agreement.* And indeed, even before I saw that first part in book form, I had ended the pause and had begun to "write forward" on this second half, the rest of a life. Or so I fondly thought.

But picking up a new book for the first time, a book you yourself have written, is an experience so exciting, so gratifying, that unless you are as high-minded as a saint, you can't go back to calm steady work on another book, even when it is an extension of the one you are at last holding in your own two hands.

If euphoria is ever justified, surely that is one of the times, and I feel sure that it has come, however fleetingly, to every author anywhere who has ever opened to page one, paragraph one, of a book he or she has written.

And like every one of those others, I began instantly to read it. There it was, that first sentence I had set down nearly two years before, on a day when I had not as yet said yes to the publisher who was urging me to write my autobiography.

It was a day in late summer of 1981, and all at once I found myself thinking, But if I did say yes, how would I start it?

In the next moment I had turned to my typewriter, and with

scarcely a moment's pause, I was writing, "The Z is for Zametkin, my maiden name, and I have clung to it through all my years because it held my identity intact before that Anglo-Saxon married name of Hobson."

Reading it again from the first page of a new book, a sudden burst of pleasure came as I remembered that when, a week later, I did say yes to the publisher, I had impulsively added, "I've written the first couple of paragraphs—do you want to hear them?"

On the phone I read him those lines and the few that followed, about my being born with the century. It took less than a minute, and then there was silence, the kind that makes you want to say, "Are you still there?" I wondered if I'd been a fool to obey my impulse to read him those lines. We had exchanged letters and had talked on the telephone, but we had never met.

"If you ever change a word of it," Don Fine said, "I'll kill you."

I think I knew then that I could really do it, but now as I read on beyond that first page, I remember, too, how often I was to feel, I can't write this part, nobody could write this part, it's too painful, it's too personal, it's something I can't live through again while I put it into words. And I would come to a full stop, dismayed and uncertain.

But on the third page of my book, I read again a promise I had set down, for myself as well as for any possible readers, a promise that was to jump alive at me each time I decided that I simply had to skip over *this* episode or that.

I had been talking about the novel I had written about "my radical childhood," and the mysterious amalgam of fact and invention that had gone into it, so that people would ask me, "How much of it is true, and how much is made up?"

> In this one nothing will be made up, nothing invented, nothing knowingly shaded to put a better light on some crisis, no special pleading to exonerate me in some quarrel or misfortune. I don't mean that I will permit myself no reticences, or that I will feel obliged to weep in public over whatever griefs and disappointments and sorrows there have been, along with the delights and joys. I simply promise that there will be no invention. If it is written here, it will be true.

And as I read on past page three I kept thinking, Well, it *is* true. There was my childish yearning to "be like everybody else," and not have parents who did what seemed like crazy things to me and my twin sister Alice, things like draping our whole front porch in black bunting, as a protest against the flaming deaths of scores of young workers in the Triangle Fire, or temporarily taking in two bedraggled little girls whose parents were caught up in the winter-long textile strike in Lawrence, Massachusetts.

"Everybody will laugh at me," I used to cry out in an anguish of desire to have parents like my friends' parents, one a salesman, another a plumber, yet another a policeman. *My* parents were intellectuals, Russian-Jewish, old-fashioned socialists, my father an editor of the *Jewish Daily Forward,* my mother a regular contributor to *The Day,* both agnostic before ever I was born, both forever involved with the politics of labor unions, with free speech, the right to oppose injustice, things my friends' parents never even talked about.

I read on to my adolescent diaries, teeming with signs that that kid I was in my teens was going to be a writer. I read of my struggles to get to college, not Hunter, the city college where I had started, but a real away-from-home college, Cornell. And then I read of my first job, in advertising, and of my first great love in an arrangement that today would be lightly enough dismissed as "a live-in affair" but sixty years ago would have created scandal and immediate dismissal from my job in the pious world of Madison Avenue, a disaster we avoided by telling everybody we were married.

Tom Mount was already married, though he and his wife, who lived abroad, had an "open marriage," where each was permitted to have "other interests." I was Tom's other interest for half my twenties, and he was my only interest, with me beseeching him to write the great novel he was so sure he could write while I earned enough to support both of us, pay his growing debts and even send money to his absent wife and her children.

And then, of course, there came the desperate experience of an impossible pregnancy and the bungled abortion that then seemed inescapable, with a second abortion still to come. I read on to the predictable ending of that kind of first love, with separation and heartbreak and the conviction that I could never be happy again.

Through all of my twenties I was writing and finding that I could earn a living by writing not only advertising copy, but several articles that were published in national magazines. I even took a year out to do newspaper reporting, and I seemed to have some natural bent for it, getting the high reward of frequent by-lines. "By Laura Mount."

It was as Laura Mount that I met Thayer Hobson, a young publisher, and came to find that I *could* be happy again. I read on about my happy marriage, finding myself in the world of books and publishing, so different from the world of advertising, getting to know the authors and editors and publishers it was so natural for my husband to know, his own classmate at Yale, Harry Luce, of Time and Fortune; the beautiful Clare Boothe Brokaw who was to become Harry's wife; Harry Scherman, founder of of the Book-of-the-Month Club; Dick Simon of Simon and Schuster; Sinclair Lewis and Dorothy Thompson and so many other gifted, even fascinating people.

I read, too, of the recurring bouts of sadness and defeat because it now seemed impossible for me to attain the pregnancy I so much wanted, as if I were being punished for the two abortions that had once seemed unavoidable. I read of my endless visits to a sterility expert, Dr. Virgil S. Damon, of the tests and schedules, the cruel seesaw of hope and despair, until we finally decided that by our fifth anniversary if I still were not pregnant, we would adopt a baby.

And reading on, I came to some other lines I was never to edit or rewrite.

> And then, suddenly came divorce. I put it that abruptly because that is how it came to me. There was no warning, no preparation . . . Falling in love at first sight may be a myth, but annihilation in one moment is not. It was like . . . a bullet to the inner brain . . . I didn't behave well.

Behave well or not, I did what most of us do in sudden misfortune. I intensified on my work to get through the days, and took sleeping pills to get through the nights. I had never before taken even one sleeping pill.

In the matter of work I had just had some good fortune, for I had just begun working for Harry Luce and his magazines, and found that he liked my particular style of writing promotion. Harry always showed his approval by assigning new tasks for the people on his staff, and I was only too glad then to be swamped with work.

I would stay at the office far into the night, wanting not to go home to the apartment I had moved into as a bride. And I began, for the first time, to try to write fiction, and sold my first short story to Collier's, and then another and another, each time wondering whether it was just a fluke, or whether I might, some time in the future, become a real writer, not just a copywriter or a hobby writer.

It was during my five years at Time that political matters began to be a real part of my life. During my twenties, I had scarcely been political-minded at all, except to share in the sense of outrage of all liberals over the Sacco-Vanzetti case, and to vote *for* Al Smith in the presidential campaign of 1928, largely because of the outcry that he was a Catholic and would be under the thumb of the pope. My own real interest in politics dated, almost too neatly, from the burning of the books in Nazi Germany and the election of Franklin Delano Roosevelt in the depths of the Depression.

But at Time I really began to *feel* about what was called news. Time's section on foreign affairs was then written by a man who could write "Jew Blum" about the premier of France, Léon Blum, and who could not write "Franco and the Fascists" about the war in Spain; instead he called them "Franco and his Falangist forces" and called the Loyalists, the duly elected government in Spain, the "popular front," or more simply, the "reds."

This kind of slanting of the news aroused many of the top editors and writers at the magazine, people like Archibald MacLeish, Russell Davenport, Ralph Ingersoll, Eric Hodgins and others. I was soon feeling myself a minor satellite of these major stars, many of whom were my friends. There were others at Time that I began to argue with because they seemed to me to be doing some slanting of their own in the other direction—they apparently felt that Russia could do no wrong.

In my private life too I did the same kind of arguing—only it became so bitter at times that the true word was not argue but fight. My sister Alice and I could barely begin to talk about the news without our voices rising, our emotions heating up—she was convinced that the Soviet Union was right and I equally convinced that it was wrong, in nearly every issue we discussed.

It was during those years at Time that I had my first battles with red-tape worshipers in my own government, over affidavits I tried to provide for Drs. Richard and Editha Sterba, whom I had never met, two Viennese analysts and their children, who fled Austria after Hitler's conquest, not that they were Jewish, which they weren't, but that they would not stay on, comfortably practicing their profession when Freud, the father of psychoanalysis, was forced by the Nazis to flee.

I read on with some long-ago pride, too, about my deep involvement in another battle with the rich and powerful of New York over Freedom Pavilion, an anti-Nazi exhibit planned by a large group of distinguished refugees for the World's Fair of 1939. Thomas Mann had gone to Dorothy Thompson over this, asking her to suggest some American who could help them with publicity and promotion for their wide-ranging plans; Dorothy had turned to me, knowing about my work at Time, and in the course of one brief luncheon I became part of the whole thing, with half-the-night meetings at my house for a year, with constant phone calls and discussions, and with me spending a dozen nights writing the official pamphlet that went to all the newspapers and would-be or might-be supporters and sponsors.

It was all to end in defeat by the wary, the cautious, the let's-not-provoke-a-foreign-government folks, and our collective hearts were broken. But for me it meant my first writing, and publishing in The Nation, of an exposé of those political naysayers, of social naysayers, of that invisible force that closes the doors in foreign consulates, those who jeer at youthful protesters, marching against idiot wars and endless nuclear arming, those who look away from the poor and unemployed, saying "They could get work if they wanted to," and those that say "I'm not prejudiced but . . ."

Reading that part of my young womanhood, I saw it as a training school for so much of what was to come in my life, and it was oddly reassuring, as if I were just now learning to know some of the early patterns in my own development, not while I was writing it two years before when I was so absorbed by the struggle to set it down, but now as I sat back, easily reading page after page.

And then I came to that special part of my life that will always give me a heightened pleasure, the adoption of my first child, my son Michael, when he was at the advanced age of eight weeks.

I had waited two whole years after my divorce before setting forth on the wonderful and scary quest among the better adoption agencies, waiting until I could be sure that I wasn't seeking out some tiny baby as a companion, a pet, a prop for my own broken life. By then I was beginning to see people again, even to care for some of them again, I had had several raises at Time, and at thirty-six I was still young enough to be considered a likely parent—even in those benighted days when single-parent adoption had hardly ever been heard of.

And my ultimate success, after months of waiting, was then, and has remained ever since, one of the high points of my life, one of those rare instances where the unfolding reality, despite occasional problems, always surpassed the secret hopes of what it would be.

But crisscrossing my happiness about those first years of my escape from a childless existence was another kind of experience, one that had brought me to the cruellest full stop in the entire writing of my book, that had made me wish almost desperately that I had undertaken only to write "memoirs" and not autobiography.

I have always felt a slight mistrust of any book called *Memoirs* or any synonym thereof, for in it the author agrees only to write what it suits him or her to reveal about his or her life. Tennessee Williams, in his *Memoirs,* barely mentioned the homosexuality that was the driving force of both his genius and his inner struggles, and Lillian Hellman, after writing repeatedly about her thirty-year love affair with Dashiell Hammett in earlier of her recollections, could actually write, in *Scoundrel Time,* "I am fairly sure that Hammett joined the Communist Party in 1937 or 1938. I do not know because I never asked . . ." Writers of memoirs, after all, may pick and choose, they may *edit* their own lives.

But that page-three promise of mine that nothing would be "knowingly shaded to put a better light on some crisis . . . or misfortune," had taken on some force of its own as I had continued writing, and as I came to that particular full stop I knew I could not simply skip over those next four years of my life, nor even gloss over the love affair that ran through nearly all the four, an affair that later on was to fill me with chagrin, admitting I had been a spineless ninny, unable to put a swift enough end to what was clearly a "neurotic love."

After my book was published I was asked by Arlene Francis on a long radio interview, and by other interviewers as well, why I had used so harsh a term as "neurotic love." Perhaps it was only immature love, she suggested, or infatuated love, even compulsive love, the kind so many young people have, but why label it, myself doing the labeling, "neurotic love?"

"I've been through analysis," I said, "and I *know* what's neurotic and what isn't neurotic. When you are terribly hurt by somebody and then go back to him again and again so he can hurt you some more—*that's* neurotic love."

Here I will write with some exactitude, because of a surprising development that happened recently, which I'll come to soon. Back there, in my thirties, of course, I hadn't the faintest idea that there was anything but delight in my finally falling in love again, at first lightly, with one of the top people at Time, Ralph Ingersoll, a man whom many other Time Inkers thought ruthless and an egomaniac, but whom I found fascinating for his shoptalk during daytime lunches and exciting and attractive during evenings at the theater or "21" or dancing.

19

As in most affairs that begin with mutual assurances that "we'll steer clear of too much involvement," that one proceeded to grow deeply involved, particularly after Ralph, who was also childless and who had had some fear that he was sterile, came to me one night "replete with bad news," as he put it. In a brief weekend resumption of an earlier affair with a girl I called Ruth in my book, he had got her pregnant, only to have her refuse to have an abortion.

Three long months were to pass before Ruth at last gave in and had her abortion, and inevitably there was plenty of involvement, with Ralph and me talking about not having had children, of my adopting little Mike—he was wonderful about that—of the possibility still ahead of having children, of marrying again to have children, of me saying I would never marry any man who wanted children unless I were to find out, after all the years, that the time had come again when I *could* have children.

And there I was once more, after that three-year lapse caused by my divorce, going back to Dr. Damon to start all over again on the quest I had abandoned. Ralph knew I was going to Dr. Damon, and even sought a check on himself, though I wondered why he even thought of it after that weekend with Ruth.

More months were to pass and then I did become pregnant, and joyfully told Ralph. In those hours of exultation I never imagined that within ten days I would enter upon a shock so harrowing that it would send me into the three years of psychoanalysis I probably should have had years before.

For some time Ralph had been engrossed by his one ambition—to start his own newspaper, *PM;* he had left Time to plan it and to seek the millions of dollars to fund it; he was obsessed by it, and his friends were all drawn into his efforts for this paper that was to be his "life's greatest accomplishment."

I should have known that our hours of exultation would be brief. Exactly eight days later Ralph asked me to his office. He'd been thinking and thinking, he said somberly—and a hammering began within my ribs. This was the worst possible timing, he said; for this year, for several years, his whole life had to be devoted to the paper, *only* to the paper; there was no way to fit in getting married, having a baby . . .

A thousand hours were to pass before those words of his stopped crashing at my brain cells, but in the very minute of leaving his office I knew I would go ahead anyway. Something in me said, I'll never void my body again, never.

For forty-four days I did go on, and for forty-four nights, taking sleeping pills, losing weight, taking sedatives for my day's work at Time, down the hall from Ralph. And then came miscarriage, and the hospital and Dr. Damon trying to comfort me and a visit from Ralph, and me, a few days later, going to an analyst for the first time, crying out, "What do you do when you can't *bear* it?"

You do bear it, of course, but me, I had to go further, had to begin to "understand" Ralph and find excuses for him. One definition of neurosis is that you *have* to. And so before long we were back together and I again believed there was a future for us.

Despite his obsession with his paper, there was some reason for me to believe. For two whole weeks in July of 1939 he abandoned everything else and came to stay with me in my rented house in Bermuda, and when we got back to New York we got engaged, "officially, publicly, ring-on-the-finger" engaged.

The date books I had begun to keep while I was married to Thayer Hobson recreate that period for me even in their one-line jottings.

August 14, 1939: Engaged to R.
August 19: Dad & Tante. (Tante was Ralph's stepmother. I had never met either parent before.)
August 27: Dad & Tante—cocktail party for us. Lakeville.
December 29: Quebec with R.
January 10, 1940: Paper fully subscribed—dinner H. R. Luce— Stork Club—Davenports, John Gunthers, Thurbers, etc.
January 11: Marshall Field's; Lil Hellman, Shumlin; Hawes & Losey, etc.
January 15: Off to Cat Cay & Nassau with R.
February 14: R & I, President Roosevelt, 11:20–11:50.

For this momentous event in the Oval Office, Ralph decided to give me my wedding present early, my first mink coat. (My wedding gift to him was to be a tennis court for his place in Lakeville, Connecticut.) Tante went shopping for the coat with me; in those days Jaeckel and Revillon Frères were still separate stores, and we shopped at both places, but ended up ordering a custom-made beauty at Bergdorf Goodman.

I was to wear that coat only a few times before spring came, and with spring the growing realization that once again we were doomed, the way most neurotic love is doomed, by hurt feelings, by resentments, by quarrels, by too much time spent apart. I was ill again, in the hospital again, and we broke again, this time for good. June 1, 1940 says, "Wrote R—breaking off."

That need for exactitude arose because as I sit here, in the late winter of 1984, in the very act of rereading those painful pages of my autobiography, and of writing about them once again, I learn that in a book now being written about Ralph there will appear his denial of just about everything.

It was a "pretend engagement," he would say; the ring-on-the-finger was a diamond-and-gold ring he had once given to Arny, his nurse; his father and Tante never gave us that cocktail party, and the mink coat was a gift from Tante so I "would have something nice to wear to the White House."

Before I ever wrote a line about the Ingersoll part of my book I had asked my editor and publisher, and my attorney too, "What if he denies it? He probably will."

What I couldn't imagine was that the brilliant Ralph Ingersoll wouldn't come up with something a little more plausible than all the above. Would anybody anywhere believe he would introduce a pretend fiancée to President Roosevelt? As for Tante and the coat, what stepmother anywhere ever gave anybody a custom-made mink coat after meeting her twice? As a gift for a pretend engagement at that. It beats me.

Exactitude be praised! Those blessed little datebooks of mine that I originally kept only to record social matters while I was a publisher's wife, and which I didn't throw away because they contained names of people who had entertained us and whom we would have to entertain in turn—how could I have dreamed that the habit of keeping them would persist, a row of years on a bookshelf in a closet, and that half a lifetime later they would emerge as my most reliable advisers and companions, my private little Library of Congress for the "investigative reporting" I would be doing of my own life?

If I *had* suspected it, they might have turned into self-conscious little exercises in diary-keeping, with comments and soul-searching and attempted aphorisms. Instead, their brief jottings remained the bare bones of the continuing tissue and flesh of my life, my writing life as well as my private life.

After that June of the final break there was no private life to record for a long time; there was, though, a spate of entries about numbers of pages written, titles of stories, voluntary writing of full-page newspaper ads signed by groups protesting that isolationist part of the press that constantly assailed Roosevelt and Churchill for trying to "drag this country into a foreign war." There was also something brand-new: job interviews by the dozen.

I was no longer at Time—one further casualty of that neurotic love. I was the only woman in the newly formed "Senior Group," a profit-sharing group of thirty people selected by Harry Luce and his cohorts; our weekly meetings often dealt with future plans for the magazines, possible innovations. Nobody at Time considered *PM* or Ralph a conceivable rival, but there I was in those meetings, engaged to be married to a man many of them disliked and even mistrusted. Inevitably an awkwardness developed, and about the time of the visit to the Oval Office I had resigned.

So, having given up (for love) my $20,000 salary and $11,000 bonus, I was left with no job, no love, and at the age of forty a new start to make. In my analysis, together with my rage and grief, I would often say, "It's all *my* fault—I always fall in love with a man who's going to kill me."

Well, my typewriter was never going to kill me, and again writing was the anodyne I could truly rely on. After the long months of summer and fall and winter, I even began to see people again, to have a few dates, including one light affair, amiably ended in early spring, without regret for either of us, and soon part of the past, and later that year an affair that was neither light nor quickly ended, with Eric Hodgins, one of that liberal group of top editors at Time and Life and Fortune who forever tried to get Harry Luce to realize how much his magazines were slanting the news.

And then two things happened, almost simultaneously, things that took me and my life and shook them up and about and around.

One was an offer from Dick Simon of Simon and Schuster of a $5,000 advance to write my first novel. I had written a storybook for children and it had been published, but I had never even thought of a novel. At Dick's offer I was flabbergasted, flattered, frightened all at once. I had written my little storybook in less than an hour, but a novel might take years. I asked for time to think about it.

And the time I needed was provided by the second great and unlooked-for event, something that also flabbergasted me but never frightened me for a minute. The light and amiably ended affair had also ended in another way. At the beginning of June I suddenly realized I was pregnant. I was forty-one.

And in the minute of knowing it, I knew I would go ahead. This time there would be nobody to cause me nights of anguish, this time there would be no miscarriage, this time nobody would even know about it except me, and I could rely on me.

And there followed the intertwining of those two creative forces, writing my first book and giving birth for the first time.

The baby was my son Chris, just five years younger than Mike, born a thousand miles away from Evanston, Illinois, where I had adopted Mike, and having the same "blood strains," as they were called in those distant days. Mike's original parents had been, they had told me at The Cradle, two intelligent, college-educated people; the father British, Protestant, of English, Scotch, Irish ancestry; the mother American, of Russian-Jewish ancestry. And now Chris, the father American, Protestant, of English, Scotch, Irish ancestry and the mother, me, also American, also of Russian-Jewish ancestry. I never did get over the coincidence of all that: if I hadn't been an agnostic, I would have believed those two births had been arranged by God, or at least by some beneficent and smiling angels.

And the book I had begun, and which took more than twice as long as that blessed pregnancy, was *The Trespassers,* published late in 1943 when we had been at war in Europe and the Pacific for nearly two years. I myself thought of it as a modest success, for it earned me just about what I would have earned in four months during my final year at Time; many a first author, however, would have thought it a huge and shining victory, for it appeared on the best-seller lists for several weeks (on the lower rungs) and sold some twenty thousand copies.

My life as a novelist had begun. It was not to be an easy life from publication day onward; there would be debts and freelance promotion jobs to pay some of them, and loans from friends; there would be two trips to Hollywood as a salaried employee of Columbia Studios, each time moving out my two kids and Rosie, their nurse and a member of our household, each time hoping to put aside enough money to support my little family while I tried to write a second novel.

Interlaced with all the debts and freelancing and dashes to the payrolls of Hollywood was an insidious fear that I would never again get an idea as good as the one for *The Trespassers.* Worse yet, when I finally did think of the idea for *Gentleman's Agreement,* was the discovery that Dick Simon at Simon and Schuster took an instant dislike to it, tried to persuade me to drop it, and finally wrote me a four-page letter listing for me in graphic terms the assorted kinds of heartbreak that would be mine if I were stubborn enough to go ahead and write what I had begun to call "my obsessive idea for a novel that would never sell to the movies, never sell to any magazine and most likely never sell to the public."

While I was writing that final half of volume one of my life story I found myself racing along with a kind of grateful pleasure in that old stubborn compulsion of mine, and when my book appeared, many of the reviews made a point of calling that whole section perhaps the best part of the whole, for it managed to reveal the inner story of what authors may go through as they shape and develop any book they deeply believe in.

And now as I was rereading that same section, priming myself for the beginning of this part of my autobiography, I also raced along with a kind of gratitude, all the way up to the surprising news that Twentieth Century-Fox had bought it for a Darryl F. Zanuck movie, and beyond that to publication day itself, in February of 1947.

No voice from on high informed me that "this day is the turning point in your life as a writer," nor did I suspect it myself, not even when my then editor phoned me early in the morning to say, "You better get yourself down here right away—you'll never see anything like this for the rest of your life."

By noon 10,000 copies were sold, *Gentleman's Agreement* was off to its first official day in a life whose length nobody even then could predict, and I had been given—though I wasn't to know it until thirty-six years later—a most natural place to say that I had come "not to the end of my story, but only a brief pause in the telling of it."

Ten days after that pub day I made a quick decision: I had to get out of New York, for the sake of my kids if for no other reason.

The incessant ringing of the telephone, the telegrams, the bursts of mail, the jubilant talk when my friends were there—all this told my children that Something Big had happened, a something that left them out. It was as if the only person in the house that mattered was mommy.

As I remember it, I tried from the start to turn it into something "good for all of us," something that meant we could go off on a trip, buy new toys, even get a new car, though new cars were still hardly attainable since Detroit was still retooling from the war years of tanks and airplanes and everything else in what President Roosevelt had called "the arsenal of democracy."

But that concept of "good for all of us" must have been a bit beyond the boys' grasp—Mike was just ten and Chris just five.

And then there occurred one of those excesses that made me decide, Enough! It was only the delivery of some flowers, but Mike turned it into a dramatization I could not ignore. In those days, just before television made its first tentative entry into everybody's life, there was a radio commercial that was heard a thousand times a week. It was for Philip Morris cigarettes, with a pageboy chanting in choirboy tenor, "Call for Pheel-ip Mawr-ees, call for Pheel-ip Mawr-ees." Though he was invisible on radio, endless magazine ads in full color showed a kid in the red and blue and brass buttons of a page boy uniform, so young his voice could not yet have changed.

That day, the tenth after pub day, Mike answered the ring of the front-door bell. A florist's messenger handed him an elongated box of American Beauty roses.

The box was not only long, it was heavy, for it contained not the normal dozen but the Hollywood *two* dozen of long-stemmed flowers.

Mike hoisted the box up so that it lay flat across his two uplifted arms and came strutting through the living room, calling out in that same choirboy tenor, "More flahrs for Mees-is Hob-sohn, more flahrs for Mees-is Hob-sohn." When he handed them over to me, he bowed low—he had seen enough movies for that gesture, though he did refrain from the slyly extended palm.

I laughed, but I didn't think it funny. Something was all wrong. If this sort of attention kept up, some sort of farce-picture would form in my children's minds, as if mommy had turned into a movie star.

Parenthetically I should say right here, as I did early in volume one, that when I set down a short sentence, like Mike's "Flahrs for Mees-is Hob-sohn," it is as if a tape had been made all those years ago that I could now run again on my recording machine; being blessed with a good memory, I can still hear that choirboy tenor of Mike's saying those precise words. They are verbatim.

But when it comes to conversations that run for some length, there is no pretending from me that they are verbatim. Being a novelist, however, it comes more easily to me to recreate a scene in dialogue than it would if I were to use the narrative past tense.

And it wasn't only the flahrs and Mike that made me want to get out of New York and away from all the fireworks. My own life was suddenly all hectic flush, like a face in a high fever. Fira Benenson, a famous designer, had given me a large party on the night of pub day, and this was followed by many other celebrating parties, even one cocktail party Sigmund Freud surely would have frowned upon, given by my analyst, Dr. Gosselin and his wife, with me as guest of honor.

And there was still another motive for leaving New York that I don't think I recognized or acknowledged at the time. I had some inner need to see for myself the people who now held the fate of the movie in their hands, in their minds; would they stay true to the book or think first of "entertainment" and dilute it or shift away from it to please "the front office"?

But Darryl F. Zanuck *was* the front office; this was to be his one personal production of the year; I had some conviction that if I could meet him and talk to him before he got too far along I just might strengthen his determination to make it a movie that met all the issues head-on.

I had no author's "right of approval." I was not well-known enough, had no such status—until then I had been the author of a medium success called *The Trespassers* and had no leverage for making special deals with movie moguls about author's rights.

But I did have some protection, actually, written right into the contract with Twentieth Century-Fox. Most movies open with that awful phrase, "Based on the novel by." Even in so famous a film as *The Maltese Falcon,* the opening announcement, called the "card" in movie lingo, says, "Based on the novel by Dashiell Hammett." That little "based on" gives the producer an open license to change, invent, concoct whatever he wants, no holds barred. Only in rare cases was that open license withheld, contractually and legally withheld, and only with world-famous writers. There is no "based on," for example, in one of the great movies of the early forties. Its card reads:

Ernest Hemingway's
For Whom The Bell Tolls

I had only the vaguest notion about these matters at the time, but one thing my agent Bert Allenberg had done for me was to ask for, insist on and finally get the opening card that was regarded as a valuable asset. In much smaller letters, it is true, my own name heads the card that opens the movie.

Laura Z. Hobson's
Gentleman's Agreement

But despite this legal protection against wanton change, invention or concoction I still felt impelled to talk to Mr. Zanuck myself, to meet Moss Hart and Elia Kazan, as if—as if—I couldn't put a name to that "as if," but it made me think about going out to California as soon as I could, before everybody's intentions had fully jelled.

About this time I had met Lenore Cotten, the wife of Joseph Cotten, already famous for his role in *Citizen Kane*. At lunch one day I told her why I wanted to get away from New York's hoopla, and even confided my notion that meeting Zanuck and Hart might somehow "protect" the picture.

She was kind enough not to laugh at me; instead she offered me their house in Pacific Palisades, plus free use of their Lincoln, plus her blessings. She wanted an honest movie too.

I started packing that same evening, but then spent two days shopping for what I thought of as "clothes suitable for Hollywood." That tells me now that I was apprehensive about meeting all those personages out there, no longer as a job-seeker but as the author of a book they were actually staking their own reputations on.

I met Moss Hart first. He and his wife, Kitty Carlisle, had rented Otto Preminger's house for the duration, and even as we three sat down together on the porch I saw that he was holding a clipboard bearing a sheaf of pages of his manuscript—the first few scenes he had written, using the pages of my book in whatever way he was planning to use them.

The small talk of preliminaries between all of us went pleasantly and easily enough, but when Kitty rose to let us get down to the script itself I was suddenly nervous on a brand new level. Here was this famous playwright, author of such smash hits, with George S. Kaufman, as *Once in a Lifetime, You Can't Take It With You, The Man Who Came to Dinner,* and, by himself, *Lady in the Dark*—here was Moss Hart about to read aloud to me for my approval his version in dramatic form of what I had written in that novel I had thought of three full years before. Suppose I didn't like what he had done?

He began to read. With the greatest economy he managed to set the scene, and through the dialogue between my hero Phil Green and his small son give the audience the background for Phil's character—his serious mind, his loneliness as a widower, his recent move from California to New York to become a staff writer for a national magazine, and that, as a newcomer and a stranger, he knows nobody except the man who is his editor.

All this Moss had taken from my book, of course, but what I had written as exposition he had turned into dialogue and some action, and I listened with admiration for his skill as a dramatist.

But then he began to read the next scene, and now the words the characters were speaking were *my* words, just as they had been written by me, words he had lifted unchanged from the pages of my book. I forgot all about his skill as a dramatist and heard only my own words being read aloud by him to me, now part of the script of a "major motion picture" in the process of being born.

My breath caught, my eyes filled, listening, not even trying to hide my face from Moss, thinking obscurely of myself writing those words in uncertainty and solitude so long ago. At one point he looked up and saw me, and all I said was, "Oh, Moss," and he understood, and we became sure of each other, I think, in that moment.

Actually, as I was soon to learn, Moss Hart, for all his worldwide fame, was a touch nervous himself, and when I did offer one suggestion after our first session he instantly accepted it. One or two of his own phrases, I thought, were ambiguous and might possibly suggest to the audience that Phil too was a little mixed-up about anti-Semitism, in the same way Kathy would later show herself to be.

"It's sort of dangerous," I said, "because it might say to the audience, 'Well, isn't everybody?' "

Moss at once took my point; without pause he struck the phrases, nodding as he did so, one nod for each phrase he took out.

About four years later, long after the movie had been made, Moss did something a little ambiguous on his own. By then he and Kitty had two young children, Christopher and Cathy, one still an infant.

"How old do kids have to be," he asked me casually one day, "before you tell them they're Jewish?"

"You should never have to *tell* them." I remember thinking of Mrs. Walrath at The Cradle the day I adopted Mike. "There should never be 'the moment of revelation,' " she had told me. "He should hear the words *adopted* and *adoption* as early and as often as he hears the words *bottle* or *diaper* or *love.*"

I can't remember how tactfully I relayed Mrs. Walrath's advice to Moss, nor how he received it, but I do remember from another time his burst of laughter when he told me a story about his brother Bernie, whom he loved. Bernie was a witty man, as Moss was, and though he couldn't write plays, his working life was largely devoted to the furthering of Moss' plays as producer, publicist, general factotum.

"I'm going to start a new organization: J.A." Bernie announced at a party after he had read *Gentleman's Agreement*. "It's for Jews Anonymous, and the idea is, if you're Jewish and one night at three in the morning, you can't stand it any more, you call up another Jew and you both go out and get plastered."

But there was no joking between me and Moss in that first session when we had met to talk about the script he was doing. He was as anxious as I that it be an honest picture, that it be strong and challenging—and a hit. We had another two-hour session the very next afternoon, and a longer one the day after. Though he told me he was still unsure about how to end the movie I was positive he would solve every problem.

He had never written a screenplay; stories in Variety and the Hollywood Reporter had it that Zanuck had had to come up with $150,000 to induce Moss to do this, his first one. After all those stimulating hours with Moss, listening to him outline the entire thing scene for scene except for that troublesome ending, I for one was convinced that Zanuck would never be sorry.

And then came my appointment with Darryl F. Zanuck himself, one of the great ones in filmdom. I had read or heard such farfetched stories about him and the legendary polo mallet he always swung while he talked to people, about his love affairs with successive movie stars of Europe, about his princely life in general on the throne of power, that I half-dreaded the moment of meeting him. When I was ushered promptly into his office without the usual wait, I felt that I had passed some unknown test in my own right.

His office looked about as big as Grand Central Station. Way down at the end of it, rising to his feet behind his vast desk, was Mr. Zanuck, tan and slim but, at that far distance, looking about three feet tall. The famous polo mallet was there somewhere—I saw it, leaning against something—but he was not swinging it. He was dressed in tweeds, the pale tweeds of a warm climate, a good-looking man in early middle age, and as he came forward to greet me, full of praise about my book, I wondered what unseen thing it was that exuded a sense of power in him.

I had known men of power—Harry Luce, for instance. But to me, as employee or friend, Harry had never exuded that mysterious aura that said, I am the king. Yet right there, despite Zanuck's gracious words, I was aware that some unseen voice was announcing, I am Darryl F. Zanuck, and you know what that means for the future of your picture.

He seated me at his side, took his place behind his desk, and started to cast the picture for me. *Gentleman's Agreement* is about anti-Semitism in America right after World War II; its principal character, Phil Green, is a young writer who does research on anti-Semitism by saying he's Jewish when he isn't.

Gregory Peck would play Phil, the perfect choice. He was young, handsome, himself a decent man detesting prejudice, but Zanuck had one more reason for choosing him. Peck was already a major star because of his roles in *Spellbound, Duel in the Sun* and other hit pictures, and soon he would be commanding huge sums before accepting any role. But he had one more picture to do under his first contract of $50,000 per film, and Zanuck had him for that final deal.

I was of course delighted at the choice and at the other names he gave me; the only uncertainty he showed was who was to play Phil's closest friend, Dave Goldman, an army captain just being demobilized and returning home from the front. He wanted John Garfield, Mr. Zanuck said, but some people were arguing against that choice, saying that his speech had something of New York in it, something Jewish, and that the audience might not believe they had been boys together growing up in California.

Of course it was John Garfield and no other. Much later I heard—though this may be apocryphal—that Garfield was already commanding a million or so for doing a picture, a sum that had kept Zanuck from making any move toward an offer, but that Garfield had taken things into his own hands.

"I want to be part of that picture," he supposedly told his agent. "I'll do it for nothing."

Somewhere I read that he finally did it for scale, the lowest legal fee, and what he actually was paid or whether he was ever paid at all I never did find out. But I liked the story so much that I have repeated it a hundred times, with no denial ever forthcoming from anybody. And I will go right on believing it and repeating it.

Sitting there at Mr. Zanuck's desk, I knew nothing as yet of this and doubtless would have been too awed to ask him about it in any case. Yet my awe couldn't have been too dominant, for I suddenly interrupted him with a question he clearly hadn't expected.

"Mr. Zanuck, why did you buy it?"

I said it quietly, I remember, so quietly that he hardly took it in, and went right on with what he was saying about the other people he was casting. Then he stopped.

"Why did you buy it?" I repeated. "You only had the galleys—"

"Why did I buy *Gentleman's Agreement?*" He sounded astonished.

"I've sort of wondered why," I said. "Before it came out, before the wonderful reviews began, before anybody knew for certain how it would go."

His whole manner seemed to alter. His voice changed to a man's ordinary speaking voice, without that slight ring of authority I had heard before. He stopped being the Hollywood power and became just a person, like me. He didn't answer at once; he seemed to be searching for the words he needed, or even to be thinking it out for the first time for himself.

"I have three children," he finally said slowly, "Darrylin and Richard and Susan." He was looking past me, as if he were looking at the faces of his son and two daughters, then all in their teens. "If this country ever did go fascist," he went on, "and they said to me, 'Well, pop, what did *you* do to stop it? You had the studios, the money, the power—what did *you* do to fight it off?'" . . . I can't remember precisely how he put it, but that was the gist of it, and he went on in that ruminative, thoughtful voice. "I want to be able to say to them, 'Well, I made *Wilson,* and then I made *Gentleman's Agreement,* I made *Pinky* . . .'"

Wilson had been his big picture the year before, and a box-office failure. It was about the League of Nations and Woodrow Wilson's famous Fourteen Points. I knew that *Pinky* was to be about "Negro" soldiers in World War II—they were not yet called black soldiers— so I understood that he was telling me he was not going to be held down, as most producers were, by the Hollywood sneer, "If you want to send a message, go to Western Union."

I can't remember much about how I responded but he must have sensed that I was impressed by what he was telling me. He talked on a bit about story values and conflict and then again he paused. . . . "Anyway," he said, and now his ruminative tone gave way to a good practical one, "I felt in my bones your book would be a sensation, and I wanted to be *in* on a sensation."

That put a cap on everything he had said so far, and if I ever were to find myself a bit skeptical about all the higher motives, I never once doubted this one.

CHAPTER

TWO

THERE IS ONE THING about the movie version of *Gentleman's Agreement* that has remained very nearly a secret for all the years since it first appeared in 1947: one of the major scenes in the film, the next-to-last one, a scene I like very much, is not in my book at all. I have often wished that it were.

And yet it was I who wrote that scene for Moss to dramatize, writing it eight months after I had finished my book, writing it because Moss, even after our three long sessions, was still searching for the way to end the film.

I could see why it should be so elusive. In the book, about a hundred pages follow Kathy and Phil's quarrel about why she won't rent her vacant house in Darien, Connecticut, to Dave Goldman and his family.

> "It would just be so uncomfortable for Dave, knowing he'd moved into one of those damn neighborhoods that won't take Jews."
>
> "Kathy!"
>
> "I loathe it, but that's the way it is up there. New Canaan's even worse—nobody can sell or rent to a Jew there. But even Darien—well, it's a sort of gentleman's agreement—"
>
> "Gentleman—oh, my God, you don't *really*, you *can't* actually —you won't buck it, Kathy? Just going to give in, play along, let their idiotic rules stand?"

In my book I could take all the time I needed, and all the episodes, to show Kathy probing into her hidden feelings about the anti-Semitism she deplores as much as Phil does. But Moss had to find some way to telescope those hundred pages into some swift, dramatic resolution, and finally he issued a specific invitation to me to come up with any idea that might help him solve his problem.

I was still in California but no longer in Beverly Hills where we could meet and talk. After two weeks, I had decided that the hullaballoo was even worse than in New York; at home it had been about my book—here it was mainly about Zanuck and the movie and who would play what part and when it would start actual filming and the like.

I had gone out, alone, to the desert, not to fashionable Palm Springs but to what was then a small resort, La Quinta, near Indio. My datebook, which by then I was calling my work log, or simply my log, says "$26 a day," perhaps in open confession of my sin of extravagance in treating myself to so opulent a place.

Moss had lent me an old portable typewriter, and driving out in the dry desert heat, I kept reviewing everything in the last chapters of my book. Somewhere there must be one special bit that could do the trick, maybe buried in some stretch of exposition, easy to overlook. I had a copy of my book with me—I would read every paragraph of those hundred pages.

I had told Moss that if I did arrive at anything I thought he could use I wouldn't try to put it into screenplay language. I would have to pretend that I was still writing my book and do it exactly as if it were an extra chapter in it.

And of course, when I did find what I wanted, it *was* buried, in a short paragraph just before the final chapter. Kathy is at a dinner party, where one of the guests tells a joke of pure bigotry, about "kikes and coons," laughing uproariously as he does so, while most of the guests, and Kathy among them, listen in appalled silence.

> Kathy waited for the waves of heat to stop running through her.
> . . . Illness was in her and shame for all of them. They despised
> him and they kept quiet. They were well-bred and polite, so they
> kept quiet. Just as she did. Not making fusses was also part of the
> gentleman's agreement. To rise and leave the room was not in her
> knees and muscles; to call him to account was not in her vocal
> chords.

In my book it was narration—the omniscient author revealing what is going through a character's mind. A movie is dialogue; this would have to be acted out, made into a visible, vital scene. How?

I might have Kathy turn to someone in her distress, spill out her shame and guilt. It couldn't be Phil—it might be Dave Goldman; she might ask him to meet her at some bar or restaurant—I began to write.

For a whole weekend I wrote. I would take a swim and then write; I would sunbathe and then write; I would eat and write, sleep the happy uneasy sleep I always know when I think something is going well, and then write again. I didn't begrudge a moment of it; it was like those heady days of the final rush to finish my book. I wrote interim notes to Moss, keeping them till I was done.

Dear Moss, you brute,

I've done everything I can do, unless I were to work another week, rewriting the stuff, expanding the elliptical parts, etc. It may be lousy, it may be good, it probably is part good, part lousy, like most first-draft stuff—but I pray it will be helpful . . .

But after each interim note to Moss I returned to Kathy and Dave in that newly imagined restaurant.

Kathy got there first, and when Dave arrived she waved all preliminaries aside. "Dave, help me, you've got to help me. I've got to find a way to get this straight with Phil."

Dave nodded slowly . . . He beckoned to the waiter . . . "What happened just before you called me, Kathy?"

"Nothing. That isn't the point. Dave, you're so close to Phil . . . you can tell me how—"

"But what did happen, Kathy, just before you phoned?"

She made a gesture of impatience. "That hasn't anything to do with *this,* Dave. Please don't go off on a—"

"Suppose you tell me anyway."

"Oh, Dave." She waved it away with an impatient hand. "It was just a—well, a sort of dirty joke—it hasn't a thing to do—"

"Take it easy, Kathy. Maybe it has. I've never heard you so near hysteria as over that phone. What kind of joke?"

"But, Dave, it's Phil I wanted to talk about—I've got to get him back, I've got to make him see that I'm just the way he is about these things that keep pushing us apart."

He patted her hand. . . . He was interested, ready to help. But apparently Dave could be stubborn, in his quiet . . . way. "This joke, Kathy. I can take dirty words, you know."

"Oh, not that kind. It was a horrible man, a vulgar, aggressive, money-money-money, profit-profit-profit kind of man named Lockhardt Jones. He told some awful story about getting all the —oh, Dave, it hasn't one solitary thing to do with the way I sounded over the phone."

"Getting all the what, Kathy?"

"Getting all the kikes and coons out of the country. I despised him—everybody at the table despised him. It was like—oh, it was so—" She broke off, shuddered, looked at Dave, then away. Dave was smiling now, gently, as at a sick child.

"What'd you do, Kathy, when he told the joke?"

Kathy stiffened. Increased agitation tightened her lips . . . fought her breathing.

"Me?"

"Yes, Kathy. When he finished, what did you say?"

She sat staring at him . . . at the calm, persistent gaze he gave her . . . unable to find words.

"Or what did you *do,* Kathy? Forgive this, but I had a hunch that something besides Phil had upset you, something newer than your parting from him—on the phone, you were so—"

"Dave, oh Dave—I *wanted* to yell at him. I *wanted* to get up and leave—I *wanted* to say to everybody else at the table, 'Why —why do we just sit here and take this? Why do we all live by this—this—gentleman's agreement not to make a scene, when everything we believe in is attacked by people like this?' " She put her hands over her face. Dave watched her, his eyes old with his own feelings. "But I didn't, Dave. I just sat; we *all* just sat. I felt so ashamed, and I just sat—"

"Then you left and got me on the phone?"

"Later, when dinner was over. I said I was ill—it's true—I'm sick all through—"

There was a pause. When Dave spoke, he spoke softly, without rancor, without scorn. "I wonder if you'd feel so sick now, Kathy, if you *had* nailed him?"

"Oh, Dave."

"There's a funny kind of elation about socking back, Kathy. I learned that a long time ago; Phil's learned it."

"And me? I haven't?"

He raised his eyebrows as if he were asking her the same question. But he said nothing.

36

"Dave, you mean, I'd feel square with myself if I *did* something when the thing came up? . . . You mean that you feel sick and cheap if these things happen and you just sit and take it?" She reached toward his hand as if for help, then withdrew her own. "But Dave, Dave, it's so ghastly to fight and—"

He looked down at his uniform. "Lots of things are pretty rough, Kathy."

"It's a different kind of war, you mean. . . . you mean that if anybody crawls away from this kind of war, he's a deserter just as much—"

"I didn't say that. You did."

"It's true." Suddenly she was intense, excited. "I know it—it's the long war, Dave—the longest war this country's ever had. And it isn't over—and I'm not fighting it . . . I'm just waving the flag and *talking*. Is that it? Is that what you think?"

Again Dave said quietly. "I didn't say that, Kathy."

"But *I* did. Phil did. You know it. We all know it. Oh, God, Dave, it's so easy to forget that there is this long war—there are no uniforms to wear, no flags waving, no brass bands—"

"The toughest wars, sometimes, haven't the show and the bands and the technicolor—"

"You mean I've just been getting sore at Phil for expecting me not to desert, instead of getting sore at the people who help the war along, like Lockhardt Jones tonight."

"Not just old Lockhardt—at least he's out in the open. But the other dinner guests—they're supposed to be on *your* side, and they didn't act much as if there were any war on, either."

"No. No, they didn't. And I didn't. We never do." She fell silent. She stared at him as if he were new. . . . "It all links up, you mean. Phil can fight; he does fight; he always will fight this. If I can't do anything but sit there and feel sick, then I'm not a fit wife for him? Not a soldier's wife?"

Dave smiled, as if at some victory he had won. "A man wants his wife to be more than just a companion, Kathy, more than his beloved girl, more even than the mother of his children. He wants a sidekick, a buddy to go through the rough spots with—and she's got to feel the same things *are* the rough spots, or they're always out of line with each other."

"You're saying Phil couldn't feel I *was* a wife, the way I am."

"You're not cast in bronze, sweetie. . . . you're nice and soft and pliable and you can do anything you have to do—or want to do with yourself."

"I can?" She looked at him . . . pondering something . . . as if she were planning something. "But it's got to be better than talk. Maybe if somebody starts shifting over from talk to *doing* —maybe, Dave, it might get easier with practice?"

"Could be, Kathy." Dave saw that her face was changed— harder, more determined. Almost cunningly he said, "Now, about you and Phil. You wanted me to dish out some brotherly advice about that?"

But Kathy was standing. "Not now, Dave, thanks. I—well, thanks, but not right now."

She started to put on her coat and Dave signaled for the check.

That was it, just as I wrote it, with its schoolgirlish plethora of dashes between phrases, its repetitions of Daves and Kathys. I sent it off to Moss without editing or making a clean copy on that miserable portable with its worn-out ribbon, and despite my multiple disclaimers about its being only a first draft, I must have felt fairly sure of myself, for some of my remarks as I ended each day's work sounded pretty sassy.

> I've been writing for hours, you slavedriver . . . why the hell couldn't you have a typewriter with a new ribbon on the spools, with rubber caps for the keys, and a few comforts like that? And then, why the hell can't you keep the typewriter and do all this drudgery yourself, and let me have my vacation without you in my hair, on my conscience, in my mind, unconscious and so forth. WHY? . . .
> Thirteen pages—holy smoke.

My restaurant scene occupied less than half the thirteen pages; Moss had also asked for ideas on some secondary scenes, and I had done my best with those as well, in a hodgepodge of ordinary letter-writing style interlaced with bursts of dialogue. I was astonished at how thick the manila envelope was when I finally mailed it.

For all my sassy tone I began to wait for the telephone to ring. Instead, the telegram that finally came was delightfully elongated, and typical Moss, starting with a phrase he lifted from my book and used in the movie.

> DEAR LAURA   FIRST AND FOREMOST YOURE QUITE A GIRL.   I JUST RECEIVED WHAT I CAN ONLY TERM YOUR MANUSCRIPT AND I AM DELIGHTED WITH IT AND YOUR FULFILLMENT OF YOUR PROMISE.

Half the long wire said he understood what I meant about his proposed Phil-Anne scene, and that he wanted to read everything I'd written "two or three times very carefully."

> THIS IS JUST TO TELL YOU HOW REALLY SWELL I THINK IT WAS OF YOU TO CUT INTO YOUR VACATION . . . IF IT IS ANY CONSOLATION ITS GOING TO BE MOST HELPFUL EVEN FROM A QUICK FIRST GLANCE AND LASTLY AGAIN YOURE QUITE A GIRL.

As it turned out, this wasn't just polite praise. When the movie appeared, that scene between Dave and Kathy appeared in it just about word for word. Moss had introduced it with some brief dialogue of his own, and with his great skill had used some lines from other parts of the book, for transitions, for tightening the scene. My amateur stage directions about pauses, gestures, tightening of the lips, Dave's mean-ingful glance down at his own uniform—all this, of course, had disappeared, transformed into Dave's and Kathy's acting.

It was Moss, not me, who told Zanuck where that scene came from, and the last time I saw Zanuck he offered to pay me for it. But I declined, saying I wanted *not* to be on his payroll in any way, so I could feel free of constraint about the movie; he had the studio send me two heavy gold-link bracelets and earrings as a thank-you present.

Moss also told our friends about that extra scene, but somehow it never got into the newspapers or movie columns, so it has indeed remained a secret from the public until now.

Recently I saw that *Gentleman's Agreement* was scheduled for its thousandth rerun on television, and I asked my son Chris to come on over with his tape recorder and take down the dialogue of that one scene. Then I had it transcribed to manuscript form, so I could compare it, line for line, to what I had sent Moss from the desert so many years ago. (The tape-recorded scene from the movie is included at the end of this book.)

Again I wished that this extra scene of mine had appeared right in my own book, in print instead of on film. And suddenly I thought, Well, it can appear in print in *this* book.

That telegram from Moss wasn't the only one I was to receive at La Quinta. Back then, telephone service to a small resort with the phone number Thermal Main 3 was apt to be tricky, so people wired instead of calling you.

The first was from my Simon and Schuster editor, Lee Wright.

The week after, she wired that it was eight thousand and number four.
And a month later when I was home in New York, there was an
exchange of wires between Dick Simon and Zanuck whose carbons I
pasted up in my large press portfolio. The first was from Dick.

I HAVE JUST HEARD THAT GENTLEMANS AGREEMENT
WILL APPEAR AS NUMBER ONE FICTION BEST SELLER IN
NEXT SUNDAYS TIMES STOP THOUGHT YOU OUGHT TO
BE THE FIRST ONE OUT YOUR WAY TO HEAR THIS EX-
CITING NEWS STOP WE ARE BOTH TO BE CON-
GRATULATED ON HAVING THIS WONDERFUL BOOK.

Zanuck's answer was in kind, each congratulating the other. I must
have thought back to that "heartbreak letter" Dick had written me
three years earlier, listing the various heartbreaks lying in wait for me
if I were stubborn enough to go ahead with my obsessive idea for a
novel.

Today the phrase is, The best revenge is living well, and for authors,
the best revenge tends to be the best-seller list. I can't think I was noble
enough to be above some such yah-yah-yah feeling about Dick and
all the others who had so insistently advised me to drop my book, but
with great kindness my unconscious has suppressed all memory of such
pettiness.

Any triumph I do remember was quite different—a shock of delight
whenever I got on a bus or a subway or a commuter train and saw
somebody sitting there reading my book. It was all I could do not to
stop and say, "Do you like it? How far in it are you? I wrote it!"

The only time I ever did anything of the sort was one night
returning to New York on the famous train, the Superchief. When I
went to the dining car the first night out I saw that every table was
taken, but that at one, only three of the four seats were occupied.

I asked the headwaiter if I couldn't sit there, and he looked at me
with surprise. "Are you sure, miss?"

"If they wouldn't object. Please ask them."

There sat Lena Horne, still in her twenties, wearing a cashmere sweater-set in a pale beige, setting off her beauty like stage floodlights. Two men were with her, one white, one black, and as I joined them, saying, "Sorry to be a gate crasher," we all laughed, and the laughter drowned out our names as we introduced ourselves.

But on the broad windowsill a book was propped up, leaning against the pane of glass, and it was mine. I saw it instantly and looked away as instantly.

We began to talk about what we'd been doing in California. Lena was already famous for the Cotton Club and her first movies, like *Stormy Weather,* which I had seen and could talk about. When they got around to me, I said I'd been out discussing a screenplay being written for Twentieth Century-Fox.

"Oh, are you a screenwriter?"

"No, I just—"

"What screenplay?"

I remember a flash of embarrassment, commingled with pleasure and, I confess, vanity. I said nothing, but I reached for the book on the windowsill, turned it to show the back of the jacket with its photograph of me, and faced it toward Lena, holding it below my chin.

The commotion was marvelous.

I couldn't wait to get home to Mike and Chris and my regular life, but soon after I did so an unexpected thing happened.

My old familiar foe came home with me, stealthily at first, and then with open boldness. Inexplicably I began to feel sad, empty, discontented. Everybody I knew thought I was on top of the world, and in public I smiled and chatted away and behaved as if I were.

One friend said, "You ought to have your special table for lunch every single day at '21' and queen it over the world," and I found myself wishing it were in my character to do just that. But the old heaviness stood inside me, ragged-edged, out of reach, but there.

I was sure I knew what was wrong and sure that I could cure it: it was a year since I had done any real writing, though I spent hours every day answering letters from people who had read my book, feeling that if it had moved them enough to make them write me, I couldn't be too busy or self-important to let them wonder if I had ever even read their letters.

I did have a project going that I thought would absorb me, writing a possible movie treatment for *The Trespassers,* because several people out in Hollywood had assured me they were "dying" to see it. They were the very people who had fiddled around for weeks when they could have had it, suddenly rereading my first novel with glowing eyes.

I had a possible title for the screenplay I was working on, more suitable, I thought, than *The Trespassers* on a marquee; I was going to call it "The Lifted Lamp." But I had to force myself to keep working at it; I knew it would go nowhere all over again. What they really wanted was another *Gentleman's Agreement,* or a spin-off of same.

So I soon realized that this was made work, not any anodyne for my new bout of depression. In the first half of my autobiography I said that once I was well into writing a book I cared deeply about, I felt "placed." This was the opposite. I felt uneasy, restless; I knew how to cure myself, but couldn't seem to dig in to anything where I could again feel solid and firmly rooted.

I knew enough to keep active, not only socially; I never missed a meeting of the Authors Guild, and I was asked to one of the earliest meetings of the newly-formed ADA, Americans for Democratic Action, and attended eagerly. It had been organized early that year, and all I needed to know about it was that Eleanor Roosevelt was one of its charter members.

I also was invited to be a member of the National Conference of Christians and Jews, and was guest of honor at a luncheon at the Waldorf. I had gone with the stipulation that I not be asked to speak and with the promise that I would not be asked to, but somehow an insistent call from the audience when I was introduced made it too awkward and girlish to keep refusing. So I stood up, looked one person in the eye and began.

To my astonishment, it went well. I told them about my meeting with Darryl F. Zanuck, about his vast office, his style, his polo mallet and his changed voice when I asked my simple question, "Mr. Zanuck, why did you buy it?"

When I left the Waldorf, I was sure that if I truly wanted to, I could become a regular on the lecture circuit in a reasonable time. Heaven knows, I had been asked to accept lecture dates aplenty by then; I probably could have made several thousand dollars a year. One newspaper interviewer called me "that rare specimen who turns down all lectures. She says she has put all she has to say about anti-Semitism in her book."

Thinking back to those refusals I now feel sure that I must have had enough sense to know that a whole burst of new experience, rushing about from town to town all over the country, autographing books, making small talk—that none of that would in any way restore me to that sense of being placed, and happy, and fulfilled.

In any case, I stayed at home and tried to write, and tried again and tried once more, searching for an idea for my third novel. I did begin a short story, a somber one, unlike my usual light fiction for the magazines. "To Do Her Killing" was about an embittered divorcée who always thinks, I could kill him for what he's done to me. One day, in the window of an art gallery, she sees a portrait of a man, an unknown model, whose face and bearing strongly remind her of that hated ex-husband. It is far too expensive, but, compulsively, she buys it anyway, and hangs it over the mantel in the center of her livingroom. When her friends ask her about it, her careful, poisoned replies show clearly that she is letting the portrait do her killing for her.

It sold for several times my usual short-story price, and I knew at least a temporary relief from the illness of not writing. But I also became uneasy and self-conscious about my suddenly skyrocketing "popularity." There was scarcely a party in smart literary or publishing circles that I wasn't invited to—was it me or the top-of-the-best-seller-list they were so keen to seat at the right of the host at the dinner table?

I recognized that all this anxiety would vanish once I was well-started on a new book; I knew too that a new angst was rising in me because though the screenplay was now finished, Moss had not yet sent it to me. Did that mean there was trouble with it? Would it turn out, after all, to be some sleazy "entertainment" that the front office was forever seeking?

So the day came when I found myself at the telephone, calling Dr. Gosselin, explaining what I could of the way things were.

"I can't seem to handle it myself," I ended. "I wonder if I could see you, maybe for an hour or two?"

Thus began a refresher course in analysis, and of course it went on, not for an hour or two, but throughout that wonderful year when I was supposedly on top of the world.

Gentleman's Agreement stayed number one on the *Times* best-seller list for nearly six months, and in its various editions sold over a million copies in its first year. There were no dazzling paperback deals in those days; five years were to elapse before Permabooks risked the first paperback edition at thirty-five cents per copy and for an advance of,

I think, $5,000, to be split between my publisher and me. By then, apart from the movie, the book had been translated into a dozen of the West's major languages—with one notable exception.

In Jerusalem, Palestine (it was not yet Israel in 1947), the Achiasaf Publishing House gave an advance of twenty-five Palestinian pounds to publish my book in Hebrew.

I received the contract and the hundred-dollar advance promptly, but on the contract, which I still have along with all the others, there is a penciled note in my own handwriting.

Adv. pd—no books rec'd.

And no books in Hebrew were ever received. When enough time had passed, with no response to my agent's queries about the expected edition, the book was offered to other publishers in Jerusalem, and never did any one of them accept and publish it.

It's only a guess, but perhaps I know why. All my foreign contracts specify, "Abbreviations or alterations shall only be made in the text thereof with the written consent of the Proprietor," the "Proprietor" being the author.

There are two brief exchanges between Phil and a Professor Lieberman, where Phil asks the scientist for his ideas about Palestine or Zionism.

"Palestine as refuge?" Professor Lieberman asks, "or Zionism as a movement for a Jewish state?" and on Phil's reply, "The confusion between the two," Lieberman seems pleased.

> "Good. If we agree there's confusion, we can talk. I can't talk to
> a positive Zionist any more than to a confirmed Communist—
> there is no language."

And in another meeting, during the crisis about "the Palestine solution," Lieberman once more explains himself to Phil.

> "Don't let them pull the crisis over your eyes. You say you
> oppose all nationalism—then how can you fall for a *religious*
> nationalism? A rejoining of church and state after all these centu-
> ries? A kind of voluntary segregation? Always for the other
> fellow, of course."

Remember, Palestine was Palestine when I wrote those lines in the middle forties; there was no Israel. It was still a time when, as Abba Eban was to write years later in *Civilization and the Jews,* "Jews thought of themselves as Frenchman and Germans and Italians and Englishmen." And I, who had written a book about the closing barriers of the nations of the world—I still was idealist enough to believe that the only true search for an end to the "Jewish problem" was for the opening of all those closed doors, so that Jews everywhere could go on thinking of themselves as Frenchmen, Germans, Italians, Americans or whatever—with Judaism their religion, but not their state.

Many years later I was to write an entire novel rooted deeply in my own changing feelings about Israel, but I will go into that when I come to the novel itself. But though I can retroactively understand that decision *not* to publish, way back there in what was still Palestine, I am not really so forgiving.

Believing in a free press as ardently as I do, I can only think I would have respected those publishers lots more if they had criticized or even cursed me for those few paragraphs—and then brought out the book anyway.

If "chasing the fast buck" were not a phrase one hesitates to use in the prestigious world of publishing, I wouldn't find myself so hard-pressed for vocabulary just now. Perhaps it would be more seemly to write about "tricks of the trade," or "clever coups."

Whichever. In rapid succession, soon after I was back in analysis, there occurred two episodes, one on the heels of the other, both dealing with money, my money, or somebody else's horning in on it, at a time when I had the rosy notion that money worries would never be mine again.

While I was priming myself to write this part of my autobiography by reading the first part again, I often found myself thinking, How aware of money you were at that time! All those specifics about what you were paid for this story, for that novelette, how much you had to borrow, how happy when you paid it off, only to have to borrow again. And how fatuous it would have been if you had left out all those specifics on some genteel theory that nice people never talked about money, that to say what you earn is in bad taste.

This struggle was the norm for most beginning writers, and still is. Recently there was a brief item in the New York *Times* about a letter Graham Greene had written to that other *Times,* the one in London, because they had run a story about the "vast sales" of his early novels.

> Greene explained that he had been in debt to his publishers for nearly 10 years, when at last he broke even in 1938 with *Brighton Rock,* which sold 8,000 copies, emboldening them two years later to risk a first printing of 3,500 copies of *The Power and the Glory.*
>
> "Just as most young writers today, I had to find other sources of income . . . It was not until 1949, at the age of 45, 20 years after my first published novel, that I was able to rely on my novels alone. Has very much changed since those days, except that publishers now have not the courage or perhaps the means, to help support a promising young author through the lean years?"

The item in the *Times,* our *Times,* was aptly headed, "The Heart of the Matter," and I think it really is. The Authors Guild of America has done much research into this subject among its six thousand members—of these six thousand only about two hundred can live on what they earn by the writing of books, fiction or nonfiction. The others have to turn elsewhere to earn their living, usually to teaching.

Well, I had done it by writing advertising and then magazine promotion, and occasional short stories and even some salaried movie writing. But it had taken me twenty-five years, since college, to become a writer who could live and support my kids by writing novels.

And suddenly, in two episodes, I was to find myself with money problems on a different plateau, involving other people as well as myself.

The first began at a corner newsstand, where the June 10, 1947, issue of Look magazine had just been delivered. The cover glared up at me in heavy black lettering.

The Year's "Hottest" Novel
Condensation of *Gentleman's Agreement*

As I slapped down my fifteen cents for a copy, a huge delivery truck rumbled away from the curb, its whole side plastered with a colored poster shouting the same words in letters ten feet high.

Inside the magazine, under the same headline, was a bank of sub-heads, all in enlarged type. "Exclusive 5,000–word Condensation" leaped out at me, and then another.

With a picture story based on the book and produced by LOOK in the studios of Twentieth Century-Fox.

What followed was no less than nine large pages carrying no fewer than eighteen photographs of Phil and Kathy and a lot of minor characters supposedly acting out scenes from the movie. The pictures were held together by patches from my book, with transitions written by somebody at Look or at the studio.

But there was something extremely odd about those eighteen photographs. Not one of them showed Gregory Peck or Dorothy McGuire or John Garfield or Celeste Holm or June Havoc or anybody else who would appear in the film.

Along the bottom of the first page, in the same minute italic print that contained the necessary mention of publisher and copyright, there came the explanation: "With Twentieth Century-Fox Players Cathy Downs as Kathy Lacey and Reed Hadey as Phil Green." The players in the other photographs weren't even named.

Five thousand words lifted for free? I began to count them but soon quit. The usual limitation for excerpts used in book reviews or feature articles in the press was five hundred. Four very long instalments of my book had appeared in Cosmopolitan magazine, in the months leading up to pub day, and had been duly paid for, with proper contracts drawn. But here was this, eighteen stand-in actors and five thousand words all in one grand surprise appearance. It had to be some great big publicity stunt dreamed up by a public relations genius at the studio or at Look.

I phoned my New York agent, the not, I'm afraid, very capable son of the founder of a well-known firm both here and in London. He had received the magazine the day before, yes, assumed I had received one too and would be calling him. He had done nothing whatever—after all, it was already on the stands.

I phoned my other agent, Bert Allenberg, through whose Hollywood office the whole movie deal had been arranged. He was as astounded as I and instantly got himself on the phone to the studio and various lawyers.

I called Dick Simon; he went into a flame-colored fury; he had been on the verge of closing a $10,000 deal with Reader's Digest for the condensation rights. This, of course, would kill the deal.

I had no lawyer then, but Bert Allenberg phoned me soon enough. He was in no mood for pleasantries; his office had drawn up the contract. I was to get my own copy and read paragraph five. He would wait while I did.

> The Owner hereby grants the Purchaser the right to publish . . . in any form or media, (including but not limited to, press books, press notices, trade journals, periodicals, newspapers, heralds, fan magazines and/or small separate booklets,) synopses, revised and/or abridged versions . . . not exceeding 5,000 words."

The original version had read "7,000," but this had been crossed out in ink and duly initialed in the margin to read "5,000."

"That paragraph," Bert said, "goes into just about every damn contract with every studio. Everybody knows damn well that it means movie magazines, fan magazines, trade papers—nothing like this has ever happened before."

But it was perfectly legal. There was nothing Bert could do except fulminate, nothing Dick could do, nothing I could do.

Maybe I should have tried to sue Look for some sort of bonus or consolation prize, or booby prize. But of course I didn't sue—with one exception that was soon to wind up, I had never been the litigious type. Apart from my divorce, which Thayer had asked for, offering me his ownership of William Morrow and Company as an inducement, an offer I had turned down saying he didn't have to bribe me—apart from the divorce suit I had virtually been forced into, I had never brought suit against anybody for anything, nor was that to change in all the years of the future. With that one lovely exception where peanuts were involved, along with a principle I held dear.

So it never occurred to me to sue Look magazine. Yet I couldn't just meekly accept it. I kept thinking, If you're going to rear up and protest about injustice for other people, why not do a little rearing when the injustice is aimed at you?

Finally I phoned Minneapolis and asked to speak to Gardner Cowles, the publisher of Look. I had met him and his handsome wife Fleur at a few parties, and knew him well enough to call him by his nickname.

"Mike, I've just seen the new issue."

He burst into congratulations on the fine book I'd written, but I cut him short. "I know it's perfectly legal," I said, "that five-thousand-word condensation, and I think it's appalling. Maybe you didn't know a thing about it."

I listened to his attempt at explanation, sensing a certain embarrassment in every word—he was usually a nice man. Then I said there was a passage in my book he might want to read again.

"It's about publishers, Mike. Mostly Jewish publishers and Christian publishers and how publishers are just publishers, minus the adjectives. But I do think some adjectives might apply—you know, ethical publishers and not-so-ethical, fair publishers and not-so-fair. Don't you?"

I can't remember what he said and never knew whether he ever did anything about it at his office. But I felt better. Nearly twenty years before, when I was a student in Baby Greek at Cornell, with a professor who constantly mispronounced my name, calling me Miss Zaminky and Miss Zamooski and even Miss Djimorskey, I had one day said, "Sir, if we're supposed to pronounce names like Clytemnestra correctly, and Iphegenia and Aeschylus, don't you think you could say Zam-*et*-kin? It's really quite easy."

That was the first time I had discovered for myself that there was something awfully good about making a stand, and this phone call to Mike Cowles gave me something of the same feeling. When I put the call through, I had known it wouldn't do any good. But it seemed the right thing to do.

To me, that's always been "true north."

Anyway, a new issue of Look soon replaced the offending one and the nastiness began to recede. But within two weeks, in that same month of June, another episode came up in my writing life, and it too was "perfectly legal." This one involved my own publishing house, or at least its treasurer and financial wizard, Leon Shimkin.

I had had a swift little sample of his wizardry three months earlier, during the happy frenzy of pub day, when he pleasantly informed me that there was $972 still unearned on my previous novel, *The Trespassers,* and that it was customary to make up the deficit from the next one.

"Oh, sure, square it away now," I had said airily, not learning for some years that it was anything but customary, and at that time not even dreaming that it might be condemned. What I did dream of was the Internal Revenue Service out there somewhere, just waiting to get its hands on me, and as the sales mounted that dream became a nightmare.

It seems to me now that despite my ability to persuade my bosses in the business world to pay me what my work was worth, even in the prefeminist years of the nineteen-twenties and thirties, I never did manage the same thing when it came to my writing. At Time, Harry Luce had been shocked at the $7,000 starting salary I asked for, but I had held out; he had survived and granted it. From then on my pay had gone up in rather dramatic jumps for the five years before I resigned.

But in the seven years since I had left Time, I had never once held out on any price set by a magazine editor or any salary offered by a movie studio. I had always been too glad to earn it. Now the coin had flipped over in a rather sensational way, and suddenly I was facing a quite literal abundance of riches, and in those days an author could be taxed up to 88 percent in a windfall year, and starve the next.

My movie contract had specified that after 50,000 copies, the studio would pay an extra royalty of twenty-five cents a copy. Supposedly a year or more would pass before reaching any such milestone, thus spreading the bounty—and any taxes thereon.

But nine days after my book appeared, S&S ran large ads in many newspapers: "78,000 copies in print—4th printing on press." I consulted my tax expert, the first one I had ever had, and then turned to my publisher and friend. By that time the ads were saying "103,000 copies in print."

"They'll grab most of it," I said to Dick Simon, "and never mind all the loans I had to make and what I still owe."

"What does your tax man say?"

"That we can add a new section to our contract, consulting the IRS in Washington first so it is on the up and up, and then spread my book royalties over several years."

"That spreading arrangement," Dick said, "has to be in the contract *before* the book comes out, not after."

"He says it can be done even afterward in certain cases if we get to the IRS and explain why."

"I'll take it up with Leon."

Soon came the good news. There had been much consultation between Leon Shimkin and my tax man and the people at the IRS and finally a long legal document was drawn up including the welcome phrase, "commencing with the year 1947, the Publisher shall not be obliged to pay to the Author, in any one year, sums aggregating more than Twenty Thousand Dollars ($20,000)."

I was relieved and thrilled; by rough calculation that meant about seven years of security brought to me by my book. The extra movie royalties would be taxed away this year, but my book was to save my inner peace and let me write other books. I never even wondered who would get the interest all that money would be earning in seven years!

As I said, I had no lawyer. I can only imagine what he would have made of certain preliminary passages in the new addition to the contract, before that limiting clause.

> **WHEREAS,** the parties hereto have had certain differences regarding the agreement between them . . .
>
> **IT IS AGREED,** that the said agreement . . . hereby is amended in the following particulars:
>
> **1.** The Publisher agrees to expend a minimum of Five Thousand Dollars ($5,000) at its own cost, on further advertising and promotion of the work in addition to any sums already spent or contracted for.
>
> **2.** The Author agrees to relinquish the sum of Five Thousand Dollars ($5,000) out of the payments receivable by her under the said agreement and authorizes the Publisher to retain said sum with the understanding that it shall be used for further advertising and promotion.

Some years later, when I finally did sign on with a law firm that specialized in authors' problems, my lawyer examined all my contracts and then gave me a vital bit of education.

"This five thousand," he began. "*Did* they spend it for extra advertising and promotion?"

"Why, I guess so—there were an awful lot of ads, even some full-page ones."

"With a best-seller like that one, they wouldn't have held back anyway." I didn't say anything. "Do you know any other successful author who was asked to chip in on promoting his own book?"

I shook my head, suddenly feeling my skin go hot.

"The usual phrase in such documents," he went on, "runs like this." He slid a slip of paper across his desk toward me. "We've used it hundreds of times, and so has every other lawyer."

> In consideration of the payment of One Dollar ($1.00) and other good and valuable consideration . . .

I read it three consecutive times and then crumpled it into a damp, agitated little spitball.

THREE

AND THEN ERIC HODGINS came back into my life. His first novel, *Mr. Blandings Builds His Dream House,* had appeared a few weeks ahead of my second one, his also published by Simon and Schuster, also being made into a major movie. I had read all his reviews, but had held back from reading the book, fearful that the wit and irony I knew I'd find in it, so typical of Eric, would stir old memories and that sense of loss, the basic ingredients, for me, of a bout of depression. And that was *before* this depression.

It was now three years since he had disappeared into that sad world of his alcoholism, three years since we had talked or written. I had thought of him often, missed him often, but without that old conviction that somehow it was *I* who had failed. I had heard about him during those absent years, heard that he had joined Alcoholics Anonymous, that he had gone back, however briefly, to his wife, and that they had had a new baby, a girl whom he doted on. I hoped that he was happier, that AA had changed him and freed him of his deepest woes.

And now, on a sunny morning in midsummer, came a letter from him. It was handwritten on the formal stationery of the University Club, and even the fact that he had written it with a careful pen instead of dashing it off on the usual typewriter of a professional writer told me that it was a letter he had taken special pains with.

Dear Laura,

I haven't written you anything about *Gentleman's Agreement* because I thought that mine might be one piece of fan mail you might prefer *not* to receive. But with everything going so magnificently for you at the top of the heap, it seems to me that by now it's getting churlish of me not to congratulate you on having struck top stride, and putting those Marquands, Steinbecks, Roberts, etc. etc. where they belong.

I haven't read *G.A.* yet, but there's a very simple reason for that: a fear that I might find some of my own less endearing characteristics embedded in some minor character on a page somewhere in the middle of the book. But I will conquer this fear in due time.

He was just back from Hollywood, he went on, where he was "naive enough, or something, to be pleased with . . . the translating of *Blandings* from book to screen."

I have to do a little mental arithmetic to guess how old Mike is (I think it must be 11 or 12) but I have less difficulty by far, in making a calculation on Chris. I hope they and you are flourishingly well, and that you don't mind this small cheep of communication.

Yours,
Eric

He must have known that this final paragraph would heighten the charge of memory for me, back to the very beginnings of our relationship, six years before, back to that day when I risked grieving him, even losing him, by telling him that I was pregnant, and already in the third month.

Not that he had wondered for a moment whether this could be his child—our own affair was less than two weeks old. But the whole question of pregnancy and childbirth, for Eric, was still one to arouse every anxiety and misery in his own being, for his first wife, Catherine, had died in childbirth years before, and he had never got over the pain of it.

But risk it I did, on the very day I knew of it myself. And though my news had rocked him, Eric was man enough to be happy for me in my happiness, and help me through the long months of waiting and "hiding out." So of course he could now "make a calculation" on Christopher's age, probably to the very day.

The one thing I had not told him was who "Hugh," Chris' father, was, nor did he ever want to know. Though Hugh had been out of my life for two months or more, I'm sure Eric didn't even wish to acknowledge that there had been a Hugh. But that seemed to be his only reluctance. He knew I would have to go ahead with this last chance, at the age of forty-one, to give birth to a baby for the first time in my life, and he also had been full of understanding when, a little later I told him of a plan I had been working out for after my baby was born.

"Mike will be five-and-a-half by then," I said. "I can't risk hurting him." I never wanted Mike to feel "different" from the new baby, I said, never wanted him to feel jealous, perhaps to be taunted later by a kid brother who said, "You were adopted, but mommy *had* me."

The one way I could prevent it was to duplicate what I had gone through with Mike years before—go through court proceedings for a legal adoption. I would adopt my own baby.

I had told Dr. Damon I would go out to The Cradle in Evanston to do it, but he had assured me we could arrange a private adoption right here in the courts of New York, and that he would have one of the city's best-known law firms take charge of it for me.

"Of course I will tell Mike and Chris," I had assured Eric. "Years from now, I don't know how many years—maybe when they're adolescents, maybe not until Chris is twenty-one and Mike a man of twenty-six, when they'd both be mature enough to handle whatever it is they're going to feel about it."

And now, six years later, in this unexpected letter, Eric was remembering backward to those weeks and months of my happy and secret pregnancy, back to those good days of our being so close.

Except for his drinking, he had from the start struck me as one of the most original and decent people I had ever known. He was nothing like any of the men I had known; there was nothing light or romantic about him. He was homely, with a good intelligent face; it would never have occurred to him to take you to a nightclub or out dancing; he loved music, as I did, and books, and we were always on the same side about politics; never was he one of the people who seemed so sure Russia could do no wrong, as my own sister Alice did, and so many of my friends and Ralph Ingersoll's friends.

I remember reading that letter of his again and again. I waited a week before answering, and then I did what I rarely did, wrote a first draft of my answer on my typewriter, and then copied it out by hand after it reached what I regarded as the right tone. I have that first draft still, and see that in those days I affected a blue typewriter ribbon in my machine.

Well, Eric—

That was a bolt from the blue, all right, and far from "minding," I was pleased. Last fall, I'd had the impulse to write you my congratulations about the Book of the Month Club selection of *Mr. Blandings* and your own movie sale, but I guess I'm the timid type because I let it slide.

So, as I read your letter, I thought how mature and self-contained you sounded, and decided that your analysis must have come lots closer to being 100% successful than mine. That depressed me, but then I came to the part about your not having read *G.A.* because of your fears of finding something uncomplimentary to you in it—and at once I cheered up and felt less inferior . . .

I wish you had read it, because then this letter would have told me what you thought of it. If you want to, you can start in, minus the fears and tensions . . .

I haven't read your book either (I'll read yours now if you read mine) . . . I was, and am, uncomplicatedly glad for you about the great success you've had with the book. What queer things have happened to each of us as writers!

There followed a couple of lines about my two boys and good wishes for his two children. I remember that I tried two or three separate versions of a suitable ending.

Which seems to bring me to a full stop. It was strange to hear from you, and strangely nice.

Five days later, he wrote once more, this time in his more usual fashion, by typewriter, single-spacing two long pages, again on the stationery of the University Club, that all-male (at that time and for many years to come) bastion for members distinguished in one field or another.

Laura,

I'll tell you just how "mature and self-contained" (your words) I was when I wrote you my letter of congratulation: all I expected was the snub of no answer at all. So when I got to New York yesterday and found the blue envelope with the so-familiar handwriting, I was affected in all sorts of ways.

It's a deal: I will start reading *G.A.* tonight if you will tackle *Mr. B . . .* In one respect I think I can guarantee you will find it interesting: it is an unrelenting attack on its principal character, which is me . . .

Having the letter in my hand again reminds me that the one phrase that caught at me most in his delightful beginning was, "So when I got to New York yesterday." He must be living out of town, in the "Dream House," no doubt, up in New Milford, Connecticut, with his wife and son and daughter. So he had returned to family life for good. In the intervening years I had never been sure; some of my friends who knew him kept indicating that there was a sadness in him about this second marriage.

I kept pondering that *got to New York yesterday* and then went back to his letter.

As to the fascinating subject of analysis (psycho) I wouldn't have the faintest idea how to calculate the percentage of success that applied to mine. Very low, I often think, so you can be cheered accordingly. The most consistent thought I have about it is that it helps in ways you do not expect, and hadn't asked for . . . What I wanted out of mine, and what I prayed for, was some measure of serenity, and this I did not get.

Many times, in the years since, I have quoted those words of Eric's to people asking about analysis, at the beginning attributing them only to "a wonderful, troubled man I know," and then, many years later, after his death, directly to him. What he did get, he wrote, was the "courage to quit [his] increasingly hateful job in the Time Inc hierarchy" and go back to writing, finding there "a sort of irregular and not-to-be-counted-on serenity."

He was funny about the best-seller list: "I think *Blandings* had a toe-hold on ninth place . . . so I felt a flash of good high-minded professional jealousy," and went on with another full page. And then came the last paragraph.

Getting your letter makes me very much want to ask your permission to pay a call on you, during this week that I am in New York. I'm afraid you will regard this as a ferociously bad idea, but I'll be god damned if I'll be so timid as not to record it.

Pay a call. It was so formal, so old-fashioned a locution. Was he telling me that he knew perfectly well that there could be no resumption of our long-abandoned closeness? Was he assuring me that this would be just a visit, a little spot of talk and laughter, and nothing beyond that?

Was that what I wanted him to mean? I don't know why I can still remember so clearly that I was filled with uncertainty, but remember it I surely do. *When I get to New York.* A sailor arriving in port for some rest and recreation? That analogy did me in.

Again I treated myself to a first draft on my blue-ribboned typewriter, retaining the first draft along with the other, and reading it again a couple of times even after I had mailed it.

Dear Eric,

This second letter led me along pleasantly, with me full of complimentary reactions to your wit and grace, and then I came to that last paragraph about . . . "paying a call."

At once I found myself, if not in a State of Panic, at least in a State of Conflict, (my two candidates for admission as the 49th and 50th States of the Union.) Which explains why I have (timidly) let two days go by, so there wouldn't be enough time to make "a call" possible this week anyway.

Having thus artistically arranged to evade the issue for now, I am left with the shilly-shallying, non-competent plan to postpone everything, read *Mr. Blandings,* which arrived this morning, write you about that, and count my beads in a state of innocent suspension until somebody forces my hand or something else helpful occurs. (Which ought to give you a fair grading on *my* analysis.)

. . . This isn't even supposed to be an answer to your letter. As you see, that last paragraph screened off all the rest.

Yours,
Laura

I began *Blandings* that same day. The inscription was pure Eric.

From Mr. B.
To Laura Z.
A novelist of lustre
With whom I share
As far's I dare,
The firm of Simon-Schustre

And with gratitude and deep
affection to
Laura,
from
Eric

His next letter began, "I think it is a very calm and judicious decision, the shilly-shally." He was already reading *G.A.*, he said, "reading on two levels at once: 1) *it* is a novel; 2) I know *her.*" He added, "All right, now tackle *Blandings*. You will find it completely inconsequential." It was his final paragraph that I read several times over:

> The letter of critique you have promised to write me will not mildew at the Univ Club; I "get down," as they say, every fortnight or so. It seems inevitable to me that I will renew my request to pay a call on you, so tell your beads and tell them good.

As I read his book, also reading on two levels—*it* is a novel, I know *him*—I was conscious of a third level, that of wondering whether I really wanted to risk resuming our old relationship. I was not enough of an innocent to think that this time everything would be platonic: I knew Eric and I knew myself. He had never been happy with this second marriage of his; even through the charm and humor of his new book, it came through clearly that there was a good deal of stress and irritation between husband and wife. But I knew it also from people who often saw the Hodginses.

And I knew myself; I was already in a period of letdown, of uncertainty; more than that it seemed that I hadn't been in love with, or loved by, anybody for long lonely ages. I was trying to handle it, trying to accept the deficits in my life along with all the still-surprising abundances.

When I answered Eric, of course, I said nothing of this, nor of his "call." I permitted myself to be a "fellow writer," talking about his book. *Mr. Blandings Builds His Dream House* is about a young couple, city-bred, who come upon a marvelous old antique house in the hills of Connecticut, become obsessed with the notion of remodeling it, and then fall heir to the thousand trials and tribulations that seem inevitable enemies of such dreamers. It made a delightful moving picture, starring Cary Grant and Myrna Loy.

> I had already read *Mr. Blandings* before you . . . informed me that it was "inconsequential" so I missed that fact entirely. I found it all the things I'd read it was—clever, amusing, beautifully written, but I also found it deeply touching because it is—for me —informed with the sadness that lies in the vast disparity between the dream and the reality.
>
> For me that disparity is one of the big themes for any writer, whether he be a humorist as you are, or a solemn crusading type like me. . . .
>
> I suppose every reader always finds in any good book the things he carries to it and places there; certainly in *Mr. B.* I found, under all the urbanity and funny situations and skilful writing, many things I know of you and me and of all people like us.

I had not been prompt about writing that letter, and I knew perfectly well that I was stalling for time, willing to keep on hesitating, putting off decision. I was still seeing Dr. Gosselin and talking it out with him, but as for any specific advice from him about what to do, nothing. As usual from him.

It was being a busy summer anyway. I had rented a too large, too expensive place in Wilton, Connecticut, complete with *en tout cas* tennis court and natural swimming pool—no real estate broker would even show me a modest little place, saying I had started house-hunting months too late for any such lucky find.

Just before moving out for the summer I had made a fancy backhand swoop after a tennis ball on the city courts where I used to play, had torn the Achilles tendon in my leg, and was on crutches while all my weekend guests and neighbors made use of my tennis court before my envious eyes.

I began once more to fret a little about what all the upsurge of talk about my book and the coming movie was doing to my children. Mike's vocabulary had changed. Not yet eleven, he was constantly relaying questions to me from his schoolmates and summertime friends: who was to star in the movie, was it already filming, at the studio or "on location," where would it officially open on Broadway, and when?

Chris, going on six, also threw a dart of worry at me one summer evening. I was having five or six friends over for dinner and the weekly poker game that would follow; it was a traveling game, going from house to house, and that week was my turn. I remember that Norman Cousins was there, and Clifton Fadiman, and other devotees of the game, all strong players.

Norman Cousins was to tell me, long years later, that it was I who had made a winning player out of him so he could join our games. I had gone over to his house, he told me, for an entire evening, dealing out hands for him to play, hands of stud, straight five-card poker, seven-card high-low and the rest of the serious repertoire—no deuces wild, spit-in-the-ocean or other childish variations. I made him play three of the hands while I was in charge of two, teaching him the odds, when to raise, when to fold, when to see. According to him, we two sat there for about four hours, dealing hand after hand, round after round, stacking our chips as if they represented hard cash, "buying" another stake when one of us was cleaned out.

But he doesn't remember that one particular evening before our Saturday night poker game when Chris threw me that sharp little dart of worry.

The boys weren't yet old enough to sit in on dinner when I had guests, but at one point Chris wandered in to the dining room and said his hello to each guest in turn. Then he spoke to the room at large, making an announcement.

"Tomorrow mommy's book will be number one."

"How do you know that, Chris?" somebody asked.

"Because it's Sunday," he answered blandly.

Everybody laughed, but I didn't think it was all that funny. I redoubled my efforts to play things down, at least when Mike and Chris were around, and never knew for certain whether I was succeeding. Any more than I knew for certain what to do about Eric.

And when the summer was over and we were back in New York again, I suddenly had a perfect reason for further procrastination, a reason I welcomed not only for itself, perhaps, but also for the escape it gave me from personal dilemma.

All at once I was in a storm of work on a political matter, the very kind that seized me to the bottom of my being, because it had to do with communism on the one hand and freedom on the other.

A famous Broadway star telephoned me one day, asking me to sign a protest to appear in the newspapers about the "Hollywood Ten." Even all these years later, I do not like to name names, so I'll let him be anonymous.

"I never sign anything," I said, "without reading it first and seeing who else is signing it. So could you mail it to me?"

"I'll rush it by messenger—we want to release it tonight."

The Hollywood Ten was the latest and largest of the many communist-hunts that had taken permanent lodgings in the era of the "cold war," after the close of the hot war in 1945. They were all flourishing in the acid atmosphere of suspicion and hatred where not only actual communists but every liberal who had ever sent ten dollars to some group opposing racism or poverty or injustice was suddenly in black jeopardy from anybody who pointed an accusing finger and said, "Communist," or "Fellow-traveler" or just plain "Commie." Guilt by association became a national phenomenon overnight.

Actually it wasn't all that sudden. The Martin Dies committee had begun early in the thirties to investigate the New Deal's Federal Theater for "un-American propaganda activities"; one Elizabeth Dilling had begun a catalogue, "The Red Network," listing such as Theodore Dreiser, Sinclair Lewis, Upton Sinclair, Eleanor Roosevelt and even the YMCA and the YWCA as potential or practicing enemies of the nation; the radio demagogue, Father Charles Coughlin, and other self-appointed defenders of the U.S. of A. from atheistic communism—all were holding forth incessantly in print, on the air, from the pulpit, anywhere.

But the Hollywood Ten hearings, starting their business in the world of glamor before moving on to Washington, made all their predecessors seem like bit players. Their chairman was Representative J. Parnell Thomas (later to be indicted for payroll-padding) but he was aided by such luminaries as young Congressman Richard M. Nixon and Congressman John Rankin, who had become part of my writing life nearly four years before when, in the House of Representatives, he had referred to the columnist Walter Winchell as "the little kike I was telling you about."

It was Chairman Thomas who proudly announced that he had compiled a list of "all motion pictures . . . in the last eight years . . . which contain communist propaganda," and who sent subpoenas forth to over forty filmmakers, film-writers and film stars to come and testify before HUAC. About half of them refused; they were promptly labeled unfriendly witnesses, a title guaranteed to atomize one's career on the lush payrolls of the studios.

There were lots of friendlies, though. Ronald Reagan appeared, with Robert Montgomery, to assure the committee that there were *no* communists in the Screen Writers Guild; big folk like Adolphe Menjou, Walt Disney, Gary Cooper, Ginger Rogers' mother Lela, Jack Warner and other studio heads all showed up with alacrity. Mr. Warner testified that Elia Kazan was "one of the mob," because he had directed *Boomerang* for Twentieth Century-Fox, and was now "going somewhere to make another picture for them."

"What picture?"

"*Gentleman's Agreement.*"

It wasn't only in the movies that the frenzy was on. In the radio world, the still young television world as well, the cloud was building and bursting; through every network, every advertising agency producing radio or TV shows, among the sponsors of those shows and the agents for the actors and writers and directors. Though *Red Channels* had not yet appeared as a published book, with its index of thousands of names, one slight whisper over a thrifty one-martini lunch was enough to get people blacklisted—and suddenly without a job or a contract or any prospect of ever getting a new one.

As for the Hollywood Ten, most of whom were writers and all of whom would go to jail, their professional lives in the fields of movie-making were vaporized.

Yet when that famous Broadway star telephoned to ask me to sign the advertisement being planned, my request to have a look at what it said and who would be signing it was in no way merely a delaying tactic, no ploy to stall off an answer.

Way back at Time magazine, where I had very nearly signed up with many other Time Inkers for membership in the Spanish-American Anti-Fascist Committee, only to become convinced that there was an interior purpose in that committee that was not *my* interior purpose, that their basic aim was not so much to further the Loyalist cause for a democratic Spain as it was to further the Communist Party's desire for a communist Spain—back then, about eleven years before, I had begun to read not only the names of committees I was asked to join, but also the names of the people comprising the committees themselves. When I saw names of people who I knew would never sign any protest I might write about the loss of freedom-to-oppose in Russia, about its labor camps, about its various trials and purges, I always declined to go along with that committee, no matter how fine and idealistic its stated purpose. Always I felt, underneath all the words, their purpose is not *my* purpose.

By early 1941, my polite declining had been transformed into something more active. On April 7, 1941, I carefully wrote a certain letter that I've kept in my files along with others which were to follow; they are all in a large folder marked POLITICAL. This first letter was to the League of American Writers, asking that my name be removed from its mailing list. The group was about to hold its fourth "Congress of American Writers," and I was being bombarded with requests for donations and invitations to attend the Congress.

Pearl Harbor had not yet happened; we were not yet in the war; the ten-year nonaggression pact between Nazi Germany and the Soviet Union was still in effect; the war itself was still called the "imperialist war" by all of the Russia-can-do-no-wrong people; the changeover to the "people's war" was still a few months off, after the Nazis attacked the USSR.

I knew a good deal about the league. I owned a book about its first congress, in 1935, and the book had fascinated me. Not all the members of the league were famous writers, but most of the leading names were. A few of these were perfectly open about being communists or being sympathetic to communism, but more than a few fiercely denied anything of the sort. But that first congress, said the book about it, had opened with an address by Earl Browder, the Communist Party's candidate for president of the United States in the 1936 and 1940 elections:

It is with these thoughts that the Communist Party greets this historic Congress of American Writers. We are all soldiers, each in our own place, in a common cause. Let our efforts be united in fraternal solidarity.

The congress was a long one. It ended in song, said the book's final paragraph, proposed by a famous writer. (Again I will let him remain anonymous.)

When the applause died down, —— arose and suggested that the Congress conclude its final session by singing the "Internationale." This was done.

The letter I wrote, I see now, was far too long; it made too many points to explain my position about communism itself and why I had concluded that the league supported most of its basic tenets. But it did get down to business in one or two sentences that I was to make use of in the years ahead in polite discussion, heated arguments or passionate fights.

> I could never conceivably accept any theory of government based on the assumption that open opposition to a government's platform is treason—not to a platform but to one's country, and thus punishable by prison or death.

I wrote about why I disagreed with the thesis that the end justifies the means. "Means *shape* ends ... you can't, fifty years hence, turn a switch on and endow men with a beautiful freedom and democracy—men in whom the capacity to think independently and freely will have atrophied by then." And then I explained why I didn't do the simple thing and throw their many letters and invitations into the wastebasket and forget them.

> I think that most democratic liberals have let themselves for too long be hamstrung into demure silence on the Communist issue ... because we know that to call something "Communist" is the glib weapon of red-baiting reactionaries everywhere. But I think that now more democratic liberals must be ready to challenge those groups they see supporting the party line, lest the only challengers *be* the reactionaries.

This letter was, in some ways, to be the prototype of many future letters. Each time, my letter grew shorter, tighter; as time went on I was less careful to explain what a fine liberal I was and how I detested red-baiting.

After Russia was attacked there was a vast proliferation of "popular front" or "united front" groups all over the country. The most famous in America was known as ICCASP, the Independent Citizens Committee of the Arts, Sciences and Professions. I was a member, along with many thousands of better-knowns.

Like every other member I received many an "Action Bulletin" and a less frequent "Emergency Bulletin" urging members to write or wire the White House or Congress on this or that matter. Those bulletins began to interest me, and I began to wonder why they also worried me.

They're always right on the party line. When this conclusion lodged itself in my mind and in my political awareness, such as it was, I began what turned into a several-months' correspondence with the executive secretary of ICCASP, saying I might want to resign, but in order to help me decide, would ICCASP tell me who constituted the committee that decided on the content of these various bulletins, and how large a segment of the membership was consulted before policy was arrived at.

Two months went by before an answer arrived, naming all the people on the executive committee and ending, "I am sure you will agree that the importance of maintaining . . . ICCASP transcends by far the occasional difference that all of us are bound to have on one or two issues." When I replied, I said I was not troubled "by occasional difference . . . on one or two issues."

> I have received, as all members have, over a hundred action bulletins in the past two years. In them I have found ICCASP criticizing—and rightly—the errors, mistakes, stupidities, imperialisms of this country, of Britain, of individuals and parties. But never, as I recall it, has there ever been one word of criticism of anything done or favored by the USSR. . . . never . . . one bulletin calling for the expression of dissension, disapproval or even careful examination of anything done or favored by the USSR.
>
> If I am incorrect, or my memory faulty, would you send me copies of such bulletins which were at variance with the party-liners' position? . . .
>
> If I am correct . . . you will see why to me this seems a dangerous lack of independence indeed for an Independent Citizens Committee.

For some years, because I was so often asked to write full-page newspaper protests on political matters, I had made it my business to *know* what the party line was. I not only read the anti-Roosevelt, isolationist press on the far right—the Hearst, McCormick and Patterson newspapers—but also the *Daily Worker* on the far left, and I knew from week to week what the CP's often-changing position was.

Indeed it was because I did know the party line that I once got a tongue lashing I've never forgotten. It was while I was still engaged to Ingersoll and having lunch with one of his close friends, Lillian Hellman, that all hell broke loose. We were in the handsome high-ceilinged Edwardian Room at the Plaza Hotel, and it was near Christmas, with the war only three months old.

But another war had just broken out between Russia and her small neighbor Finland. The USSR had demanded that Finland demilitarize her fortifications facing Leningrad and relinquish certain military bases. Finland refused and Russian troops had invaded.

The pro-Russian press was full of the war over Finland's aggressive move, and of course, at lunch that day, Lillian and I were soon talking about the latest news. She said something about Finland's aggression against the Soviets, and I'm sure my eyebrows flew up. I remember protesting that it was hardly likely that tiny Finland would start fighting mighty Russia, and added that, of course, she had every right to see it that way, since she was sympathetic to communism while I was not.

"Don't you dare say I'm sympathetic to communism." Her voice rose in fury. "I never said that—how dare you say it?"

People at all the adjacent tables stopped eating and stared at us as she berated me. I tried to placate her, to calm her down. The waiter was arriving, ready to serve us, so neither of us could get up and leave. I managed somehow to get in enough words to explain my position.

"It's like a surveyor doing a job," I said. "Checking one point and then another. If a man thinks Jews are terrible, I call him an anti Semite, but not a Nazi. If he thinks the Versailles Treaty was too harsh against Germany, I don't call him a Nazi. If he thinks Germany really needs more *Lebensraum* as Hitler demands, I still don't call him a Nazi. But if he thinks all three things simultaneously, then I decide he's a Nazi."

Lillian Hellman was no shrinking violet when she was in a temper. Neither am I. If this were my sister Alice, I'm sure I'd have been shouting too—or bursting into tears as I often did in a bad quarrel. When I could go on with Lillian, I extended my point. If a man hates capitalism, I don't say he's sympathetic to communism; if he's a Marxist, I don't say he's a communist; even if he thinks Stalin was justified to gain time by making that nonaggression pact with Hitler, I still don't. But when he's on the button on all three points, then I do say he's at least a sympathizer . . .

Mercifully, my memory doesn't tell me how we ever got through that lunch and out of that handsome and dignified Edwardian Room. But I felt I could rely on my little surveying method, and it had served me again on all those action bulletins and emergency bulletins constantly sent out by ICCASP.

So when I wrote to ask for any bulletins I might have missed, I ended my letter very politely.

> In the next weeks I will try to decide one way or another—and
> either resign or try to be more useful *as* a member.

This time there was no reply. I waited a couple of months and in January 1947 I resigned. By the time the messenger came with the ad about the Hollywood Ten, I had already put in several years of clarifying my own positions. I read the copy swiftly and its famous signatures slowly. Virtually every one was a celebrity of the first rank. I will not name them either, but I knew, alas, that these were people I would never, could never, enlist on my side in any of the bitter dissensions of the day.

I went to the phone to call the Broadway star and tell him I could not add my name to all the others. But before dialing, I paused. What kind of thing would I be writing if it were *my* ad in protest of those Washington hearings?

I began jotting down phrases, bits of copy, headlines. After my years as promotion writer for Time, Life, Fortune, for groups like Friends of Democracy and the Fight For Freedom Committee, for the election to a third term for Franklin D. Roosevelt in 1940 and many other political matters, I had enough reputation to feel certain that if I wrote something cogent enough, there would be some group somewhere willing to sign that protest and put up the funds to see that it appeared in the press.

> We are against
> "party-liners"
> We are *also* against
> witch-hunts
> The undersigned are political opponents of communists and
> party-liners and fellow-travelers.
> We fight them politically.
> We are also enemies of inquisitors in the police-state tradition.
> We fight *them* politically—or, as now, by public protest.

I felt, even with that much written, that I could indeed write something other people would support. I wanted to finish the entire copy, but the messenger was sitting there in my living room. I dialed the man who was waiting for my decision.

"I can't sign your ad," I said, "because I recognize too many people who wouldn't sign any protest I might write about other people whose freedom I want to defend, like the Moscow Ten or the Warsaw Ten. But I'm going to write an ad about this, and I'll ask you and every one of your signers to sign my ad. I just jotted down the headline and a couple of opening paragraphs. Let me read it to you."

And I did. As I remember it, there were a few murmurs and some silence, and the boy left with the proof of his ad, and then I went back to my copy and dashed off a first draft of the rest of it.

Came the question: who would underwrite it in the papers? The Fight For Freedom Committee was war-born and war-oriented. I think it was no longer active by late 1947. I thought of other committees I had worked with; they had become less active too. But I thought of the young new committee that had just come into being, ADA, which described itself as being on "the uncompromising, non-communist Left."

I called Jim Loeb, then unknown to me, its executive secretary in Washington. I told him about the other ad, about my reasons for being unwilling to sign it and about the piece of copy I had just written.

"It's still very rough," I said, "but could I read it aloud to you? I know I can get lots of well-known people to sign it—but would Americans for Democratic Action be willing to be the overall sponsor, where people could send in contributions and know who was backing the whole thing?"

I read the headline and stopped. He made a sound that I felt I could interpret as approval. Then I read him the rest of it. Those opening paragraphs had set the tone for the whole.

> The whole nasty business of the present Washington "hearing" and the rest of the "red witch-hunt" that hides behind loyalty pledges needs to be fought. Fought in the name of the civil liberties which all police states deny their citizens.
>
> The Hollywood people being "investigated" by the Thomas-Rankin committee are citizens of the country which boasts free speech, free political opinion, free thought. If *their* civil liberties can be taken from them, then civil liberties for all Americans no longer are guaranteed.
>
> We have no love for communists and party-liners. We refuse

to work with them in political committees, we campaign and vote against them. But these are *democratic* methods. Witch hunts are the methods of hysteria.

Is hysteria to grow—without challenge? Are men and women in this country to live in fear that tomorrow they too may be yanked up "under suspicion" by some busy committee, department head or employer?

IT DOESN'T TAKE
BURNING FAGOTS
TO STAGE A WITCH HUNT.
BLAZING FLASH BULBS AND
KLIEG LIGHTS WILL SERVE.

The ad ended with the statement that the undersigned, members and nonmembers of the ADA, the sponsor of the advertisement, were asking for contributions so that it might appear in every city in the land.

When I read the copy to Jim Loeb in Washington that day, it was not yet in this final form, but even so he said at once he thought it could be arranged. He would have to take it up with other people, but I wasn't to wait for formal permission. Send him the final copy and go ahead in the meantime with the signatures.

And here I *will* name names, sixty-seven names, men and women who were in the theater, in Hollywood, in journalism and publishing, in the very fields that were already the most threatened and harassed in the nation. I am impressed once more as I read those names again, many of whom were to be characterized by some as "frightened liberals," the "scoundrels" who did nothing, who could be excoriated even thirty years later as those intellectual, weak scaredy-cats who stayed silent, while only one or two heroic souls stood up to fight.

Those names were signed, remember, five full years before the heyday of the McCarthy Committee.

Franklin P. Adams	Aline Bernstein	Norman Cousins
Agnes Rogers Allen	Harry Brandt	Thomas Coward
Frederick Lewis Allen	Louis Calhern	Russel Crouse
Theodore Amussen	Bennett Cerf	Homer Croy
Maxwell Anderson	Thomas Chalmers	Dorothy Fields
Lemuel Ayres	Hector Chevigny	Herbert Fields
Peggy Bacon	Dorothy Claire	Wolcott Gibbs
Maximilian Becker	Vincent Connolly	Alan Green
Ulric Bell	Allan Correli	Harold K. Guinzburg

John Gunther	Elizabeth Janeway	Sol Pernick
Robert Haas	E. J. Kahn, Jr.	Bill Robinson
Philip P. Hamburger	MacKinlay Kantor	Richard Rodgers
Oscar Hammerstein II	Fred C. Kelly	Bella and Sam Spewack
Moss Hart	Chester Kerr	Isaac Stern
Helen Hayes	Rollin Kirby	Dorothy Stickney
John Hersey	Howard Lindsay	Rex Stout
Laura Z. Hobson	George Macy	Barnard Straus
Quincy Howe	Leopold Mannes	Edith Sulkin
Charles Jackson	Dolores Martin	James Ramsey Ullman
Bessie Rowland James	Dorothy Norman	David Wayne
Marquis James	Donald Oenslager	Jerome Weidman
Eliot Janeway	Paul Osborn	Kurt Weill

It was Bella Spewack, of the playwriting Sam and Bella, who rounded up an awful lot of the signatures, but I did a wholesale business, too, of telephoning everybody I knew in publishing and screenwriting and novel-writing, saying how the ad came into being, reading it aloud, asking for support of their signature.

The ad duly ran, and it proved to be a milestone in my life—my first statement, in public, of my commitment to what Louis Fischer, the author, had once labeled the "double rejection," or which, to go further back into my own past, had been a lifelong principle of my father's, always a Marxist but never a communist.

In an important book, *The Forging of Socialism in America,* published by the University of South Carolina Press, Professor Howard Quint had written about a "group of oppositionists" who had broken away from the Socialist Labor Party to found the *Jewish Daily Forward,* with my father as "its first editor in April 1897."

"Zametkin . . . vigorously opposed both the reactionary right and the revolutionary left," said Professor Quint.

And here was I, fifty years later, carrying on that principle and openly accepting both sides of that same equation. Because each of the sixty-seven people signing my ad had to be told all about it, it soon became common knowledge that it was I who had written it.

That plus *Gentleman's Agreement* and the coming movie had a profound effect on my next years. Soon I was invited to meetings of the New York Board of the American Civil Liberties Union and not long after became one of the members of the board, remaining one for decades.

And the very week that the movie finally did open on Broadway, I was one of the guests, seated on the dais, at a dinner given by

Americans for Democratic Action in the Grand Ballroom of the Waldorf-Astoria. To be seated on the same platform with Eleanor Roosevelt was honor indeed; one of her sons was also there, Franklin D. Jr., and the famous labor leader, David Dubinsky, president of the International Ladies Garment Workers Union, who gave me a delightful surprise by coming up to me, putting his arms around me and saying "I knew your father."

One other guest was there, unknown to me, the young mayor of Minneapolis, who, people said, would soon run for the United States Senate. He seemed too young to aspire to so great a post, for he was only thirty-six. His name was Hubert Horatio Humphrey and I took to him right away, never dreaming that I would ever see him again, certainly not in my own house.

---- CHAPTER ----

FOUR

AND THEN, AT LAST, came the movie itself. I first saw it in the morning, in a private showing in the projection room of Twentieth Century-Fox, way over on West Fifty-seventh Street near Tenth Avenue.

My log for October 27, 1947, says at the top, "Zanuck not coming," and below that, "Moss and Kitty Hart, Elia and Molly Kazan, 20th Century people. '21.'"

Down below, on that same page: "God, it's good!"

I cannot, try as I may, remember Moss and Kitty there, nor Gadge and Molly; I do not remember our going to "21" afterward, presumably for lunch and champagne.

All I do remember, in a primal memory that is free of later associations, is myself sitting there in a large screening room with big fat plush seats, perhaps two hundred of them, nearly all empty, sitting there in a small cluster of people, waiting for the overhead lights to dim and the film to begin.

Vaguely I think John Garfield was in that small cluster of people, that I met him and congratulated him afterward, the only member of the cast. I had met Gregory Peck some months before when they were doing a scene over on Beekman Place, near the East River; I had taken my two kids with me to watch, thinking that they would like to see a movie being made, though all they saw and all I saw was a dozen different takes of a yellow taxicab sweeping to the curb before an attractive private house where Kathy was supposed to live, with Gregory Peck exiting from the cab and disappearing into the front door. (Even that much had thrilled me—it was *my* book being made into a movie, but years later Mike and Chris told me that after the first taxi or two they had been bored to death.)

Those minor taxi scenes had long since departed from my mind as I sat there in that projection room, watching the opening "cards" come up on the screen, hearing the music, watching Peck and his young son begin their walk from the fountain in front of the Plaza Hotel down Fifth Avenue to the statue of Atlas at Rockefeller Center, to meet Phil's mother at Saks Fifth Avenue.

Each moment gripped me, and I admired Moss Hart's ability to use dialogue to set the entire background of Phil's character, but it was not until my own words began to come at me from the screen that there was a quantum jump to a new plateau of emotion for me. It is an early scene, where Phil tells his mother at the breakfast table of his reluctance to accept his new assignment from Smith's Weekly, and his son idly asks, "What *is* anti-Semitism, anyway, dad?"—it was then that my eyes stung with heat and tears, and the hammer of pride began its beat against my ribcage.

The public press screenings began the next morning, and I went to several of them, each time taking some of my friends—my editor Lee Wright and her husband, the Whedons, Dick and Andrea Simon, my sister Alice, and once my son Mike, who seemed absorbed in it, though I was sure it was no film for an eleven-year-old.

I couldn't be sure though. Once I did ask him, "What do *you* think 'prejudice' is, Mike?" and he thought it over for a minute or two, his forehead wrinkling.

"Well, I guess it's when you decide a guy's a stinker before you even meet him."

He was eleven at the time.

The press screenings were only part of the fortnight that followed. Zanuck, we were told, could not carry out his plans to give some large parties in New York because a two-million-dollar lawsuit of some sort was hanging over his head the moment he crossed the state line into New York, so he had commandeered Moss and Gadge Kazan and me to take turns giving black-tie parties for favored folk, especially those connected with the press, the theater, publishing, or café society, as the "beautiful people" were then called.

Gadge could do little; he was in the midst of directing a new

Tennessee Williams play, *A Streetcar Named Desire,* so the hosting duties fell to me and Moss.

The first one was at my house, first the screening and then back to my house for the party. My log lists about twenty names, close friends, many of whom fitted Zanuck's specifications, like Harry Scherman and his wife Bernardine; Charles Jackson, author of *The Lost Weekend,* and his wife Rhoda; Raymond Massey and Dorothy; Joseph Lash and his wife Trude, close friends of Eleanor Roosevelt. (Joe was later to write many books about the Roosevelts and win a Pulitzer Prize.) And of course Moss Hart and Kitty.

If ever praise from one's guests sounded genuine it did that night, and Moss and I openly reveled in it. At what Zanuck calculated to be the proper time, he telephoned from California to get everybody's reactions. He held me on the phone for a good fifteen minutes, then Moss took over and was connected for an even longer time.

There was, however, one blight for me on that wonderful evening. Dorothy Massey and I had gone to my bathroom to touch up our makeup. She had been my friend for years, though we differed on politics; Republican though she was, and normally not a whit interested in things like Freedom Pavilion, she had nevertheless quickly put up her own two hundred dollars to pay for seven pages of newsprint for The Nation in order to let them print an article I had written about those "people of status and power" in New York who had combined to kill it off in its final stages.

Dorothy had raved about the movie, predicting it would be a smash hit; every time she did so I winced, for she kept saying how great Julie Garfinkle was in it.

"John Garfield," I would say each time.

"Julie Garfinkle," she would repeat a moment later.

"You mean John Garfield." I said it quietly enough, I remember; there we stood, two women in evening dress, each getting angry and trying to remain polite.

I must have thought of my own line about not wanting to make "a fuss, a mess, an inconvenience," for after about the third Julie Garfinkle I asked her why the special name?

"It's just old habit," she said.

I knew it couldn't be old habit. It was early in the thirties, at the beginning of the Group Theater, that he had changed his name, and Dorothy at that time was married to a lawyer and knew nothing whatever about the theater that she couldn't see from an orchestra seat.

"You might as well call him Julie Jewboy," I said, and for the first time in my life I knew what it meant when somebody said, "She bridled."

"We will never discuss this again," she said frostily.

I still tried for another minute to make her see that though she agreed with what I wrote about the unconscious revelations of anti-Semitism among nice people, it was only when I was talking or writing about "other people." When it came to my own friends, I was dead wrong.

But it was no use. I was supposed to go over to her house to play bridge on the following Sunday; I called it off by a note and it was twenty years before we ever saw each other again.

The very next night Moss Hart was host at his first party, and his list of guests would have lighted up half the marquees on Broadway. George S. Kaufman was there, and Lillian Hellman; Greer Garson; Max Gordon, the producer; Elsa Maxwell, hostess to the rich and famous; Arlene Francis and Martin Gabel and a dozen others.

And so it went, night after night, until the official opening at the Mayfair Theater on Broadway (with a whole row of seats roped off for us) and the Apollo in Chicago. Zanuck had made it in time, just under the deadline for the Academy Awards for that year.

Moss and I saw it once more, the first public showing to a movie audience. He could tell better than I what that hush meant, but amateur though I was, I felt it too. And when the audience streamed out, I heard all the comments around me, just as Moss did, and out in the street once more we hugged each other and we both knew everything was going to be good.

The reviews next morning were unanimous.

Extraordinary achievement . . . one of the finest films of this or any year. (Cue)

The screen version of Laura Z. Hobson's eloquent and indignant novel, has clothed a subject of portentous meaning in terms of irresistible entertainment. (Tribune)

The spectacular critical, popular and financial success of . . . [the book] Gentleman's Agreement should be repeated in Darryl F. Zanuck's brilliant and powerful film version. . . . a milestone in modern fiction, the picture is one of the most vital and impressive in Hollywood history. (Variety)

They all went like that, all over the country, and Variety reported that all records for attendance had been broken at both theaters for the first week.

And when, some weeks later, it was selected for the New York Film Critics Award as the Best English-speaking Moving Picture of 1947, I feel sure you could have heard a soft brushing sound in Hollywood as well as in New York while dozens of people murmured, "My cup runneth over."

And just about the time of that award I received a great personal honor—and made a great mistake about it, though of course, at the time I was positive it was not a mistake at all.

My book was selected by the Jewish Book Council for their National Jewish Book Award as the Best Jewish Novel of the Year.

Pride and pleasure rose in me—but so did principle, that uncomfortable commodity. Religious labels were anathema to me—Jewish bankers, Jewish publishing houses, Charles A. Lindbergh's infamous reference to Jewish owners of press and radio and movies. I remembered one of the final scenes in my book and opened to it and read it again.

A famous publisher meets Phil in the office of John Minify, editor of Smith's Weekly, to clinch the deal he's offered to bring out Phil's series in book form. He asks if Phil has an agent and is pleased when Phil says that agents aren't much good for articles, but that he would get one for a book.

> Jock smiled. "Sure as hell [an agent] would send it to the wrong house and pin a neat handicap to the book to start with."
>
> "How do you mean, 'wrong house?' "
>
> "From the point of view of the book's reception; wrong that way."
>
> Phil glanced at John. He was looking at Phil.
>
> "It's just better publishing, to have a house like ours do a book of this type," Jock went on.
>
> "Why?" John asked. He wasn't looking at Phil now. . . .
>
> "If one of the Jewish houses put their imprint on it, people might think it was just special pleading, and of course, it's not."
>
> "Jewish houses?" Phil asked. "You mean, Jewish publishing houses?"
>
> "You must mean," Minify said lazily, "whatever firm publishes the *Jewish Daily Forward.*" To Phil, he said, "It's a daily newspaper, published in Yiddish."

The publisher looked at him, ready to laugh if he were smiling.

"You see," Phil put in smoothly . . . "Mr. Minify and I never heard of 'Christian publishing houses' and 'Jewish publishing houses' except in the Third Reich." He smiled. "Even firms run by men who are Jewish—we just call them 'publishing houses.' In a way, that's what the whole series is about."

That's what *I'm* all about too, I felt as I came to the end of the scene. Can I just accept this award for the Best Jewish Novel of the Year?

No, you can't. The words spoke somewhere in my mind, firm and sure. There was no give to them, no maybe, no elasticity. I could not.

I began to write a letter to the Jewish Book Council. It would express my thanks at being elected for this honor and somehow explain why I felt forced to decline it.

It was hard going. I couldn't bear to sound self-righteous; it would never do to proffer a small lecture on the theme of religious labels or ethnic pigeonholing.

Somehow I managed a letter that met, at least, with my own approval and sent it off. About the same time I was named as the arts winner of the Thomas Jefferson Award for the Advancement of Democracy, and I accepted it without hesitation. In my pressbook is the newspaper item telling about that, but I have never listed it in any of my entries for *Who's Who*. I'm not sure why I feel uncomfortable when I read some of my friends' entries that sedulously list every single honor ever bestowed on them, but it's not for me.

And I began to feel uncomfortable, some years on into my life, about my own polite rejection of that award for the Best Jewish Novel of the Year.

For a long time I set the discomfort aside, to be thought through later at some more convenient time. But of course there is never any convenient time for facing up to one's mistakes, and the years drifted by with me behaving like some archetypal Scarlett O'Hara: "I'll think about that tomorrow."

But somewhere along the stream of time, I began to realize I had indeed made a mistake. I had let myself be too doctrinaire in my decision, indulging in a touch of pedantic piety about my principles. I began to wish I had accepted the honor, perhaps allowing myself some small liberty of expression to the Jewish Book Council at the same time, to the effect that I could wish the award were called Best Novel about Jewish Affairs, or Best Novel on Jewish Themes. I might

77

even have said something to that effect in the newspaper interviews that would be sure to follow their press release.

Then, after Saul Bellow won the Nobel Prize for Literature in 1976, there was an interview with him by Herbert Mitgang in the New York *Times* that contained one sentence that said everything for me. Mr. Bellow, he wrote, "underscores a point that has been frequently misunderstood in this country: he is not an 'American-Jewish writer,' but an American writer who is Jewish."

Instantly I thought of that award I had been unable to accept. My book wasn't a Best Jewish Novel or any kind of Jewish novel. It was a book about an American problem of special interest to Jewish people.

I began to wish I had kept a copy of that particular letter to the Jewish Book Council, and in 1983 I telephoned its director, Ruth S. Frank. I explained who I was and why I was phoning, in the hope that that my letter might still be buried in some old file. I talked about the mistake I had made, and my feeling "doctrinaire," and that if it were happening now, I would not be such a fool.

She was wonderfully responsive to the whole story and everything I said; we talked for a long time, and I told her I was going to write about this woeful little episode in this book. Though their files never did yield the letter, she asked if I would tell my story to an interviewer she would send up, a librarian and a writer, Esther Nussbaum.

I did, and it was printed in the 1983 fall issue of the Jewish Book World, a council publication with a large circulation, and also excerpted by Ruth S. Frank herself in the "Circle."

It felt good to see the whole damn mistake right there on the record at last. But it feels even better to "write it down" in my own way, for my own record.

There was no uncertainty, nor any mistake, about the "one lovely exception" when I did become the "litigious type" and institute a lawsuit on my own that was destined for the Supreme Court of the State of New York.

I sued Thayer Hobson.

My divorce, also brought in New York, had not been "on my own," anything but. So unwilling was it, from my point of view, so exclusively done at Thayer's insistence, that it might fairly be termed a "divorce under duress," with his stipulation that it be not an ambiguous Reno divorce with the usual bland explanation of "incompatibility," but a New York divorce, where the only grounds were adultery, as if he felt driven to a public *mea culpa* over his plans for a fourth marriage while still in his thirties.

I hadn't fought him, hadn't even held out for alimony, and had been roundly lectured by practical friends like Dorothy Massey and Clare Boothe Luce for being such a softy.

But all that was my personal life, private heartbreak and how you coped with it. This concerned my professional life as an author, as a member of the Authors League of America.

Marriages could be broken, and too often were, but copyright was inviolable.

I didn't even know anything had been violated for ten years after that sudden divorce. But one day, in the summer of 1945, during my second and last stint for Columbia Studios out in Hollywood, I had gone into one of those drugstores that sell not only drugs but candy, sunglasses, alarm clocks, newspapers, magazines and paperback books.

There on a counter was a ten-inch stack of a western, *Outlaws Three* by Peter Field. I stopped, stared, bought a copy for a quarter and stood there seething.

Thayer and I had written *Outlaws Three* together. It was during the Depression, just after he had spent all his capital to buy control of William Morrow and become president of the company. I was doing fashion copy for B. Altman and my salary went into our common exchequer, but, like everybody else, we were hard pressed for money.

It was Thayer who had thought of writing a book his own firm would publish; he had plotted it, and then had allotted the scenes he would write and the ones I would do. He had done the first chapter, I the second, he the third, I the fourth, all the way through, and then he had edited it to give it one voice.

It was the kind of book that was bound to sell even in a Depression, a western complete with cowboys, hosses, saddles, saloons, fastest-draw-in-the-West and the lot.

It sold for $2, got some rave reviews and earned us about $500. You could live for quite a spell on $500 back there in the Depression, and we were so tickled with ourselves that we immediately started a second, *Dry Gulch Adams,* doing the same trick of alternate chapters. That one earned $500 too.

And now here was the first one, a reprint. Nobody had told me it was to be a paperback; nobody had notified my agent, and if there were any royalties from this new edition, nobody had sent me one red cent.

That was still the time I had no attorney, but I did have very close friends, Carly and John Wharton, who, like the Schermans, had helped me mightily through my happy unmarried pregnancy. John Wharton was a partner in a law firm too large and too prestigious for me even to consider as "my attorneys," Paul, Weiss, Wharton and Garrison. (It was the law firm that Adlai Stevenson would join a few years later after he lost the presidency to Dwight D. Eisenhower.)

When I got back to New York and checked with my agent, I found that he not only knew nothing about it but was obviously disinclined to bother over what would be peanuts in royalties, and ten percent of those peanuts as his only reward for getting into a sticky situation.

I turned to John Wharton, told him what had happened and said I wanted to bring suit for "infringement of half a copyright." John was the attorney not only for the regular kind of big-time client, but also for the Playwrights Company, which he had helped to found, and for many of its famous members, so he knew how I felt about any infringement of any author's rights.

"Have you anything in writing," he asked me, "any letter, any document, any memo to prove that you actually did collaborate with Thayer on the book?"

I did not. But I had something I thought was just as good. I showed it to John and watched his face break into a smile.

"This would stand up," he said, "in any court of law."

It was a copy of *Outlaws Three*. Inside the cover Thayer had drawn, in pencil, an elongated, angular beast, whether hoss or longhorn nobody could decide, with its rear quarter branded in true western style, a heart pierced by an arrow.

"To Peter from Field," he had inscribed it.

"That's evidence enough," John repeated. "He's conceding right there."

"Whatever my half of the royalties come to," I told John, "you get all of it as part of your fee. What I'm after is my half of that copyright."

The first legal steps began with courteous letters about probable oversight and the usual assurances that this could be amicably resolved. Thayer's attorneys were equally courteous: it was perfectly absurd. The signed contract, dated some twelve years previously, was "between 'Peter Field' (Thayer Hobson) . . . party of the first part, the Author . . . and William Morrow and Company . . . party of the second part, the Publisher."

Clause after clause bore out this singularity of authorship:

> **THE AUTHOR** hereby bargains, sells, grants, conveys, transfers
> and sets over unto the said **WILLIAM MORROW AND**
> **COMPANY. . . . THE AUTHOR** hereby guarantees . . . **THE**
> **AUTHOR** covenants and agrees. . . .

And so on and on and on to the AUTHOR'S signature, "Peter Field."

Off and on for two years, negotiations went on between John
Wharton and Thayer's attorneys. Courteous always, the message from
Thayer remained the same: Go sue me.

So, in due time, my "borrowed" attorneys announced the "institu-
tion of action in the Supreme Court, New York County . . . re *Hobson
v. Hobson.*"

But the night before the hearings were to begin, or perhaps the trial
itself—I was never clear about the various steps taken in the leisurely
proceedings—exactly one night before the set date, there was suddenly
a change of heart.

Thayer Hobson would settle out of court.

A full rendering of royalties would be made, and a check for one
half the total amount would be sent me at earliest opportunity. In the
interests of clarity, perhaps total copyright on one of the two books
should be assigned to me, while total copyright of the other should
be retained by Thayer Hobson.

I no longer remember which of the attorneys made this latter
suggestion, nor whether I bothered to protest when it turned out that
Thayer was retaining our first book, *Outlaws Three,* as his, while I was
to have the second. I do know I had no impulse to raise any new query
about his grabbing off the first and ceding me the other, and I also
know I was delighted to have the two-year litigation over and done
with.

Reading those old documents now, I am amused by two unrelated
things. The first is the official opening of the Assignment of Contract.

> **KNOW ALL MEN BY THESE PRESENTS, THAT I,**
> **FRANCIS THAYER HOBSON** . . . in consideration of the
> sum of One Dollar ($1.00) and other good and valuable consider-
> ation to me in hand paid . . .

That gives me a chortle in view of the small lesson I was taught earlier
that same year about my changed contract with my own publisher.

The other is my own admiration—I freely confess this—for the letter I wrote when I received my attorney's bill of $383.49 for services rendered, together with my royalty check for $451.38.

On the back of the check I wrote, "Payable in full to Paul, Weiss, Wharton and Garrison," and then sent it with my covering letter.

> Herewith the check in the *proper* amount, and please, Sir, never undercharge me again under any circumstances, as it brings out the worst in me. As I said . . . on the phone, either you take this full check, or, by God, you can sue me for the lesser amount— and as you know, I have such excellent legal counsel I have never lost a lawsuit. So I advise you to take the 451.38 and forget this nonsense about 383.49.

I ended up with my deepest thanks for "your endless patience and your stubborn interest in seeing this idiotic case through to a victory."

But I never did think it an idiotic case, and have a sneaking fondness to this day for a small square of heavy bond paper attached to the final document.

> This is to certify that the attached instrument was recorded in the assignment records of the Copyright Office, Vol. 655, pages 147–148 on January 19, 1948.
> In testimony whereof, the seal of this office is affixed hereto.

And in the raised letters of an official seal it says,

Library of Congress
Copyright
Office
United States of America

My copyright was registered as No. A 77251 of the year 1934. I never bothered to know the copyright registration numbers of any of my thirteen other published books, but that one I know by heart.

Two more ineradicable memories belong to that staggering year of 1947, both occurring on the heels of the official opening of my movie.

One came two weeks later, when I told my sister Alice that I was driving the kids up to Cobb's Mill Inn in Connecticut for Thanksgiving dinner.

"Come on over with them afterwards," she said, and it was a date. I don't remember a single Thanksgiving or Christmas that we ever spent together, or birthday either after we had grown up, perhaps because her husband Milton and I were never fond of each other, and often at loggerheads.

On this Thanksgiving I was only too glad to be asked over *after* dinner. Alice had been generous and loving about my book and the movie, in sharp contrast to her dead silence about *The Trespassers*, when we had been separated for some time over one of our bad quarrels about Russia. I had thought to make up by sending her one of the first copies, inscribed, "To Al, because blood is thicker than— ——Love, Laura," but she had never even acknowledged receipt of it.

But with *Gentleman's Agreement*, she was everything any sister could have hoped for. She praised the book, she loved the movie, saying, "I'm so proud of you," in various versions, to me and to her friends and neighbors.

When the boys and I arrived at her house in Croton-on-Hudson there were several other guests already there, people I had never met, though I recognized one name, the editor of the *Daily Worker*.

They had all read my book and either had seen the movie or read the reviews, and for a few minutes I was everybody's heroine.

But inevitably the talk turned to the hot issue of the day, formally known as the European Recovery Program, but familiarly as the Marshall Plan, after our Secretary of State, George C. Marshall, once a five-star general, who would later win the Nobel Peace Prize because of it.

It was our government's plan to help our Allies recover from the devastation of World War Two by arranging economic and material aid to help them back to normal existence. Greece and Turkey had already been slated, earlier in 1947, to be the recipients of massive foreign aid; now Marshall proposed extending it to many other countries, Austria, Belgium, West Germany, Denmark, Italy and others.

Everybody also knew—and neither President Truman nor Congress made any secret of it—that interwoven with this altruism was another motive, the "containment of growing Soviet influence" in Europe.

The Soviet Union blasted the Marshall Plan the moment it was announced; it was dollar diplomacy, imperialism, expansionism, and everything else ugly and wicked. *Pravda, Tass,* and all Soviet diplomats throughout the foreign capitals of the world forgot, of course, to mention their own seizure, by force and invasion, of Estonia, Latvia, Lithuania, certain sections of Finland, parts of Poland, and at the end of the war all of East Germany.

The Marshall Plan hadn't even been implemented yet, but it was all over the front pages of every newspaper. In any group interested in the news, it was Topic A for sure. So there I was in my sister's living room, me alone against about ten opponents, my brief status as heroine instantly forgotten, and me transformed, by the magic of political crossfire, into some sort of betrayer of the people.

Voices did not rise to shouts, as in the splendid Edwardian Room of the Plaza during that tongue-lashing luncheon, and I may have imagined the tone of condescension I always felt from my opponents in this special area. In the early days, I had often been informed that it was too bad I didn't understand dialectical materialism, and that I could so easily overlook the fact that every revolution included some harsh measures, including arrests and prison and even bloodshed.

But these people were too intelligent and sophisticated to hand out such treatment; nevertheless they formed a solid bloc of refutation to anything and everything I said.

At last I got out something of what I really wanted to say but hadn't been able to organize even in my own head. "You would all, every one of you, be outraged if this country started a shooting war against Russia, wouldn't you?" I suddenly demanded.

They looked at me as if I'd blurted out obscenities.

"So would I," I went on quickly. "Outraged as hell. But nobody's mobilizing even one regiment, nobody is starting even one embargo. What we *are* doing is using economic means to oppose the Soviet Union, political means, even propaganda if you will. What's wrong with that?"

There were voices, but by now I wasn't going to be silenced until I got it all said. "It strikes me that what you all *really* want is that we should do nothing—just lie down supinely, just let Russia go merrily along, moving in on, or widening her hold on, any damn country she has her eyes on."

It didn't come out neatly, like that; it was disjointed, it got interrupted, not only by Alice and Milton, but by the *Daily Worker*'s editor and his wife and some of the others. But it got itself said.

And it didn't make a dent in their perfect sureness that they alone were right, and that I was that most unworthy of creatures, a "liberal," something a few grades lower than a reactionary or even a fascist.

Perhaps I was too sensitive—I was forever being accused of being too sensitive when I felt battered, as I did then, but certainly I couldn't wait to collect Mike and Chris and drive off into the cold November twilight. Nor did they ask me to stay.

It probably was months before we saw each other again; our quarrels always ended in a stretch of silence and distance. Again I vowed that I would never again talk politics with my sister—and of course, the next time we did get together that vow would go out the window. It was like some chronic ailment, recurrent and flouting all efforts at permanent cure.

The other ineradicable memory of that year of 1947 came just six days after that political Thanksgiving. This one concerned my son Chris, and it was far more harrowing.

Not that he was already a political being at the age of six—lucky for me that he was not. He was already a child with a will of his own on all matters—in volume one of this book I had said that from the first he was a "handful as a baby; in a tantrum he would bang his head on the floor until a purple welt stood out on his forehead; now, as a toddler, the tantrums were fewer, but he was still the 'no-I-won't' kid."

Long before six he had stopped being a headbanger, but he was no easy tractable child either, and for all my so-called insight because of my analysis, there were plenty of times when I wished I believed in spanking, and even more vigorous punishment. Once I did shout angrily that he was being impossible, pounding on my desk as I did, and when I saw a sudden frightened look on his face as he burst into tears and ran to his room, I felt that I had turned into an ogre.

It must have impressed him. One afternoon I came into the living room and stopped dead in my tracks. Chris was banging away with a hammer at the then-fashionable latticed radiator-covers running under the windows. It was not a toy hammer he was operating with, but a hefty grown-up one, full-size and most effective; with each blow of his sturdy pounding, shingles of ivory-toned paint flew off onto the carpet.

"Chris," I called out, "what in heaven's name are you doing?"

He looked over his shoulder, still hammering. "Being impossible," he said amiably.

I couldn't help myself; I laughed, but I did grab the hammer. It was so typical of young Chris—he was so bright, and could be so disarming, that you forgave all the difficult times. (Read, that *I* forgave, etc.)

The harrowing memory began simply enough with me going to the theater for the opening night of *A Streetcar Named Desire*. It was one of those long-awaited first nights; "everybody" in New York was there. The only reason I was there too was that Elia Kazan, its director, had arranged for me to buy two house seats.

During the intermission, I phoned home. Chris was coming down with a cold, and if Rosie were still with us I wouldn't have bothered to phone. But Rosie's ten years as a member of our family, helping me with the children, had ended the year before, when she had had her first baby, and now there was nobody assigned to the care of the boys, except afternoons and weekends, when teenage students from Columbia College acted as sports-companions, taking them to the park, playing ball, skating and so on.

We didn't have a maid. We did have Norman Gibson, a kind of combination cook, chauffeur, general factotum, who was to stay with us for years. He was goodness itself to the boys, but he had no training for dealing with sickness.

When he answered the phone, I knew something was wrong. "He seems worse," Norman said. "He has a hundred and two."

"Kids always hit a hundred and two with a cold."

I stayed for the rest of the play, but begged off from the big first-night party that was to follow. When I got home I knew in one instant that it was no cold.

It was scarlet fever, a second bout of scarlet fever.

There was no mistaking it. If ever you have seen one case of it, you can identify it forever. "A bright red Benday," is how I thought of it—my years of dealing with promotion and printer's proofs had educated me. In printers' terms, Benday means those microscopic dots of black ink used in a seemingly solid black picture in a newspaper.

My child's entire body was an unbroken spread of red pinpoints. His skin was burning. The thermometer said 104. I phoned our doctor and asked him to hurry. "I thought once you had it you were immune," I said.

"Only about once in a hundred thousand cases," Dr. Cobb said, "is there a recurrence. Are you sure?" But he knew I was.

The year before, in the late spring, just after I'd come back from a house-hunting trip to Bermuda to find a place for the summer, Chris had come down with scarlet fever. I had been in that tempestuous and joyous rush of the final pages in my book that nothing in the world could possibly bring to a crashing halt—except the one thing, the serious illness of one of my children.

But instinct told me now that this attack was far more serious than the first one, and Dr. Cobb agreed. He spent far more time examining Chris; he was calm as all good doctors are calm, but I knew that he wasn't going to tell me it wasn't anything to worry about.

"There's no use sending Mike off somewhere the way you did last year," Dr. Cobb said. "He's been too thoroughly exposed. Keep him out of Chris' room, and we'll have to wait it out and see whether he comes down with it too."

At once I moved Mike to my bedroom, until I could send Norman Gibson out the next morning to buy a folding cot to set up in the dining room. I moved into Mike's bunkbed across the room from Chris, though any real sleep for me was to be nearly nonexistent for many days and nights.

Despite the wonder of the new drug, penicillin, all the old-fashioned treatments were still prescribed too, and I spent the hours giving Chris cool baths, cool compresses, trying to get him to take one swallow of food, listening to his breathing.

About the third night there came one of those moments I had never lived through before and was never to forget. I watched Dr. Cobb's face as he again examined Chris' throat, again palpated his blazing little chest, again held his wrist for what seemed like far too long a time. The only sound in the room was Chris' panting breath.

Fear rose in me, strangling, so I could hardly draw my own breath. As the doctor turned toward me, I beckoned him into the bathroom. In the tub, still slightly caked with cornstarch that went into Chris' repeated cool baths, were a couple of his inflatable toys, also whitened by a layer of the powder.

I looked at Dr. Cobb. He had been Benjamin Spock's colleague for years, while Ben was our family pediatrician, and when the Spocks moved to Shaker Heights in Cleveland he had taken over Spock's practice. I didn't know him as I had known Ben Spock; I wasn't yet sure that he would tell me the entire truth.

"Will he make it, doctor?" It seemed to take me minutes to get those words spoken aloud.

"I would think, yes. He's a fine strong little boy, and yes, I would expect him to pull through."

"Oh, Dr. Cobb."

"There's no *certainty*," he cautioned me. "But I do think he will make it."

He did make it. Until it was over, everything else in my life stood still—no writing, no thought of the movie, of seeing friends, of anything whatever but caring for Chris and watching Mike for any sign that he was coming down with it too. It was a time of total concentration, on one pure theme: please let Chris make it, *please.*

During Chris' slow convalescence, it was Mike who began to go crazy at being kept in—the bright quarantine sign on our front door kept any possible friend away, and he was an eleven-year-old prisoner, far from the center of attention.

When the poor kid was at last permitted to go out, the very morning the quarantine was lifted, he scampered down the street like a frisky young colt, racing to Central Park. In a moment he was stopped by a policeman.

"Hey, kid, you playing hookey or what?"

"No, sir, I'm not."

"Then why aren't you in school? Any truant officer—"

"Because my brother had scarlet fever—I'm just out of quarantine."

The cop took off briskly enough, and Mike thought his first brush with the law was pretty neat.

As soon as I could think again, I returned to my quest for my next book, for an *idea* that might develop into my next book. I don't mean a "plot," but something far less distinct than that, and, to me, far more important.

I was never one of those authors, fortunate or not, who could suddenly be possessed of an entire plot, sprung from their minds like Athena, springing full-grown from the head of Zeus.

Sinclair Lewis, I've been told, was one of those, and perhaps that is why he wrote a novel a year for thirty or more years, most of which were well below his best work. And Pearl Buck too, and Anthony Trollope and many more of the novel-a-year authors whom I so often envied for being so prolific, even when I was sadly disappointed in one or another of those speedy books.

When I wrote light fiction for the big magazines, I could sometimes start with no more than a phrase I liked, "Lucky at cards, unlucky at love," and end up with a two-part serial called *Lucky Streak.*

But when it came to a book, which I knew would take two or three years of hard continuing work, then I needed something far more basic than a "cute idea." It had to be something worth those two or three years; it had to have some special interior appeal to whatever it was that made me me.

It still would be just a shred of an idea, not something I could jot down in a tidy outline for submission to an editor or publisher. My first novel had revealed that much to me; it had begun with one notion: I'll write about one family trying to get visas for America. And my second had begun a thousand miles away from what it was to become; my first plan was to write a book that showed that a nation was *happy* during a war; little did I dream that it would end up as a novel about "anti-Semitism among nice people."

For my third, an idea had been skittering around in my mind in embryo form, perhaps as far back as the time when I was daydreaming about sudden success for *The Trespassers*. I would write about what I already thought of as "phony celebrity," the kind I saw so much of in our culture, where people's ambition was not so much to *do* something as to *be* somebody.

But that idea was struck down by my own experience with *Gentleman's Agreement*. If I wrote it, it would end up as first cousin to those distasteful books of instant journalism, published three weeks after some news event or public scandal; inevitably it would come out as an exposé of authors who did go in for autograph parties in bookstores, who did go the entire route of lecturing at lit'ry lunches, who were willing to tout their own wares across the nation for the sake of publicity and sales. In other words, an exposé of authors less noble than I!

But though I recognized perfectly well that I ought to abandon— or delay—that idea, my log early in 1948 had stubborn entries:

> *Maybe* got the solution to celebrity novel. Made notes on new approach.

That solution soon turned sour, and my restlessness deepened until another entry appeared.

> Different idea for the new novel? Fathers and daughters, mothers and sons? Wrote page X.

This was followed two days later:

> Wrote 2-page outline father-daughter idea. *Maybe*.

Then came a few evening dates, the first since the scarlet fever, and one highly volatile one, with assorted punctuation marks.

> My new mink coat! $5,500, custom-made, Insured at $7,200!
> Bergdorf Goodman. Began Chapter I (???)

But despite that burst of excitement, the restlessness and the entries kept right on.

> Began Chapter One again—page 1,2,3. I think *yes.* It will be so difficult.

Four days later, one swift line.

> *Mike* has scarlet fever.

Again all thinking went out the window; again quarantine, this time with Chris relegated to the dining room and the folding cot. But this time the attack was blessedly light and quickly over.

But one new development in my life just then also contrived to shunt me away from that search for a new book. As I said, I had become involved with new interests, the ADA and the American Civil Liberties Union, with their meetings and calls on you for time and effort.

And now came the news that I had been elected to the national council of the Authors League of America, with a date set for me to attend my first meeting.

The Authors League is the umbrella organization, today, of two guilds, the Authors Guild and the Dramatists Guild. Back then it also included radio writers and screen writers and people writing for television, people on salaries and payrolls.

When I appeared for my first meeting I was shy and proud all at once. There I was, with people I had heard of and read about all my adult life. At the head of the table was the president, Oscar Hammerstein, so famous for *Show Boat, Oklahoma, Carousel—South Pacific* was still a year in the future. Around the table were Howard Lindsay and Russel Crouse, of *Life With Father* and other great hits, Rex Stout, whose mysteries I doted on, Elmer Rice, Moss Hart and half a dozen other people of that stature.

It may sound naive to say I was shy, or even a touch false, but the pure fact is I did feel myself a newcomer, a freshman among university notables, as insecure as if I had somehow got there by a fluke.

Recently Peter Heggie, the executive secretary of the Authors

Guild, dug out for me a letter I had written the Guild, my first contact with the Guild or the League. It is dated 1944, and was sent from Hollywood.

> Dear Authors League,
>
> A couple of years ago Henry Pringle asked me why I wasn't a member of the Author's League, and I answered that since I'd only written a handful of short stories for the slicks, I felt I hadn't become an author.
>
> But now that I have written *The Trespassers,* and have my first book on the record, I guess I am an author. I even hoped that I'd be *invited* to be a member of the Authors League, but maybe that's not the way it happens.
>
> So I hereby apply for membership. What happens now? My being out here, by the way, may be for a few weeks only—I am trying one picture for Metro. . . .
>
> I *am* going to write more books despite all the dire predictions that I'm lost to pitchers. . . . Please let me have whatever dope I need or application blanks or an official tap on the shoulder.

The official tap came promptly and I had become a member of what I used to call the "only union that writers have." I attended every meeting open to the general membership, but not once had it ever occurred to me that I might in time be elected to the exalted National Council, and at that first meeting, nearly four years later, I still felt myself a neophyte.

It was Oscar Hammerstein who soon lifted me out of the neophyte class: after I had attended my first few meetings he assigned me to a special task, and a tough one. I was to be chairman of a new committee to study injustices to authors and dramatists in the tax laws, and I soon discovered that I was not only the chairman but the entire committee.

That there were injustices to authors, playwrights and all creative people was clear enough to all of us. Where was there any allowance for *depletion?* Owners of oil wells and coal mines could take enormous deductions for the annual depletion of their properties—what about deductions for any depletion in an author's brain or output?

Factories could deduct for obsolescence—what about an aging writer? As he or she became ill, or just felt written out, what adjustment was made in the way of lesser taxes? And what about the havoc when a play closed on Saturday night or a book sank out of sight like a stone down a deep well?

I took my assignment seriously, and found it more frustrating than any assignment I had ever had, either in the world of promotion or in my current world of writing. Futile hours went into talking with tax experts, with attorneys familiar with authors' problems, with other authors, even with an occasional minor official of the Internal Revenue System who would spare the time for an interview.

I got nowhere. "That's the way it is" was the most cogent remark I received from any of them. One positive result did emerge: I signed up as a client with one of those law firms, Stern and Reubens, on an annual retainer basis. That was hardly the outcome calculated to cover me with glory in the eyes of my new confreres at the Authors League of America, but they gently assured me that "that's the way it is" when anybody tries to improve the tax laws for creative people.

Despite all these labors, I managed somehow to keep returning to my desk and my faltering attempts to find myself again with that healing sense of being "placed."

I was still seeing Dr. Gosselin twice a week, still hoping to attain some version of that elusive serenity that Eric had so long pursued without ever reaching.

Mike and Chris, 11½ and 6½, in Westport, Connecticut, summer of 1948 (top photo), and in Stamford, Connecticut, age 16 and 11, 1953. (Chris is probably writing a *Freddy* book.)

In a rented house at Malibu Beach, California, summer of 1951—after finishing *The Celebrity*.

Something new... Something different... and... **AN IMMEDIATE HIT!**

Promotion brochure for International News Service's "Assignment America," 195

On tour for "Assignment America," summer of 1954. At Fort Riley, Kansas, with commanding general and a bashful Chris, 12½.

Publicity photo for
Good Housekeeping
columns, 1954.

The study in the East
66th Street apartment
where the author and
her family lived from
1950–55; from a
photo story in the
New York *Times
Magazine. Photo credit:
The New York Times.*

Eric Hodgins in 1954, age 54. *Photo credit: CBS-Urgo.*

One of the "Know Campaign" ads, 1957.

Clare and Harry Luce
at their home in Phoenix.
Christmas, 1957.

The kids grow up: with Mike riding his
twenty-first birthday present, 1957... and
Chris (left) with a friend in Dar es Salaam,
Tanganyika, 1964.

Jacket photo for *First Papers*, published in 1964.
Photo credit: Chris Corpus.

Aulla, Italy, spring 1965, during a vacation with Sir Francis and Lady Meynell. Francis noted on the back of the photo, "A reminder of happy sunny days."

Aboard SS *Santa Paula* to the Caribbean, December 1967. *Photo credit: Grace Line Publicity Dept.*

Taken for a Newsweek story in 1969, this
photo was used in 1975 for the jacket of
Consenting Adult. Photo credit: David Gahr.

A grandmother at last—with Sarah,
age 7½ months, September 1968.

THE CITY OF NEW YORK

RECREATION AND CULTURAL AFFAIRS ADMINISTRATION
DEPARTMENT OF PARKS
THE ARSENAL
830 FIFTH AVENUE
CENTRAL PARK
NEW YORK, N.Y. 10021
RE. 4-1000

ALEXANDER WIRIN
EXECUTIVE DIRECTOR
PETER ASCHKENASY
DEPUTY EXECUTIVE DIRECTOR

October 23, 1967

JOHN V. LINDSAY
MAYOR

AUGUST HECKSCHER
ADMINISTRATOR AND COMMISSIONER
ARTHUR ROSENBLATT
FIRST DEPUTY ADMINISTRATOR

TO WHOM IT MAY CONCERN

In view of Miss Laura Z. Hobson's dedication
to bicycle riding in Central Park, especially her
record of totalling more than 1,200 miles in the
year 1966-67, I request that she be permitted to
bicycle on the pedestrian paths of Central Park
on Weekday Mornings.

Never on Sunday. Never on Saturday. Never
on any afternoon. But on Weekday Mornings - she is
welcome.

If there are any question in regard to this, please
see the Commissioner of Parks.

Laura Z. Hobson
923 Fifth Av.

August Heckscher
August Heckscher
Commissioner and Administrator

Dr. B. Benjamin
225 E 64 St
LE5-7090

The "special permit" for Central
Park biking. It doubled as emergency ID, with the names and
addresses of the bearer and her
doctor at lower left.

FIVE

AND THEN CAME ANOTHER letter from Eric. Half a year had elapsed since he had accepted my "calm and judicious decision, the shilly-shally," and there had been not one word between us. Then, in late winter, I was the one to receive an "envelope with the so-familiar handwriting," and I was again beguiled by the Ericness of it.

> This has surely been the slowest-developing social situation I have ever found myself in . . .

I do not have that letter, but those words are as clear as if I were again copying them down for this book. He had seen my movie, he wrote, and thought it splendid, and then had gone right back to see it a second time, and found it even more impressive and powerful. Surely by now the shilly-shally should end, so that we could talk about it—and about a hundred other things as well?

The shilly-shally ended indeed. I was slated for a vacation in California, again at La Quinta, due to start the following week, and perhaps that helped to make me suddenly decisive. Three of the next five pages in my log have brief notations, down at the bottom where my personal life had its share of the daily jottings.

> Eric—8:30
> E.
> E.

Many years later, after a profound illness, when his life was drawing to a close, Eric undertook to write his autobiography, *Trolley to the Moon,* "more as therapy," he told me, "than as a literary effort."

He never finished it, never got further than his late thirties, while he was still managing editor of Fortune magazine, before he had faced up to the fact that he was not merely a "social drinker" but an alcoholic, before either of us had ever dreamed that we might one day actually write our first novels.

Near the end of his unfinished autobiography, published posthumously, he wrote about our first meeting. It had happened at that black-tie and champagne gala that Time Inc. had staged to celebrate the official opening of *The March of Time* on the screen. That was in 1935, so as he wrote about it, Eric was looking backward some thirty-five years to his youth and to mine.

> I was confronting a beautiful and striking woman ("beauty" was never a word Laura would concede to herself, but "striking" was) who was gracious and vivacious; an intense listener and eager conversationalist. Her looks were enhanced, for me, by her prematurely gray hair, a feature, I was later to learn, that she herself hated.
>
> Mrs. Hobson and I had perhaps ten minutes of conversation together, and no great themes were struck; we were merely interested in the fact that we had both joined Time Inc. in the same year, she as a promotion writer, and had never met or even heard of each other until now.
>
> Somehow we found it very easy to converse, and I remember thinking how rarely I met a beautiful woman who was also gracious; the beauties were cold or condescending, and the horse-faced ones were so full of graciousness that it was hard to escape them. But Mrs. Hobson was both striking and gracious, and I remember feeling disappointed when the general swirl of the party separated us.
>
> I wonder what it means, psychologically, that Laura Hobson has no recollection at all of that first meeting, in fact that she can't for the life of her remember when she first met me at all. But meet me again she surely did, for in one way or another, we have been in and out of each other's lives—with some very long lapses, it is true—ever since. She was not Laura Z. Hobson, the novelist, then; her first big success—*Gentleman's Agreement,* book and Academy Award-winning film—was still more than a decade ahead of her. So were a lot of other things.

So were a lot of other things for Eric, some good, some devastating. I think now that I value those paragraphs of his for several reasons, one a thoroughly unworthy one, his phrases about me being an "intense listener."

So often, after some evening with friends, or even with my own family, I've had a sweep of guilty feeling that, damn it, I talked too much, only to solace myself later by deciding it was only in part my fault. If *they* had done their fair share of talking, I would tell myself, I would have shut up and listened—I've always been a good listener when anybody has anything to say. But so many people are like sponges, sucking up the juices of your mind, your experiences, with no thought of offering an equal flow of their own talk in replacement. Or, to change the metaphor, so many people treat one like a bank, where they endlessly draw funds without ever making a deposit to replenish the account.

Eric knew I could listen, all his life he knew it. There were certain difficult areas he did not talk to me about—his marriage, for one—and yet I think there was always a lovely balance in what we drew from each other and what we gave to each other.

There are other reasons I am touched by those paragraphs of Eric's last writing; they remind me of his gifts, of wit, of irony, of grace. They offer me testimony that at last, through my analysis or through the long undersea process of maturing, I must have at last managed to avoid "neurotic love" in favor of something more substantial. I could be devoted to Eric, engrossed by Eric, I could love him truly without the risk of being shattered when the bad times came. The bad times did come, but somehow I was able to survive them—even when it seemed that poor Eric could not.

In and out of each other's lives ever since. Eric's life was over when I first read those lines, and I wept as I read them, wept because there was such truth and simplicity in them, wept in some depth of gratitude for the long-ago reality that had engendered them.

One black-tie gala I chose to avoid was the Academy Awards that everybody was preparing for while I was having my vacation at La Quinta.

There was no talk of anything but who would win an Oscar, what actor, what actress, what picture. One night at a party at Zanuck's place in Palm Springs, when I said I was leaving for home before the big night arrived, not one soul took me seriously. It was very much a Hollywood party, with Clifton Webb, Constance Bennett, the new young star Louis Jourdan, my old friend Clare Luce, whom I had seen little of since she became Congresswoman Luce—she and everybody else made it very obvious that they thought I was just putting on an act by saying I wouldn't stay over.

A few days after I was back home, my Hollywood agent, Bert Allenberg, telephoned me. "Better buy yourself a new evening gown and get back here right away," he said. "It's a shoo-in for Best Picture."

"I thought it was all kept a dead secret until those envelopes were opened."

"It is. But every poll shows—every columnist—everybody in the know—"

I told him I wouldn't think of being in that auditorium that night "just by accident." He grew a bit vexed, letting me hear it.

"Bert, I write books, not movies."

"That's got nothing to do with it."

"I guess not. But anyway, I'll watch it from here."

And that is what I did. Elia Kazan's wife Molly had a television set —I didn't have one as yet—and she invited me to watch with her. One of her Vassar classmates was my closest friend, Carroll Whedon, and Carroll and her husband John went with me. There were some people named Anderson and some others I do not remember, though their names are there on that log page for March 20, 1948, all of us gathered together before that small screen, waiting through the interminable preliminaries of awards for Best Original Song, Best Two-reel Short, Best One-reel Short, Best Scoring, Best Sound Recording, Best Documentary, Best Foreign Film—

We all cheered when Celeste Holm won an Oscar for Best Supporting Actress, but that was nothing compared to what happened when Kazan won as Best Director. And at long last, when *Gentleman's Agreement* won as Best Picture of the Year, there was a kind of happy frenzy of kisses and hugs and I-knew-it-all-alongs.

I can't truly recall what it was I felt in those first moments. I think it was a composite or collage of feelings, pleasure, pride, even a practicality akin to a salesman's with a big order in hand, but no inspired preview came to me that night of what lay ahead for that Best Picture.

We were all a bit let down that Gregory Peck did not win the Oscar for Best Actor, but were certain that in due time he would collect more than one for other pictures. But it hurt me badly that Moss Hart did not win for Best Screenplay, which went to *Miracle on Thirty-Fourth*

Street. Nobody, least of all me, could figure out how anything could be Best Picture if it hadn't first been Best Screenplay.

Moss and I never talked directly about this, but I think he knew that I shared whatever disappointment he kept to himself. By that time we could communicate with each other by a look, a gesture, even a silence.

But that night of the Oscars ended weirdly for me: when at last I got home I found a note in Mike's schoolboy handwriting telling me, "John wants to play jacks with you—he phoned twice."

What John? John Wharton? John Bassett, my editor's husband? Play jacks with me? Jacks . . . jerk . . . ?

It hit me suddenly. It had been an obscene telephone call and my Mike had received it without suspicion and dutifully written it down.

Horror ended that wonderful evening; fear was added next morning when that same John reached me, and in a strange breathy voice quickly said he knew what Mike and Chris were at Collegiate School and that he knew where we lived—and only then began the obscene proposals. I hung up, trembling in helpless rage.

Each time the phone rang that rage roiled through me. Dr. Gosselin told me to get a new phone number, but he also assured me that obscene callers never appeared in person and that my children were safe. But the first syllable from that voice on the phone would send a rock of dread straight to the pit of my stomach.

After a few days I phoned the police to ask their help—the phone company had already told me there were no available new numbers, nor would there be any for a year or more. Two detectives came to interview me; they told me that every time a woman's name appeared in the newspapers, for a book, a play, a movie, even to open a new store—that woman's name in the phone book became the property of the obscene phoners.

There was small hope of catching my particular phoner—I would have to listen for eighteen solid minutes while notifying the police on another phone to give them time to trace the call.

The only cure was to get an unlisted number and stay out of the phone book forever.

And that, dear friends, and not snobbery nor self-importance, is how and why I became one of the people "not in the book."

Whether it was the movie and the Oscars or primarily my book I do not know, but my log began again to be sprinkled with those stylish little *D*s and *Don't D*s that had been part of my life through my

97

marriage and through the Ingersoll years, when people said "Dress" or "Don't dress" as they invited you for a party, or a first night at the theater, or even just an evening of bridge.

The war had stopped all that, at least among the people I knew, but soon after publication day it was back for me once more. Quite a few of those *D* evenings were to stand out, as I look back to that era of my existence through all the years that came afterward, for a variety of reasons. One that does was at the Fadimans', where I first felt the steel Edna Ferber could slash you with if it occurred to her to make a cutting remark. Clifton Fadiman, called Kip, had for years been a household word, not so much at that time for his extensive literary achievements as editor and writer, but as master of ceremonies of the widely popular radio program, "Information Please."

It was a large dinner party, though my log gives me no names of the guests. All it offers, apart from "Fadiman, 7:30 D," is, "Edna Ferber's nasty remark re 'late dates.' " Below that is the notation, "E–12."

Edna Ferber, so famous for her novels and plays, was also noted, among those who knew her personally, for her acerbity and ability to hurt you whenever she felt like it. Some people said it was because she had never married and felt some sort of stigma about being an "old maid"; others said it was because she was anything but beautiful and envied anybody attractive. I think that though I was to meet her many times in the future, the first time I did was that dinner at the Fadimans'.

"I'll have to leave early," I murmured to Polly Fadiman at the table. "I have another party to look in on."

"These people who 'have another party to look in on,' " said Edna Ferber, enunciating very clearly at my hostess' other side, so that half a dozen people could hear her. "What they're really doing is boasting that there's romance in their lives."

I can still remember my quick embarrassment as a couple of other people laughed, can feel again that painful flush of resentment at Miss Ferber. When I opened my front door to Eric at midnight and told him about it, I offered it as a great joke, but he knew at once that I didn't find it at all funny. He talked about embittered people, and from there he talked about unhappy people and unhappy marriages. Never once did he mention his own, though I believe that by that time he was living apart from his family, living at the University Club on Fifth Avenue and Fifty-fourth Street, which was to be his chief address for many years to come.

But that was only one party. In my life the preponderance of "great parties" of that era could be called "Bennett and Phyllis Cerf parties," and they were subtly different from all other black-tie parties I had been to. Never were they for half a dozen or so people; the Cerfs liked to do dinners for twenty-four, seating them at three round tables in their large dining room, and then going upstairs to their two living rooms on the floor above.

I had first met Bennett years before, met him as another of New York's young publishers in the early thirties who were Thayer's colleagues and friends. He was married then to Sylvia Sidney, the actress, but not once had Bennett ever invited me to anything, not even after his marriage to Phyllis in 1940. Now I found myself on their guest list to just about everything—and I confess I loved it.

I think I must have been a good bit dazzled in those days by parties at the Cerfs'; I did write down names of the other guests when I got home, and it tells me that I must have been a little stage-struck. Ginger Rogers, Phyllis' cousin, was at the first one I went to, and Billy Wilder, the Hollywood producer of *Ninotchka, The Lost Weekend* and so many others, Anatole Litvak, another movie great, as well as Moss Hart and Kitty, George S. Kaufman, John O'Hara, Martin Gabel and Arlene Francis . . .

At other parties at the Cerfs' Ethel Merman and Mary Martin were often guests; Robert Sherwood, the playwright; the young Truman Capote, then in his early twenties, and already famous not only for his first novel, *Other Voices, Other Rooms,* but for the publicity photograph Random House used again and again, showing him as a slim, blond, beautiful youth, half-reclining on a Madame Recamier sort of sofa.

The Cerfs became part of our weekly poker games, and we became good friends, apart from parties; any time I gave one of my own much smaller parties I asked them, though I never did have any stars of stage and screen on my own guest lists.

But on those very pages in my log where all the glamorous jottings took up the bottom half, there ran, in the upper half, a steady and abundant stream of notes about me and writing.

March 13: Began work again (on novel.)
March 15: Tried dictating on Soundscriber; p 8–20
March 19: dic to p 43—(started music lessons again.)
March 20: dic to p 69

That was the morning of the Academy Awards, and I must have been in something of a dither, but, as I've said before, once I begin on a book I do manage somehow to stick to it, if only for a paragraph or two, without missing a day.

The Soundscriber was a precursor of today's tape recorder; you had a small square machine, bound in tan leather, like a miniature record-player, and you used small green discs, like six-inch phonograph records, so light and thin that you could mail them for a single stamp. These I mailed to my absentee and part-time secretary, whom I had supplied with a counterpart of my Soundscriber so she could play back the discs at her own speed and transcribe them to pages of manuscript.

My son Chris recently told me that he still could remember back to that Soundscriber in my life, and that he used to listen to my slow, careful dictating. Then, with some relish, he made up a gibberish example of how I sounded:

> Paragraph. The general plan, comma, agreed to with alacrity by the others, comma, was the equivalent of a sit-in strike, dash, a well-mannered, comma, even jovial, comma, rebellion, period, paragraph.

The daily recording of progress went on, through p. 80, p. 96, all the way to an entry on a certain irritated Sunday:

March 28: dic to p. 102. Dic is NO GOOD.
Began rewrite on typewriter from p. 1

It was perplexing and frustrating, this inability of mine to dictate even a first draft of a chapter and have it appear later in manuscript form as something I could pencil-edit and be satisfied with. At Time Inc. I was swift and sure when I dictated a letter or a memo; I rarely had to do anything over, and often found myself pleased at some bit of phrasing that I, if no one else, found felicitous, even amusing.

But trying to dictate anything like a story or a novel always ended in failure. It was stiff; it sounded forced; there was nothing natural about the dialogue.

Yet I was plagued with the knowledge that many authors were able to dictate, attaining a speed of production that made me envy them. During my marriage, on a trip along rutted mountain roads in California with one of Thayer's most successful authors, Erle Stanley Gardner,

I had heard directly from him, how he could tour the country in a small retinue of station wagons, outfitted like offices, with two or three secretaries travelling with him, while he dictated to his dictaphone long stretches of his Perry Mason books, going so rapidly and surely that all the secretaries were busy just keeping up with him as they transcribed to manuscript form.

I didn't yearn to write the Perry Mason genre of books, but from time to time that story haunted me and made me wonder whether I too could learn to dictate a novel. That March 28th entry was my final declaration of freedom from that delusion.

No doubt one part of my mind still put it in terms of Soundscriber technique: Dictated to page one-oh-two, period. Dictating is, all caps please, NO GOOD period. Next line, Began rewrite on typewriter from page one, period, paragraph.

And then, in early summer, and in a minor way, I entered the arena of national politics. The Democratic National Convention of 1948 was about to start in Philadelphia, and a rather casual friend of mine, Dorothy Norman, a columnist for the *Evening Post,* invited me to go there with her to see if I could help draft the civil rights plank in the party platform.

I had never been to a national convention, except for one single hour back in 1924, when I used one lunch break during my first copywriting job to step into Madison Square Garden, which at that time was right near Madison Square, on Fourth Avenue at Twenty-sixth Street. Apparently I just walked in off the street. The papers were full of the unheard-of deadlock that had lasted for two full weeks, with the delegates split between Alfred E. Smith, New York's governor, a Catholic and favorite of Tammany Hall, and William G. McAdoo, once Secretary of the Treasury and later to be senator from California.

They were also full of the equally unheard-of, rocklike immobility of the delegation from the sovereign state of Alabama, with its single unchanging response—through no less than one hundred and three successive roll-calls of the states. "Alabama casts her twenty-four votes for Oscar W. Underwood." I am sure that the line went into a little more specificity than that, perhaps, "Alabama, the Cotton State," or even "Alabama, the Heart of Dixie, casts her twenty-four votes for Oscar W. Underwood," but that minute detail I didn't think rated further research. I do know that when the deadlock was finally broken on the hundred and *fourth* roll call, the compromise candidate, John

W. Davis, only went on to total defeat in November by Silent Cal Coolidge.

But that brief excursion of mine into Madison Square Garden scarcely prepared me for what I was to find a quarter-century later in Philadelphia. My various surprises and confusions began the very night we arrived. Dorothy Norman invited me to dine with the owners of her paper, Dorothy Schiff Thackrey and her husband Ted, together with the *Post* columnist Earl Wilson and his wife. Their talk dumbfounded me; it was all about a letter that had gone forth a few days before, to round up support from Democrats to "dump Truman," although they put it more politely.

Their preferred nominee would be that war hero, General Dwight D. Eisenhower.

Behind this move was the strangest little set of political bedfellows one could imagine. Not only were the anti-civil-rights "Dixiecrats" endorsing it, under their banner of States' Rights Democrats, but also the liberal ADA, of which I was so proud to be a new member.

The signatures on that letter not only included the Dixiecrat governor of South Carolina and several others of his convictions, but also two of FDR's sons and—I was staggered—Hubert H. Humphrey, now running for the Senate, and several others of *their* convictions.

I did already know, before that evening, that another group of Democrats had formed a separate ticket, the Progressive Party, and that their nominee was to be Henry A. Wallace. That together with this new information gave me my first private lesson about what people meant when they said that at every national convention Democrats always split into factions and fragments. At that time I wasn't amused, only bemused.

At any rate I determined to do whatever little I could to help with the civil rights plank, and was delighted when the first person I encountered was none other than Hubert Humphrey. I forgot all about the letter he had signed on the "dump Truman" issue, and was glad that he remembered me from that ADA dinner the year before. I think he was also pleased to see me, for he knew virtually nobody among the New York newspaper or magazine people covering the convention and I was happy to introduce the ones I knew.

I was a little surprised myself at how many I did know, some going all the way back to my one year as cub reporter on the *Post,* and others more recent. But it was Dorothy Norman, still a member of the working press, who introduced both of us to just about everybody wearing a press badge.

The most surprising encounter, to me, was to find my old friend Clare Luce there, also as a member of the working press—pro tem member, at any rate. She was no longer in Congress, and was there on special assignment for the Scripps Howard chain of newspapers, covering all three conventions—the Republican one had preceded this one, and the Progressive Party's was to follow. Even in the mob of press people, she stood out as a special personage, with many reporters covering *her* in sidebar stories.

I had seen little of Clare since she became Congresswoman Luce, though from time to time we still exchanged letters, some happy ones, like the one she had written me about my first novel, some deeply unhappy ones, like the ones we had exchanged after her only child, Ann, had been killed in an automobile crash, when I had thought not of Clare's politics but only of the one tragedy I could not imagine anybody surviving.

I was to have a "sidebar" story of my own about Clare, one that I have never written, but that did not come about until all of the group I was with had put in two twenty-hour days and nights of struggle with the intricacies of that civil rights plank. There were differences between the Truman plank and the ADA suggestions, but they really came down to a matter of emphasis and phrasing, and if I contributed anything at all, it was nothing more than a matter of phrasing here and there. It was Humphrey, in my opinion, who was the clearest and strongest on each issue that arose; he was to make an electrifying speech to the convention that week, supporting stronger civil rights action on all fronts, repeal of the poll tax, a federal law against lynching, reestablishment of a federal Fair Employment Practice System, and abolition of segregation in the army, navy, marines, and air force.

One year after Jackie Robinson and Branch Rickey of the Brooklyn Dodgers had "integrated baseball" for the first time, there were still all-black units throughout the armed forces—even three years after that convention night speech in Philadelphia there were three hundred and eighty-five all-black units with two hundred thousand black soldiers in their Jim Crow ranks.

No wonder that Hubert Humphrey's speech won him his first national prominence. To me he became a special figure, and when I heard, from Dorothy Norman and others, that the southern caucus was preparing its own civil rights plank, the first person I told my news to was Humphrey.

I was dying to hear their discussions, which were taking place in the Benjamin Franklin Hotel, where their hosts were the Texas delegation, and it took about one minute to realize that Humphrey was equally eager to know what they were planning and how much of a split they were apt to cause in the convention.

The caucus was not a closed session. I already had a press badge that could take me into any open session; without ado I arranged to "borrow" another press badge for Humphrey.

Thus equipped we went to the southern caucus. At first I could not believe what I was hearing; I kept glancing at Humphrey to see whether he was as skeptical as I. His face was set, and he was that rarest of all things, silent, perhaps for the one time in his life.

The Dixiecrats were not only going to offer their own highly modified "civil rights" plank, watering down what they considered the worst nonsense of the northern liberals; they were not only planning to run their own ticket, with Strom Thurmond their candidate for the presidency, but they were discussing a possible masterstroke, a walkout from the convention floor. They had two states committed to act with them; they were still hoping to convince Texas and some of the others, as well as some of the border states, to join forces.

I could not believe it would ever happen; if Hubert did, he certainly never told me so. We both left in a kind of worried daze.

Two nights later it did happen. Try to imagine it yourself, as if you were seeing a national convention tonight on your own television set. The Dixiecrat civil-rights bill has been roundly defeated, and the Humphrey-Biemiller bill has passed.

Quite suddenly a member of the Alabama delegation rises, gets the eye of the chair, and addresses the crowded floor of the Philadelphia Municipal Auditorium, jammed to the rafters.

"We bid you goodbye." A hundred microphones amplify those words.

Thirteen members of the Alabama delegation and the entire twenty-three members of the Mississippi delegation rise at once, and, holding their state standards aloft, march out en masse. Their blocks of empty seats make gaping rectangular holes in the expanse of the auditorium, looking abnormally large even on your nineteen-inch TV screen.

Later I learned that the Dixiecrats had offered the bandleader a fee of $500 to play "Dixie" as an accompaniment to their walkout, but that he had turned them down.

Whenever I see turmoil and furor now, at anybody's political convention, I find a small thin memory coming back to me, of that night of the Dixiecrat secession. I have one other abiding memory of that week in Philadelphia, but this a frivolous and private one.

104

Of course it concerns Clare Luce. When we were young together, there were many special memories of things Clare did, and I found a lot of resurgent amusement as I wrote about them in volume one. But this was of something I myself did, and though I am again amused, I think I really ought to be a bit ashamed.

It happened on the opening night of the convention, a heat-wave night at a time when most hotels still had no air conditioning, except in a few deluxe suites. One such was Clare's.

What's more, back then in 1948, television sets were not the ubiquitous objects in hotel rooms that they are now; if you wanted a set in your own room you were billed an extra $22 per day for the privilege. One person who wanted precisely that was Clare.

But she was generous with her luxuries, and invited any number of her colleagues and friends to "stay away the first night of the convention, and listen to Alben Barkley's keynote speech on TV at my place."

I was only too glad to be one of those she asked up. Her temporary boss, Roy Howard, was there, Stuart and Joseph Alsop, the political columnists, and many other professional or pseudopress people, including Winston Churchill's son Randolph, who promptly struck many of us as being what my young researcher today calls an "oatmeal-head."

I remember that we were none too attentive to that flickering screen and the predictable words of the future Veep. At one point I became aware of eyestrain and a faint headache and asked Clare if she had any aspirin. She opened the door to her bedroom and indicated the bathroom.

As I stood before the medicine cabinet, its door still open as I poured some water and took my two tablets, an idle thought arose out of nowhere: those little drugstore bottles so neatly aligned on the middle shelf—were any of them filled with sleeping pills? In my own medicine cabinet there was always one bottle carrying at least a few for a possible emergency. Was Clare now so at ease with life that she never needed one?

Two years before, to the accompaniment of worldwide publicity in the world's gossip columns and even in the serious press, Clare had officially changed her religion and become a Catholic. People who liked her surmised that the death of her daughter Ann had caused her to search for comfort and surcease in a new religion; those who disliked her enough said her real motive lay in her fear that Harry Luce might ask for a divorce, and her vow would render any divorce forever impossible.

I had heard both of these theories and given credence to neither. But gazing at that prim little row of labeled bottles and boxes, I had only one thought. Maybe her new religion has given Clare such peace of mind that she no longer has even one of those despairing "white nights" when a sleeping pill becomes a necessity.

I yielded to my curiosity and performed my shameful little act. I took up, one by one, each bottle or box, read the prescription label, and when that was ambiguous, even looked inside.

There wasn't a sign of a sleeping pill in any of them, not even the over-the-counter brand of sleep-inducers. Why then, I thought, it must be that Clare has indeed found peace and inner quiet from her new religion. Confirmed agnostic that I was, I was impressed.

As I went through her bedroom to rejoin the others in the large living room, I stopped. At either side of her bed was an endtable bearing its lighted lamp and the usual bed-table paraphernalia. With one addition, something too valuable to be part of any hotel's furnishings, something that must have traveled along with Clare in her luggage.

It was a pair of small crystal bottles, each encased in a delicate filigree of silver. On one side of the bed the crystal bottle was filled with bright blue capsules, at least thirty or forty of them, and on the far side of the bed its mate held within its silver tracery an equal number of red ones.

I knew the blue were sodium amytal. The red were Seconal. How often, in those periods of anguish in my own life, had I taken one or the other to get me through some endless night.

And then I thought, Well, so much for one's new religion and peace of mind.

I stood still for a moment, just looking at those lovely crystal containers. Briefly I found myself wishing that those two lamps had not been lighted, so that the shining crystal beneath them would never have caught my eye.

Ten days after Truman won his surprise victory and Humphrey his Senate seat, I received a six-line letter on official stationery headed "City of Minneapolis, Office of the Mayor."

I had sent a wire of congratulations the day after the election, as thousands of others must have done, and had expected no answer beyond a gracious-sounding note signed by a secretary. The one that came was no form letter.

Dear Laura,

Thanks for the message of congratulations! I am to be in New York Tuesday, November 16, on "Town Meeting of the Air." Hope to see you. I'll tell you about the election then.

Sincerely,
Hubert

"Town Meeting of the Air" was broadcast from Town Hall, no part of officialdom, but a medium-sized auditorium on West Forty-third Street, which I thought of as a small Carnegie Hall, for every time I had been there it was to hear a concert.

I asked Carroll and John Whedon to go with me, and we all discovered, as did the entire audience, that Humphrey was that rare lecturer, one who could hold his listeners word for word to the end.

Not yet did people make jokes about Hubert's loquacity; it was too early for boredom or even much criticism. Later it would become smart and sophisticated to say that Hubert never had an "un-uttered thought," or to label him a political windbag, but in those first weeks of his career in Washington, he struck most people as a warm, even fiery, speaker, and never more so than when he talked about injustice and human rights.

After the lecture, the Whedons and I went backstage to congratulate him, and he invited us to go to one of the famous New York places he had always heard about but never seen. The Whedons declined but Hubert and I went first to "21" and then on to the Stork Club. He had never been to either, but during my Time Inc. days and the Ingersoll years I was known to the owners or major domos at both places, so there was no trouble getting past the front door of one, nor the velvet rope of the other.

Hubert was a fascinating face-to-face talker, too, about election night and his intentions for his future in the Senate. Before we parted, I asked if there was anything I could do for him and his new career, and he said without hesitation that indeed there was.

"If you could manage to let me meet some of the New York press," he said, "I'd really appreciate that."

"I'll give you a party, and ask all the newspaper people I know, and book publishers, and some people on Time and the Saturday Review."

There was no need to coax him, and we began to discuss possible dates. Three days later I wrote him my first letter.

Dear Hubert,

This is to thank you for a grand and stimulating evening at "21" and the Stork and at Town Hall. . . . I am in your debt for all three parts of it.

I meant it, about a party for you and your wife. This being New York, I should start calling up the people I want pretty damn soon, so do let me know whether the eighth, ninth or tenth or whatever would be good for you. Also whether you and Mrs. H. will have had time to press a dinner jacket and long dress, or whether I tell people not to dress.

I'll ask the Laskers, since you want to meet him, and the Bennett Cerfs and the Quentin Reynoldses and the Thackreys of the *Eve. Post* and Norman Cousins and heaven knows who else —people who will be fascinated to meet you and whom you will like. A few for buffet supper first and more later—any suggestions of people you *want* me to ask?

Anyway, it will be just fine to see you again, to meet your wife, and to have you as near as Washington instead of all the way out there in Minnesota.

Affectionately,
Laura

It was December first before he answered; obviously he did not realize that in New York you needed more than a few days notice to round up the people he most wanted to meet.

Dear Laura,

Just a quickee. Been busier than all get out. Just left the Mayor's office today and am in new quarters. My correspondence has been stacked to the ceiling and your letter seemed to have gotten lost somewhere around the upper rafters.

I will be in New York the evening of December 9. I suggest that your little party be held that evening. I shall be going to Washington about December 13.

I hope that you can make some sense out of this letter. In other words, let's get together about December 9. Forgot to tell you that Mrs. Humphrey will not be along. She is under terrific pressure to get the household goods moved and the family transported to Washington, all of which must be done by December 15. She is literally heartbroken over it, but I told her that some weekend we would drop up and meet you and your friends.

It was good to have been with you in New York.

Yours,
Hubert

The party took place the night before he left for Washington, after a real scramble of phone calls and a few telegrams to the people I was inviting. I had thought to start with that buffet at "21"—hang the expense—but Albert and Mary Lasker, true philanthropists that they were, spared me from such showoff extravagance by saying they'd be happy to do dinner at their house as a start for the evening, and then have us all repair up to my apartment to join all the other guests I had invited.

It turned into a rare hybrid of an evening, social excitement bred of political excitement. We were eleven for dinner at their handsome house on Beekman Place, with Hubert the guest of honor. I had had plenty of dilemmas, deciding whom to ask to the Laskers' and whom to ask up to my place afterwards, but I had chosen the Harts, the Fadimans, the Cerfs, and as the extra man for me, Paul Gallico, so nobody could think I was regarding Hubert as my "date."

I can't remember whether Paul Gallico, the ex-newspaper man, had already published his big best-sellers, *The Snow Goose* and *Mrs. 'Arris Goes to Paris,* but I do remember one of his phone calls not long before.

"I finally read *Gentleman's Agreement,*" he said, in a voice of vast relief, "and discovered I don't have to be jealous of it." Nevertheless I liked him as a knowledgeable and well-informed person, just right for the extra-man role.

When we eleven got to my apartment, Hubert found a host of instant supporters. Norman and Ellen Cousins were there; and Glenway Wescott, the author; and Quentin and Ginny Reynolds; Max Lerner, the political columnist, and his wife Edna; John Gunther, author of *Inside Europe* and all the other *Insides,* with his wife Jane; the famed attorney Morris Ernst, and Peggy Ernst; Dorothy and Ed Norman; Russel Crouse and Anna; and a dozen other people, including my friends, the Whedons.

For a while it was just a party, introductions, drinks, small talk. But after all, they were there because of Humphrey, so at about eleven I tapped on a glass and said, "Why don't we just sit around now and ask our new senator whatever we want to ask, and let him hold forth as he pleases?"

And hold forth he did. For nearly two hours he talked about the state of the union, of what he thought about its current state and how he hoped to help improve it. He was eloquent—and wordy—on civil rights, on poverty and wages, on school desegregation, which had not yet begun, on extensions of Social Security.

There would be a question from somebody, and a twenty-minute response. Nobody left early; people sat on chairs and the sofa and the carpet, listening, prodding him, coming up with new points. His readiness was endless, his faith in what could lie ahead for this nation contagious.

Yet, at about one, when he took his leave and most of the other guests said their good-byes, Bennett and Phyllis and Paul Gallico stayed behind with me for another hour, to "talk the party over."

For a while there was nothing but praise from any of us, but then Bennett, always more of a man for puns and publishing and public appearances than for political judgment, made a remark so astute that it stuck in my mind forever.

"He's a spellbinder," he said, "but I'm glad he's on our side. Because if he weren't, you'd start to worry about his turning out to be the man on horseback."

I saw Hubert Humphrey only a few times after that evening, usually in public with many others, and once after I interviewed him in his Washington office, when he took me to lunch in the Senate Restaurant and told me to order its famous bean soup. From time to time, across the years, we exchanged letters, usually after something he had written.

I remained an admirer until the Vietnam War, when, as Lyndon Baines Johnson's vice-president, he felt he could not speak out against the escalation of that monstrous evil.

But in his last months, whenever I saw him on television, so gaunt, so frail, so old, emaciated by the cancer that was killing him, I found that my shock and grief quickly reverted to my memory of him on that July afternoon in Philadelphia, when he was only thirty-seven, filled with energy and fight, wearing that borrowed press badge so he could find out for himself about the Dixiecrats, and his distaste and distance from everything they stood for.

SIX

AND SUDDENLY I WAS fifty. I had finally finished my father-daughter novel, *The Other Father,* and it had been published the month before my birthday. I took the title from the court scene in Dostoevsky's *The Brothers Karamazov.*

> Gentlemen of the jury, what is a father—a real father? What is the meaning of that great word?

I wanted this third novel of mine to contrast a good, normal parent-child relationship with its opposite, the obsessive one. My story line, the vehicle that would explore this theme, was what we today would call a "father-fixation," its point being that father fixations and mother fixations are apt to be two-way streets, where if a father falls in love with a woman young enough to be his daughter, he may well be acting out the forbidden love for his real daughter, in which case she, his child, may in turn fall in love with a man old enough to be her father.

> But with the children he seemed to be two people. Most of the time he was the father, as Mary was the mother. Then without warning, something snapped . . . transforming him into another kind of man, another kind of father. . . .
> It was this other father who could go from love to fury in one second—the other father within him, who cared too much, who

watched and pondered and demanded too much, who hated too much and loved too much.

Part of my intention was to write the entire novel as if I were doing it before Freud was ever heard of, with not a single reference to "fixation" or neurosis or anything else in the analytic lexicon.

I may have succeeded. It got fair enough reviews, though some were what is called "mixed," it was serialized by Cosmopolitan for two-and-a-half times the price I'd been paid for *Gentleman's Agreement,* and it settled down for a while about midway on the best-seller lists.

But in the long look backward, I can see for myself that it was not what is rated a "major novel."

Neither was the one I had just begun to work on, *The Celebrity.* It was to be my first attempt at social satire in a novel, and it was that same old idea of trying to do an amusing send-up of phony celebrity. I had abandoned it years ago, but as many an author can attest, no idea you are attracted to ever remains permanently abandoned. It may be submerged for ages, but it keeps sending up its periscope every so often to have another look around.

Perhaps my desire to experiment with this different idiom of writing had been freshened by something Eric had written in one of his letters during the shilly-shally.

> I've often wondered why you never make use of that extra arrow in your quiver when you write a book, the arrow of humor that adds so much point to your letters.

But, more specifically, a few months before, on a vacation trip to London, I went through a series of events that finally decided me to go ahead and try it.

I had never gone in for that friendly advice to have my own table at "21" for lunch every day and "queen it over the world"; indeed I had changed nothing in the way I lived. I wanted it to remain just the same, though some people I admired thought it only natural that the moment you had one big success your whole life should reveal it.

When Moss Hart came to my apartment the first time, with the final script of the movie, he took one look around and said, "What luck to find a new apartment in all this housing shortage."

"I didn't just find it, Moss—we've lived here for four years."

"You mean, *before Gentleman's Agreement?*"

But as I sailed for London on the original *Queen Elizabeth,* this special series of events began. Mike and Chris had come to see me off, Mike thirteen and Chris eight, as well as the Whedons, the Simons and other friends. Not only did we find my stateroom abloom with flowers, not only was there a formal invitation to dine at the captain's table, but there was also a publicity man from one of the television stations. A new program, "Ship to Shore" or something like that, had just been launched, to do live interviews with well-knowns on ocean liners arriving in, or departing from, New York.

Alfred Hitchcock was aboard that evening, and was already scheduled for that night's appearance, just as the ship pulled away from the pier. And I, they trusted, would be appearing with him.

I was about to explain that I never went on television, but a chorus of urging arose around me. "Laura, go ahead," and "Laura, do it," and "Live a little—have some fun." Even Mike said, "Sure, mom, *do* it."

I did it. The moment we set sail, the great Hitchcock and I stood side by side on the top deck, to be televised and interviewed "live." Groups of passengers watched it all, and in five minutes everybody on that ship knew not only that Alfred Hitchcock was aboard, but that I was too.

I liked it. All five days at sea I liked it. I never had to be alone for a minute; I made dozens of friends, I never had a meal with strangers. Shipboard cables arrived, one from my travel agent telling me that I would be met at Southhampton by a representative of the Dorchester Hotel, where I was to stay, and another from my London agent, inviting me to dine the night I arrived.

I began to wonder if I hadn't been a bit stodgy and virtuous about "remaining the same," about fretting lest somebody accuse me of "taking it big."

At Southhampton, the usual chore of baggage and customs was taken care of by the Dorchester representative, who also saw me to my first tea on the train to London before demurely retiring. And I liked that too.

At the Dorchester, I was waved into the lobby and never mind about my luggage; it was being taken care of as before. I was in a glow as I announced myself at the front desk, only vaguely aware that the lobby was uncharacteristically noisy and crowded. I had been in London twice during my marriage and I had never seen any such mob in any London hotel.

There was a major convention on, the desk clerk told me, slightly apologetic at the un-English bustle and crush. He was tracing down a page of names, his finger searching for mine, and the room number that would go with it.

I was tired and eager to get upstairs; I had been assured by my travel agent that though I had rejected the suite that she thought appropriate, I would have a delightful large room, high enough for a lovely view of Hyde Park, and I was more than ready for it and its luxurious bathroom, with those heated racks for the oversize bath-towels.

The desk clerk coughed; his finger was at the top of the page once more, starting down the long list of names, this time going more slowly. Something stirred in my mind, probably nothing more than surprise at this unexpected delay.

But a moment later he was turning to the next page of reservations, and then to still another. What stirred then was annoyance and anxiety. There had been some mix-up.

"Apparently there has been some unfortunate error," He said at last. "There seems to be no reservation for Hobson at all."

"That's impossible. It was made weeks ago. My travel agent had a confirmation."

"There is not one available room—this convention—" He called for the manager, a gentleman attired as if for a formal wedding. There was a conference. The manager's finger traced downward through all those names. I waited, silent, frigid and hot all at once. By now, what stirred was indignation.

Endless apologies followed, conferences took place between two or three other members of the staff. I seated myself in the only available chair in the lobby; I thought, If they're going to start phoning other hotels I'll kill them. I'd have to make a dozen phone calls, send a dozen cables about change of address—just thinking it made me as full of outrage as an orange is of juice.

"Just for this one night," the manager was saying as he approached me. He wasn't being suave or cool; he was clearly distressed and wretched. "There is one possible solution, just for tonight, Mrs. Hobson." I later imagined him wringing his hands, but I know he did no such thing.

On the very top floor, he told me, there was a string of small rooms which, in the past, had served for lady's maids, valets and chauffeurs. They had been redecorated, and were now quite acceptable, even charming. If I would consider—of course, in the morning I would be moved to totally suitable quarters, the staff only too happy to do all the moving for me.

He escorted me himself to the string of rooms in the upper reaches of the splendid hotel, right under the eaves, if the Dorchester has eaves. He opened a door. The room was narrower than the old-time maid's rooms they used to build in luxury apartments in New York City.

There was a narrow bed, a shallow dresser, one wooden chair and a flattened oval washbasin barely extending from the wall. Between bed and dresser was a strip of space, perhaps sixteen inches of it.

We had passed the bath, down at the end of the hall. As we did, a handtruck or dolly emerged from the freight elevator, bearing my huge square steamer trunk and smaller luggage. The trunk would have to remain, locked, in the hall. It would never even get into the room.

"The very first thing in the morning, Mrs. Hobson," the manager repeated.

Another truck now appeared. It was loaded with floral arrangements from my London agent, my British publisher, from several friends in London whom I'd written to about my trip.

The manager indicated where the trunk was to be set down, outside my door. The same with the flowers; they were strung out along the baseboard of the hall, with the exception of one smaller one that he himself escorted into my room and set down on the dresser.

"The moment you awake in the morning," the manager repeated as he emerged.

I nodded, went in, closed the door softly and flung myself at the narrow single bed. There was a knot in my throat. My eyes felt hot and I closed them. I would take a nap.

A moment later a picture faded in on the screen of my brain. I saw a large glittering pink bubble, and a tiny, shiny pin approaching it, then piercing it. There was a whoosh, probably of hot air. I sat up, suddenly laughing. Thank God I was laughing. So much for celebrity! So much for being a bigshot!

I heard my own laugh, I felt my own delight. It was a wonderful joke—I couldn't wait to tell it to somebody.

And tell it I did. That afternoon, having cocktails with Hamish Hamilton, who had published the British edition of my little story-book for children, *A Dog Of His Own,* I told the whole story, from Hitchcock on to the wardrobe trunk sitting out there in the hall.

That evening I told the whole story to my London agent, again as a larky anecdote, again laughing until my disbelieving listener finally joined in.

I even told it to the press.

It did something for me, that whole ludicrous episode of grandiosity, saving me, perhaps, from falling for it again in the celebrity culture we lived in. I didn't *want* to be a bigshot or be treated like one. All I wanted to be was an author writing books.

And I went straight back to the one that had been teasing me for years. I begin to search for a story line that would take my theme and turn it into a story.

The Celebrity was begun at last. It was about two brothers, Gregory Johns, a gifted, serious novelist, and Thornton Johns, a successful insurance broker, who helps him with mundane matters like taxes but who has no gifts whatever except charm and a born salesman's gift of gab.

When Gregory's novel about world government, *The Good World,* through a fluke, is chosen by a major book club, and then hits every jackpot there is, with movies, lectures, radio interviews and the rest, it is not Gregory who becomes the celebrity but his brother Thornton, loquacious, joke-telling Thornton. He appears in his brother's place at a literary luncheon, then at another, and then begins to lecture on his own, "My Brother Gregory Johns." It's the next best thing to lectures by a "real-live author," and audiences lap it up.

And he's not the only one who suddenly is "a somebody." Harriet, Gregory's teenage daughter, lets herself become a celebrity among her schoolfriends, loving the new attention she gets; his mother, in her small town on Long Island, cannot resist passing along to her neighbors every crumb of news about her famous son, and discovers the limelight all for herself; and so does Gregory's niece, his nephews, his butcher and baker and grocer and newspaper boy. While he keeps on quietly writing, they all batten on his fame and find it sweet to be somebody who knows Gregory Johns.

This novel too had its share of good reviews and its place on the middle rungs of the best-seller list. It too made a decent amount of money, and even sold to the movies, bought for a rather low price by Paramount because there was no active bidding on it by other studios. It was to be produced by F. Hugh Herbert, who had done such comedy hits as *The Moon Is Blue, Kiss and Tell,* and others.

And yet, I was vaguely dissatisfied with both these novels, though I would have been hard-pressed back then to say why. I remember wondering if I had turned them out too quickly—never before had I written two books in less than three years. Writing them had given me good hours of work and a sense of accomplishment, yes, but not the same sort I had known as I was working on my first two books.

This was more like the satisfaction I got from writing a story or novelette for the magazines, on-the-surface, evanescent.

I was not wise enough then, I am sure, to think of these two novels as lesser works or minor novels. But I did know that I had written them largely as an observer of other people's lives, and I believe I had already begun to realize that only a novel that sprang from some private compulsive necessity, like *Gentleman's Agreement,* could give me the truest sense that I was doing work that I at least felt was "major."

I think it was Chekhov who said that the only things worth writing about are those things in one's life that are too painful to talk about. Those things do not come from watching other people's lives; they come only from the basic stuff of your own life. And so, long before I was ready to begin my fifth novel, I was once again searching for buried private material which I'd come to see was where my best writing—anybody's best writing?—always came from.

My publishers harbored no such misgivings about my last two books, and after *The Celebrity* was published in the fall of 1951, and with no prompting from me, they suddenly up and offered me a security contract of $50,000 for my next two. They would advance me $3,000 on signing the contract, and then $1,000 a month for the next forty-seven months, through 1956.

I would be fifty-six years old! For each book, an advance of $25,000! To me it was an upward leap in my professional status, and though for a while I had said I preferred small advances and had asked Dick to cut the one for *Gentleman's Agreement* back to $2,500, half of what he had offered me for my first book, I had been slowly changing my mind about "using up all your royalties before your book even came out."

My attorney and my agent and my own ego had been pointing out that many authors I knew were receiving substantial advances, that publishers often did lots more promotion and selling on books on which they had risked large advances, and by the time Dick had offered me a $10,000 advance for *The Celebrity,* I had decided to take action on my new point of view.

"There's a sort of cachet about larger advances," I told him.

"How much larger?"

"I thought fifteen." I saw him shake his head. "If it doesn't earn it," I added impulsively, "I'll pay back the difference."

My attorney was to frown at that when he examined the contracts, talking darkly about setting up precedents, and it was never written in as a clause or subclause.

But when my royalties did fall short—I never did understand how a novel that was on the best-seller list for several weeks could earn less than $15,000, but so it was to be—when it did, then, quixotically enough, I did remind Dick of my promise, and did write, in a formal and binding document, "I feel a moral, though not a legal, obligation to repay you" the unearned $3,473.97 on this book.

But that was in another contract, still off in the future, and the present was this offer of four years of security via those monthly payments. I did stipulate that the payments were not to start until I had actually begun writing whatever the next book was to be.

I was busier than ever. In addition to the council meetings of the Authors League, and to the more frequent ones of the American Civil Liberties Union, I had been for some time a member of the Writers' Board for World Government. The World Federalist movement had been formed shortly after the end of the war and in New York some twenty authors, playwrights and editors had grouped together to give what aid we could to this cause we believed in.

Gregory Johns, in *The Celebrity,* had used the theme of world government in his surprise best-seller *The Good World*, and of course my friends on the Writers Board liked having me do a novel that might spread the word. Partly as a jest, I dedicated my book to all of them.

THIS BOOK IS DEDICATED
TO
Lee and Peg and Frederica
and Ruth and Annalee
and Kip and Merle and Alan
and Norman and Bob and John and
Jerry and Cord and Kipper and
Russel and Rex and Oscar

To identify some of them, Kip's last name was Fadiman, Merle's was Miller, Norman's was Cousins, John's was Hersey, Russel's was Crouse, Rex's was Stout and Oscar's was Hammerstein.

A group of writers, everyone usually swamped by his or her own work, giving one evening every week, year after year, to the impossible ideal of world government? Looking back to those arduous, and ardent, meetings, I do not find myself thinking, What visionaries we all were, what knee-jerk liberals. Instead I think, with some nostalgia and envy, How young we were, and how decent. Weren't we, perhaps, ancestors of those young people today, marching to ban the bomb, marching for a nuclear freeze?

And were we not, in those days of the cold war and the rise of McCarthyism, risking all sorts of harassment and attack for ourselves? The voices of red-baiters were rising to new crescendos. At the Authors League there was a surge of new determination to separate the two main guilds, the Dramatists and the Authors, from the "payroll guilds" of radio writers, screenwriters and television writers; this move had been under way for some time, but now it became a lively topic of discussion. I was nearly alone in protesting that part of the motive, never spoken of by anybody, was to put a distance between ourselves and those already tainted by being listed in Red Channels or by their association with the Hollywood Ten.

This was stoutly denied at our meetings, but I was appointed as a committee—of one, of course—to look into this matter, and I went up one morning to the Columbia Broadcasting Building, then on Madison Avenue, to meet with a group of radio writers, urging them not to go along with this move for separation, not to become a splinter group.

"Whether you're on a payroll," I remember saying, "or a freelance, you're a writer, and the Authors League is the nearest thing to a writers' union we have. Splintering it five ways is union-busting, when you get right down to it."

I lost out in the end, and the separations took place, but I never regretted trying. By then I had sharpened up the letters I myself wrote to groups *I* wanted to separate myself from, and they had lost the discursive, overexplanatory flaws of my early ones.

One such was my reply to a follow-up letter from the "Civil Rights Congress"—oh, those names of committees! Perhaps I had become too cynical, but what I paid attention to was not the names of committees but the names of the sponsors or members. This letter began, "A few weeks ago, you received an appeal from DASHIELL HAMMETT, for the Civil Rights Journal." The capitalized name stood out from the lower-case letters like a headline.

I wrote pretty tersely, asking that my name be removed from their mailing list. "It will save you much postage and me much irritation."

I have tried and will continue to try, to fight for civil and human rights. But I will never join with people who raise a great hue and cry over the curtailment or loss of those rights in the U.S., but keep beautifully mum about the same kind of thing in Czechoslovakia, Poland, the USSR. . . .

Later I was invited, by a revised version of ICCASP, now called the National Council of the Arts, Sciences and Professions, to speak in Carnegie Hall, "at a public meeting on civil liberties."

I wrote politely that I never lectured, but then added very much the same paragraph, with one addition.

This is because I believe that civil liberty is indivisible, like peace or prosperity, and that [to take] a nationalist view of it, instead of an international one, is tantamount to saying that one can pick and choose . . . that *this* civil liberty means a lot but that *that* civil liberty doesn't matter.

I had taken to ending each letter with one simple sentence. "I prefer to work instead, for civil liberties and the dignity of man, through organizations like ADA and the ACLU."

And in every letter, too, I would include my plea, "If I am incorrect, if you have made public statements protesting the loss of liberty in the USSR or in other nations dominated by the Soviet Union, please send me copies . . ."

Never, not once, did I ever receive any such copies, not from one of the groups I had written to.

Still, through ADA and the ACLU, as well as in my own discussions and arguments, I went right on upholding any citizen's rights to his own political beliefs. I was appalled when Hubert Humphrey introduced a bill in Congress that would have made the American Communist party illegal, and was later to tell him so, with as much diplomatic tact as I could muster, in a personal interview in his Washington office. I detested President Truman's program of loyalty oaths; I felt that they were meaningless among those with disloyal intentions, who would easily sign anything, and that they were demeaning to ordinary citizens, as if demanding that they proclaim in writing, "I am not now nor will I ever be a traitor to my country."

And so I went on practicing Louis Fischer's "double rejection" in every way I could. It had become the parallel bars on which I exercised *my* right to say, "A plague on both your houses."

* * *

One day just about then the doorbell rang and when I opened it, there was a tall slender young man holding out a small I.D. card so that I could read it.

"The FBI," he said pleasantly.

"The what?"

"Federal Bureau of Investigation. May I come in?"

I hardly glanced at his identity card. I was so flustered that I remained silent as I stood back and let him precede me into the living room.

In those days there was no sign in the lobby of every apartment house saying, All Guests Must Be Announced, and it was a Thursday —maid's day off. Norman Gibson was still with us, and if he had been there answering doorbells, I might have had a moment to prepare myself for what lay ahead. As it was, I was robbed of any warning or rehearsal time.

So all I said, as I motioned him to a chair, was, "I'll be back in a minute," and departed for my bedroom. It was some vague instinct to change my dress, fix my hair, freshen my lipstick. I was in one of my "working dresses," this an old one in red-and-black plaid, light and comfortable, and so worn that it was out at the elbows.

But by the time I reached my room I must have decided that it was nonsensical, this reflex action of getting dressed up in a time of peril, and I did none of the above. What I did was equally nonsensical: I reached for a handsome new piece of jewelry I had treated myself to, not diamonds but a flower-shaped arrangement of pale pink tourmaline stones, oval cabochons set in gold.

This pinned to my left shoulder, I returned to whatever awaited me, shredded elbows and all. I was less flustered, God knows why.

"Yes?" I greeted him. "What's this about?"

"Your friend Joseph Than."

"Pepo?" I know I sounded surprised. I hope I didn't also sound relieved, but I may have.

"In reference to a new motion-picture program the U.S. is planning in West Germany, part of the postwar effort."

Pepo, born in Austria, had been a well-known producer and writer of films in Germany, Austria and France before the war, had served in the French Army, and after a series of Nazi-caused disasters had finally arrived in the United States, his spirit and health very nearly destroyed.

I had met him during the first of my two money-earning stints in Hollywood studios, and we had become good friends, even writing an

121

original together, *Half a Sin,* with Pepo supplying most of the plot and me doing all the writing. It never sold.

He was as interested in political matters as I was, far more sympathetic to Russian policy than I could ever be, and many times we had spirited arguments, but without the underlying hot emotion that always characterized my disagreements with my sister.

He had applied, the FBI man told me, for an important post in a projected film company being established in Germany as part of our Americanization program during the occupation. This was a security check, quite routine, before any government job could be assigned to anybody stationed in Berlin.

"A security check?"

"Only about his general political position."

"It's just about like mine," I said. "He voted for Roosevelt, so did I; he hates poverty and bigotry, so do I. I hate witch hunts and red-baiting and the tactics of the House Un-American Activities Committee, and so does he."

I had meant to keep my voice calm and equable, but I could hear it rising. My gentle-sounding inquisitor was taking notes, not steadily or copiously, just a jot now and then. I felt resentment beginning to glow inside me.

"I suppose all this is going into my dossier too," I heard myself say testily.

"Oh not really," he said placidly. "The dossier on you is fairly thorough as it is."

That rather threw me. He was so matter of fact, so polite. I raised my hands, palms facing each other, one about ten inches above the other.

"I suppose it's that thick," I said.

He measured the distance cheerfully. "Not quite."

The interview went on, as aimlessly as that, for another few minutes. Any specific questions about what groups or committees Pepo supported brought forth my same answer: the same sort I do: the ADA, the ACLU, the Authors League. What newspapers, magazines, books did he prefer? The same as I did. I named the Times, Time Magazine, The New Yorker, the Saturday Review, Harper's, the Atlantic.

"As for me," I added, "because I write a lot of political promotion, I also keep looking in at the *Daily Worker,* but I don't think he does."

He made a few last notes and rose. I remember feeling a bit proud of my last remark, as if I were daring him to make something of it.

But he let it just lie there, and as we approached the door, I added one more remark I was to remember.

"You know something? You look a lot like Alger Hiss, tall and nice-looking."

If they had a dossier on me, they must have known that Thayer was once married to Priscilla Fanzler, who later married Alger Hiss, and that years before I had met him on many an occasion, if only for a few minutes at our front door, because it was he, and not Priscilla, who would bring Thayer's small son over for his periodic visits.

This remark the FBI man totally ignored, except for what I decided was a tired smile. As I closed the door on him I suddenly felt pretty tired myself, vaguely wishing I hadn't gone in for wisecracks.

What I didn't suspect was that this little episode was going to lead me into another of the painful periods in my life. I told it to Pepo as an amusing story, and to Eric and to other friends, and then one day at lunch I told it to my sister Alice.

It was one of our good periods; we had been seeing each other and avoiding talk of politics, steering clear of those sudden quarrels that seemed part of our destiny. As I told her about the I.D. card suddenly offered me at my front door and the revealing nonsense about affixing my new tourmaline jewel to my worn dress before going back to the FBI man, her face took on the look I had come to know so well, a kind of rigid resistance that showed disapproval at least, with disdain right behind it.

"You should have shut the door in his face," she said.

"I what?"

"Should have said you wanted your attorney to be present and not even let him in."

Much later I realized that she was right. After the McCarthy hearings I discovered you couldn't give any answers at all without being in contempt if you refused to give other answers. But that was in a court trial, not in your own house—it hadn't even occurred to me to talk of my attorney or shut the door in the man's face.

"What would you do," Alice suddenly asked, "if they had come here asking about me?"

"I guess about the same."

"Would you tell them where I worked?"

She had quit teaching science in high school some years before and was now doing voluntary part-time work with a magazine or periodical that was like the *Daily Worker,* perhaps even connected to it.

"I wouldn't tell them one damn thing they didn't know already."

"But you'd confirm it if they said it first?"

We were off, then and there, to one of the worst times that had ever risen between us. Everything I said was wrong, everything I didn't say was wrong. I hadn't learned yet—as I was to learn years later—that any sudden confrontation of hostile questioning was unfair, a kind of entrapment, no matter where it came from; I didn't know as yet that I should have said, "I'm not asking that my attorney be present, but I do ask that I have some calm time to think these things over, coming at me out-of-the-blue as they are. You've had some training in this sort of thing—I never have."

I cannot now disentangle all the steps of our quarrel; I cannot even put them in exact sequence. For years I was sure I could never forget a single phrase, but after my sister's death many years later, I was given two other versions of what happened, both based on *her* account of that day, and since then, parts of those versions have fuzzed up my own memory, though not, I think, in any vital sense.

One thing that bears no fuzziness whatever is a cry from me. "I'd go to jail before I'd ever say you're a communist."

"I'm not a communist."

"You're not a—?"

"That's right. I'm not a communist and I never was."

"Al, I'm your *sister*—how can you say—? Why, once you showed me your party card!"

"I never did any such thing. I never had a card."

How we gave up, how we changed the subject, I can no longer remember, but somehow we did at last get clear of this subject. I asked about her little girl, Lizzie, a lovely child she and Milton had recently adopted after years of his refusal to consider adoption at all. And I asked about her son Paul, now a young man, very bright, on his first job.

"He just lost it," she said.

"How awful. Why? What happened?"

It was another case, so prevalent then, of running into the new business of "security clearance," and I asked how he was taking it, did he have another job lined up, was he interviewing other possible employers, did she think this clearance experience would hurt him in the future?

I probably gabbled on—we both wanted to get through that miserable lunch and go our separate ways.

*   *   *

And go our separate ways. Only after I wrote those words just now did I see how fitting a phrase it was, and how literal.

From the beginning of this autobiography I have tried to tell things more or less in their natural chronological order, but here I would like to make an exception and project far into the years ahead.

That quarrel took place during a period when I had not yet begun my next book, when I was not writing steadily, making daily notes in my log, of pages and rewrites and other important matters, and so my log for that year does not even mention this unhappy lunch with my sister.

It is not until many datebooks or logs later that there is an entry about it, this on a page headed, January 11, 1964—thirteen years later.

Alice—2 P.M.
first time since May, 1951

At the beginning of those absent years I did not even realize that we had begun this first great separation of our lives. So often, after some quarrel, we had let months elapse without seeing each other, a sort of rest period, until finally one or the other—usually it was I—would make a conciliatory gesture that brought us together again. I often said I loved her more than she loved me.

But this time, slow though I was to catch on, I finally saw that Alice was gone. The first clue might have been some birthday letter I sent with no answer from her, or some phone call never returned. But Alice was never much of a letter-writer, and probably I put down the unanswered note or unreturned phone message to neglect or something equally ordinary.

Finally I did catch on. This was no temporary absence, this was no forgotten phone call. She was through with me. At last it had got to a point where whatever could flare up so hotly between us had left nothing but ashes, at least for my sister.

Perhaps it should have been the same for me, but it was not. It hurt, it made me angry, perhaps it stirred, far down in my unconscious, the sad misery I used to feel as a little girl when she wouldn't play with me, when she would taunt me by saying, "Nobody's ever going to love you—I pity your poor husband."

Through those silent years, I would go from anger to indifference

125

to that awful sense of loss that gives people you love their greatest single power to punish you for whatever they think you did to them, their only weapon, absence.

From time to time, when I would renew my visits to Dr. Gosselin for another refresher session to cope with some new attack of depression, I would speak of Alice and the choice she had made. "It's just as well," I would say. "The hardest, the most maddening of all human assignments are family relationships."

On another day I would say, "It's like being exiled to Siberia." On still another, I would change the simile. "It's like being excommunicated from the Catholic church." And at last I found a greater immediacy: "It's like McCarthyism—I don't even know what I'm accused of."

It was not until that January day thirteen years later that I finally found out. I had written once again, a letter saying I had just finished writing a novel "about our childhood, about Pa and Ma and Jamaica." And I had ended it by saying, "If the Soviet Union and the United States now believe in 'peaceful co-existence,' why can't we try it once more?"

This time she did answer, saying she had thought we would never see each other again "in this vale of tears," and giving me her telephone number. We met and spent an entire afternoon together, for a long time not even mentioning those lost years.

Her husband had died a few years before; I told her I had heard it from a stranger, seated next to me at Roseland, of all places, during a big fund-raising dinner for the Wiltwyck School for Boys. The stranger had asked if I weren't her sister, and when he told me of Milton's death, my look of shock told him I hadn't even known about it. I asked if he knew whether she was all right, comfortably fixed. I had wondered, I told Alice, if she were in any kind of need, if I ought to call her right then and offer my help.

She laughed at that. For all of Milton's lifelong denunciation of the capitalist system, I gathered, he had left her a small fortune in stocks and bonds and tax-free municipals. She was ten times richer than I'd ever be.

Only at the end of the long afternoon did I ask, "Why the thirteen years?" We both had known it would come down to that.

I could hardly believe what she told me. It all went back to that final meeting we had had, to what I had told her about how I had received the FBI agent, how I had answered all his questions. But far more than that, it was my own behavior after she had told me about Paul losing his job, how many questions I had asked, and in such detail, about the security clearance, about his plans, whether he had any new job in mind, whether he was planning any new interviews . . .

There was something all wrong in that much interest, she had felt; there was something unnatural about it. Could it be, she began to wonder, couldn't it be that I might turn Paul in to the FBI? She couldn't risk it. Milton agreed with her.

Even writing it now makes it sound too preposterous to set down. How anybody in this world who had ever met me for an hour, who had read a page of anything I had written, how anybody who really knew me could think for one moment that I would turn over my own nephew to the FBI . . .

"If ever there was paranoia," I stormed to Dr. Gosselin, "this has to be it. She would never be analyzed—analysis is forbidden in Stalin's Russia."

How I kept from shouting my head off at her then and there, during our reunion, I can not say. But I knew that another fierce quarrel would doubtless mean another thirteen years—perhaps that halted me.

But after Alice's death those two other versions I spoke of actually extended the nightmare. What Alice really had decided was that I might turn in not only Paul but Milton and herself as well.

Toward the end of volume one of this autobiography, I said that I was beginning to have some bitter thoughts about the terrible chasms that could develop in families where there were passionate differences about politics, and I said that it made me speculate about what families must have gone through a century before, about abolition and slavery. I sometimes imagined writing a novel, I said, not about two brothers facing each other, ready to kill, on a battlefield in the Civil War, but about two sisters today, torn apart over Stalin and Russia.

Today a new dimension adds itself to those dark thoughts. I think now that the horror that had wrecked Alice and me for those thirteen years sprang not only from our lifelong differences about communism; it was also a product of the noxious suspicions of the era we were then living through, filled with accusers like Red Channels and informers like the "friendly witnesses" in the trial of the Hollywood Ten. The Rosenberg espionage case was getting under way, filling the nation's front pages just at the time of that lunch with Alice, and the chief evidence against them came from Ethel's brother David Greenglass and his wife. In Russia it had long been known that kids would turn in sister, brother, mother, father, if they thought them "enemies of the revolution." Apparently the idea that it was possible had seeped its miasmic poison into the air we breathed in decent America.

The air breathed by the sister I loved so much.

CHAPTER

SEVEN

THE "REST PERIOD" AFTER that fierce FBI quarrel back in May of '51 was filled with a rush of happier matters: my two boys and I were about to set forth on the kind of vacation we had tried once before and had found to be better than any other vacation we'd ever had, a cross-country trip by car with a summer on the beach in California.

The first time we had tried it was two years earlier, a few days after I got home from London and the Dorchester and my own experiment at living the grand life of celebrity. It had been the dead opposite of bigshotism. We ate in diners at truck stops, where hamburgers cost a dime and milk or coffee a nickel, we spent nights in motels, where room and bath went for ten dollars, we wore shirts and shorts and sneakers, drove hundreds of miles a day through the plains, through the Rockies, the deserts, to the coast, loving all of it.

And here we were starting out once again. This time we were going to include lots more territory, parts of Canada and the Canadian Rockies, and spend the summer at Malibu, but *not* so I could work for any studio. This was just vacation.

It was the end of the school year, and I was proud of my two sons. Mike, now going on fifteen, won the history prize for the eighth grade, and Chris, not yet ten, was awarded the prize for original composition in the fourth.

Mike was managing adolescence in his usual amiable fashion, with endless hanging on the phone, dating many girls, going to everybody's parties.

Chris, all too often, was still "being impossible" in various ways. Whatever troubles he had at school were what was called "behavior problems," and seemed to be rooted in his eternal rebellion at what everybody else took for granted. Was sports the big thing? Not for him; he wanted shop and drawing. And what some might call merely boyish pranks sometimes made the headmaster of the lower school ask me to come up for a conference, like his trick of abandoning the seat assigned to him in the school bus and lying down in the aisle instead for the entire trip.

At home his hobby was, yes truly, writing. Writing a book, what's more, the first one entitled *Freddy The Pig,* closely related to the fifteen or so *Freddy* books of the animal series by Walter R. Brooks, and subsequent ones dealing with a Bengal tiger named Benjy and other denizens of the jungle or barnyard.

He had begun his literary career two years before, when he was eight, during a summer we had spent in Provincetown, near Bennett and Phyllis Cerf's house, and he and Chris Cerf, also eight, had gone into a publishing partnership together, to be known as The Cerfson Company. Chris Cerf was to be the publishing genius, while my Chris was to supply all the manuscript necessary to get going. At least he acted as if he were to be sole supplier—through long stretches of his childhood he spent hours writing with a persistence that startled me. A "book" was about a hundred handwritten pages, perhaps twenty thousand words. His heroes were always members of the animal kingdom. One line I have never forgotten came early on in a book about a rhinoceros, name now forgotten. I'll call him "Rhino."

He aimed Rhino at the enemy . . .

Before Chris tired of the whole thing he had amassed half a dozen of his manuscripts; at times he was busily writing while I was struggling around for an idea for my next book, the first of the two under my security contract. I was fascinated at his choice of a hobby, matched only by his love for making model planes and ships, but the time would yet come, after he had his first portable typewriter, given by me in true innocence of what might follow, when his favorite hobby was metamorphosed into a direct challenge to me, still in my futile struggle for that elusive big idea for my next book.

"Shut your door," I would sometimes shout at him. "I can't stand that damn clackety-clack, clackety-clack, clackety-clack. You *never* stop."

And then I would be flooded with maternal guilt and hate myself savagely. It would be instantly obvious to any child analyst that he was setting himself out to rival me, but what about my theoretical insight and maturity? Was I suddenly bereft of both?

Not that I wasn't writing. I was doing fiction again for the magazines—by this time anything I wrote was sure to be bought and published. I was also writing a television version of *The Other Father,* under the aegis and with the considerable help of Worthington Miner, the producer of CBS's highly regarded series, "Studio One." This starred June Lockhart, was nicely reviewed, and earned me all of $900, the going rate at that time for an hour-long TV drama, for the book itself and the teleplay too.

CBS also bought *The Celebrity* for a TV comedy, but Tony Miner and his high standards had nothing to do with it, I was not asked to write it, and, for once, I had "author's approval," so when I saw the shoddy script that came out of it, I exercised my legal right to reject it. A rather miserable scene took place over this "unusual" decision, during a meeting with several of CBS's finest, but as my log says: "Rejection of TV version of *The Celeb* stands!"

And suddenly I was doing a new kind of writing, something I had never tried before, and immediately found very entertaining. Bennett Cerf, who had done "Trade Winds" for years as a weekly column in the Saturday Review, nominated me as his vacation replacement. I told Norman Cousins that I wouldn't even try to emulate Bennett's jokes and puns, that I'd like to try my own idea of what "Trade Winds" should be: a weekly report on the world of books, authors, editors, agents, deals, inside dope, oddments about literary personalities.

This lasted for five weeks, and went so well that I did it all over again for six weeks later that same year. My daily life suddenly changed. I was swamped not only with new books, galleys of books, uncorrected proofs, but with letters, the likes of which I had never seen. When I returned for my second stint, I wrote about those letters.

> You "Trade Winds" readers turned out to be the most articulate, informative, opinionated, cantankerous and delightful letter-writers on earth. . . . Wasn't it La Rochefoucauld who called gratitude a lively sense of favors yet to come?

The letters continued to come, from authors, critics, publishers. educators and just regular people. Two of these I couldn't resist showing Norman Cousins; he decided they should appear right in the magazine, not in "Trade Winds" but on the popular Letters page itself.

Thurber to Hobson to Thurber
I cannot be niggardly enough to keep to myself the following letters by James Thurber. First, however, as background for them, two excerpts from my stand-in columns for "Trade Winds." The first one is about my sons and books.

"The younger one, also without suggestion from me, embarked on voracious book-reading two summers ago. . . . He has just finished Hemingway's *Old Man and the Sea* and his fifteenth (approximately) reading of *The Thirteen Clocks* by James Thurber. He liked the new Hemingway also but says Thurber is still the best.

. . . Mary Welch Hemingway . . . has just turned in to Today's Woman a 2,500-word piece which will start a new series, to be called 'The Man I Married.' . . . [There will be] ensuing articles by Mrs. James Thurber, Mrs. Mario Lanza, Mrs. Richard Rodgers, Mrs. Dale Carnegie, Mrs. Eddie Cantor, Mrs. Leonard Lyons and the like."

Letter from James Thurber, dated September 17, 1952:

If you had ever met my wife, you would know that there isn't enough money on earth or wild horses in hell to get her to do a piece about me called, "My Life with James Thurber," or whatever WOMAN'S DAY calls it. (I don't know about it in caps, but woman's day is done, you know.) A guy and a doll from Time came up here two years ago, and the guy says to Helen on the porch, "Would you care to evaluate your husband's work?" Her answer was simple and wonderful; she said, "No." I would never have married a woman who would write about me while I am alive or when I'm dead. I am repelled by husband-evaluators. I am putting such a woman in a piece I am now writing and she'll make you sick. If I lived in Cuba, I probably wouldn't give a damn. Now you lift me out of that list of husbands in which you included me with a casual and calloused "and the like."! The like of that group of boys has never been known before.

Laura, you used to know me! Love and kisses just the same

to you and your boys, especially the younger one. I think he is better than Hemingway too.

As always,
Jim Thurber

To which I replied in part:

I just called the editor of Today's Woman, and asked how the hell he could have included your wife's name in his story, inasmuch as (a) he sent me the story in a signed letter, and (b) I had taken the trouble to phone him long distance, at the Saturday Review's expense, to read back the item word for word, to check its accuracy. [He said that] an intermediary had led him to believe that an article by Helen Thurber was actually forthcoming. . . . Anyway, all apologies to you, to Helen, to West Cornwall, and anybody else listening.

I then offered public retraction, asked whether I could quote parts of his letter in same and offered to send him whatever I wrote for his approval, to avoid compounding of errors.

Letter from James Thurber, dated October 2, 1952:

I think it's probably too late now, but if you want to use any parts of that letter of mine, you can do it, and you don't have to let me see anything in advance. I understand there actually is an "intermediary" who thought he could get Helen to write about me. He has met her several times and she is very sweet and gentle and courteous, and she has never fired at him at point-blank range. Where do men get the idea they understand women, for God's sake?

I have been going through a thyroid thing or I would have got this off sooner. Once again my love and best wishes in the hope that we can sit around together sometime and wonder whatever became of Barrow Lyon, Bob Potter, and such of the others that are not dead. I have one or two scandalous facts, but they are about the dead ones.

As always,
Jim

That exchange took up nearly the entire Letters page. I ended it by writing, "After which I can only add the hope that SR readers will be as delighted as I was that I committed my error and earned Mr. Thurber's scolding."

Doing a regular column was not the only new experience entering my life in that busy year of 1952. Many of my friends were giving some of their time to the still new world of television; Bennett Cerf was already a national celebrity on "What's My Line?" and frequently Phyllis would ask me to go with her to the theater where the program was done "live," as we say now. Later we would wind up at the Oak Room of the Plaza Hotel, usually with Arlene Francis, who was also a star on the show, and her husband Marty Gabel, together with Mark Goodson and Bill Todman, the show's producers, already planning their next big game show, "I've Got a Secret."

I had tried television twice already, neither effort destined for high ratings or long life, perhaps because they were on a higher brow level. One was a word-game show, "Superghosts," and what with my hobby for solving double-crostics without reference books, and for the erudite British version of crossword puzzles, I had to be good at it, and therefore was relaxed and at ease doing it. Another show, "Conversation," also came easily to me, and though the fees were only "scale," meaning inadequate for the time and effort involved, I really liked doing them both. These two were being developed by a CBS vice-president, Lou Cowan, who later hit pure gold with the "$64,000 Question," gold, to be followed some years later by some pretty hot scandal when it was charged that it was rigged.

Then I was asked to try out for "I've Got a Secret." I tried out for it, was signed to a six-show contract, quailed a little when I was told the producers hoped I'd turn out to be "the Arlene Francis of the new show," but affirmed that I was not a bit tense or anxious. Indeed, during rehearsals they told me I was just fine.

The very first time I set forth, in evening dress, to do a real show, however, my son Mike stopped me at the elevator door and said, "Mom, do you want to take both of them?" He was pointing to what I was holding in each hand. One was my evening bag, the other my big daytime purse. I gulped and handed over the big one, and knew I was in trouble.

I don't know now what induced me to try out for the Goodson-Todman type of show, so different from the ones I felt comfortable with. Maybe it was my growing need for escape from the nibble of doubt about not finding that good solid idea for my next book; the nibble showed its shiny little teeth more and more often unless I kept myself busy, busy, busy.

A weekly television show keeps you busy, getting your hair done, planning what dress to wear, avoiding last week's dress as if the whole country would notice it was the same, thinking up amusing remarks you'd make if you got a chance.

"Secret" offered three or four guests, each equipped with one secret that was revealed to the audience but not to the panel. The panel was told nothing except the general area of the secret: something done in sports, some unusual trip taken, something important being planned.

The program supposedly was ad lib, absolutely unrehearsed. Quite true. Nevertheless, as we were going through makeup for my sixth program, the assistant producer offhandedly said to me, "When the last guest goes on, and your turn comes, one line of questioning you might take would be to ask, 'Is it risky in any way?' or 'Is it dangerous?' You might even try, 'Is it something you wish you could get out of?' or 'Is it something you'll be ashamed of in the morning?' "

When the last guest appeared, it was a movie star, the leading-man type, Ricardo Somebody or Francesco Somebody. The audience was told the secret, but all the panel knew was the general clue, "It's something I'm going to do."

The audience tittered, but I began. "Is it something off in the distant future?"

"Not in the distant future, no."

"Something you're going to do right away?"

"As soon as I can." (Another titter.)

"Is this something risky you're planning?" (Laughter from the audience.)

"Not really."

"Is it dangerous?" (Louder laughter.)

"I hope not."

"Well, is it something you'll be ashamed of in the morning?" (Shrieks of laughter, with lascivious overtones.)

When my allotted time was over, movie star Ricardo or Francesco revealed his secret, which the audience had known all along.

"I'm going to kiss Laura Hobson tonight."

He came over to give me a lush and lasting kiss, the laughing changed to guffaws, and I felt like the biggest damn fool in the world.

Maybe that tawdry little bit of business helped me to recognize that big popular show-biz wasn't for me, any more than lecturing had been, or public autographing parties, or book-promotion tours, all of which seemed to appeal so much to so many authors I knew, including some I respected.

More likely I just wasn't very good at being the Arlene Francis type. Even more likely, the sponsor said nix. My brief contract was not renewed, my TV career was ended and I was back where I belonged —at my typewriter.

By that time my security contract with S&S was about eight months old, and I was still struggling and searching for my next book; I had not yet taken even the first payment under the contract, and I had begun to wonder if something had happened to me, if the big beautiful contract was some sort of new hurdle that was stopping me dead in my tracks.

I even found myself in trouble with a short story I was working on. It too kept stopping me, though every instinct told me that it was too good an idea to give up.

One night I drove over to Dobbs Ferry to see the managing editor of Good Housekeeping, Margaret Cousins, herself a fiction writer. As I began telling her my plot, I found it took me quite a long time to spell out its main lines, and its interweaving ones, and I myself discovered that there was too much already in my mind for the brevity of a short story, that what was demanded was the greater length and complexity of a novelette. There was old age in it, and loneliness, opposed to a young mother's need for more money, better living conditions, security for her tense little daughter. And so I began once more at page one of *The Reward*.

> It's not true I'm a miser, Annie Stoner thought as she pulled down the shade at the barred kitchen window. But if you're old, there isn't much, except to save.
>
> She seated herself at the table, counted off five bills, rolled them into a tight spindle, and then bound the spindle with a tiny elastic band, the kind that holds knitting needles together. This was a hundred dollars, this thin spear of green, and in an hour there would be forty-nine more spindles just like it. . . .
>
> Twenty years of life and work and loneliness lay there before her, waiting to be sorted and bound into the beautiful shaftlike spindles. They *are* beautiful, she thought, as a year is beautiful, as the strength to work is beautiful . . .
>
> If one is old, she thought again, what else? She *was* old, seventy but for a few months.

I always seem to denigrate anything I wrote for the national magazines; that pejorative word, the "slicks," always stands between me and a belief that some magazine fiction could actually be worthwhile. But as research for these pages I am now writing I just reread *The Reward*, and found a good deal of satisfaction in it, saw an increased skill in handling several threads of the story, an increasing ability to create character and situation that might hold the reader, perhaps even move the reader.

Even back then I must have had a fair amount of respect for what I was writing because as my manuscript lengthened and grew, its pages piling up, I began to think that *it* might be my next novel, and began to confide that hope to my log.

"*The Reward* a book?" was the first such entry. It was followed every few days with others.

> *The Reward* may be my 5th novel.
> Short? 50,000 words.
> To p. 46—a book!!
> Told Lee I *think The Reward* is my 5th novel.
> Sent 46 p. to Dick Simon.

I also sent it to Margaret Cousins and to Edith Haggard, my agent for stories. I told everybody that I knew I would have to enlarge it and deepen it if it were to become a full-length book, and it was wonderful when everybody praised what I had already done as a very good start. What a blessed relief to have the long search done with at last.

And right then I was interrupted by a phone call that would take me away from New York, from my two boys, from Eric, take me away for the whole fall, keeping me away until Thanksgiving and the inescapable rush of the holiday season. *The Reward* was left behind too.

For the past four years, Eric and I were indeed "in and out of each other's lives," thus far mostly "in," with none of the long lapses he was to write about as he looked back so many years later. This one lasted only a few months, but it was well-timed, for he had to be away from New York too, either in Washington or in Springfield, Illinois.

Part of his absence was indirectly due to President Truman, and more explicitly to William S. Paley, president of CBS; the other part was due to John Kenneth Galbraith and the presidential campaign of Adlai E. Stevenson.

The Washington part was because President Truman had called upon Paley to head up a new commission on raw materials for future industrial expansion, and Paley, a friend and admirer of Eric, had invited him to be a member, and, I think, to write the official report.

The Illinois one came about because John Kenneth Galbraith had an idea. He wrote about it himself, in the Afterword he did for Eric's unfinished autobiography.

> In the late summer of 1952 I was in Springfield, Illinois, helping Adlai Stevenson with his speeches. We were desperately in need of more talent, and . . . I brought up the name of Hodgins. The suggestion was immediately accepted. I phoned Eric, and he arrived within a few hours.
>
> As a ghost writer he was incredibly unsuccessful. The speech drafts were wonderful—but pure Hodgins. He could not accommodate to Adlai's political style and was, I suspect, too honest even to try. There was also the old problem of length. Minimum delivery time for a Hodgins draft would have been about three hours. . . . I remember lunching with Eric one day in Springfield. He was deeply, silently in depression over what he considered his failure. I remember my own sadness that day.

But Eric was never a failure at his own regular writing. By then he had written a second novel, a long one, *Blandings' Way,* and it had again been taken by a book club. This time Blandings wasn't building any dream house; he was commuting from that dream house to a job in a New York advertising office. It again was filled with wit, and a mordant attack on some of the ways of big business, on the cold war, and the idiocies of suspicion connected with it. And running right through it was again a fairly savage exposé of all the things that kept going wrong between Mr. and Mrs. Blandings.

When I told him I was going away for four weeks, perhaps more, he was glad that circumstance had arranged my unexpected absence to overlap his own. The phone call that had summoned me forth so suddenly was from Kenneth McKenna of Metro Goldwyn Mayer in Hollywood. There was a new book, *Snips and Snails,* by Louise Baker, about a plushy private school for boys. It was to be produced by John Houseman and star Greer Garson and Robert Ryan. If they sent me the galleys would I read it overnight and tell them whether I could come out for four weeks or a bit longer and write the treatment for it? They had already called Bert Allenberg, my agent out there, and the terms would be excellent, and all my expenses paid at the Beverly Hills Hotel.

John Houseman, at that time in his early middle age, was nothing like the ubiquitous figure you see in television commercials today, making sales pitches for everything from brokers—"they EARN it" —to low-cholesterol salad oil to God knows what. Back then he was still known as a serious director of serious plays and films. He had been one of the founders of the Group Theater in New York, during the depression, together with other incipient luminaries, like Orson Welles and Elia Kazan, and in Hollywood it was known that he would never touch anything less than first rate. Just then he was nearing the end of *Julius Caesar,* starring Marlon Brando as Mark Antony, and when I was in the studio and saw it in its unfinished version, with no musical soundtrack as yet, I simply sat there, half-stunned, for over two hours, forgetting even to light one cigarette, and I still a chain smoker.

I had met Houseman and his wife the summer the kids and I had spent on the beach at Malibu. Down the beach from us lived Gadge and Molly Kazan and their four children, ready-made playmates for my two boys, and also good friends of theirs, the Housemans. I had admired what I knew of Houseman in the theater and was glad to begin to know him as a neighbor.

The galleys came; I read them overnight; I liked most of the story about the twelve little boys in the rich boys' school—and for me too, in an exceedingly personal way, the timing was, fortuitously enough, also just right.

Michael was leaving home for his first semester at Exeter Academy in New Hampshire. All the clichés about the emptying nest had been trying to pierce the armor of my resolve to be a modern and well-analyzed mother, and every once in a while, if only briefly, they succeeded. I asked the Whedons if they could possibly let Chris live with them for the four weeks that was the probable length of my absence, and Carroll immediately agreed. For some years the Whedons had been the legal guardians of my boys, if anything were to happen to me, and through those years I had carried over a hundred thousand dollars worth of insurance, so the Whedons could see them right through school, college, vacations and any unforeseeables, if anything did. But it was our long close friendship that made it possible for me to ask so large a favor of them and know it would be readily granted.

I went off with an easy mind. John Houseman was to be my only editor and only boss. I had done treatments years before in my two stints in the movie studios and was confident that I could turn the cutely named *Snips and Snails* into a good one about little boys and their troubles at school. My frequent letters from Mike in his new world of Exeter even filled me in on the newest schoolboy slang, "It's the greatest," for anything from a hamburger to an earthquake, a brand-new expression then, "white shoe" for anything preppy, or even just plain "shoe."

A treatment is supposed to be a synopsis, something like a novelette, written in the present tense, outlining all the scenes, with a bit of dialogue thrown in here and there to set the tone, to reveal the general character and personality of each player.

John Houseman, I soon discovered, was definitely not the synopsis type; If I wrote, "Hargrave fobs her off with a sly remark," Mr. Houseman would demand, "What does he say?" It kept reminding me of what I had heard about Harold Ross and his editing of a piece for The New Yorker, constantly writing in the margins of any manuscript, *Who he? What say?* Soon I was writing dialogue all over the place, not only using what I liked best from Miss Baker's book, but dialogue I had to invent all by myself.

I soon saw that four weeks wouldn't come close to the time needed to finish my work. I telephoned Carroll; during my absence we had frequent talks about Chris, about various new problems I was too quick to blame on my being away but which I also recognized as evidence that, nearing eleven, he could still be the No-I-won't kid. I had talked to the headmaster of Riverdale School as well, as the need arose, and now I did once more. Finally it was agreed by all of us, even by Chris, that for the next four weeks he was to go and live right at school, in the one dormitory they had.

I was still out there on Election Day, having cast my absentee ballot before I left, and of course listening to all of Stevenson's speeches on television—my first experience of having a TV set right in my own room, enjoying that novelty but acutely missing all the discussion I would have had with Eric and all my friends if I had been back home. Several days after Eisenhower's sweeping victory I received a letter from Mike, also off there away from home, a letter I kept in a special folder of his school years, for it was my first sign that my sixteen-year-old son was really growing up, into manhood, into citizenship.

Dear Mom,

I'm shocked and completely at a loss for words. I heard the election last night, we were allowed to stay up to hear it, until

140

about 1:00. Hearing the returns come in left me in a state of shock. New York, conceded at 9:30, Florida and Texas and Virginia going Republican, Illinois, Stevenson's own state, California—all going Republican. . . .

I went to bed in a daze, realizing that I had never seen anything like this since I was born. I've never even seen a Republican president in the White House. . . .

I'm not going to write any more since the election has left me dead. . . . Don't be too depressed as I know you are and as I am. We'll be back in 4 years.

I dropped my treatment and Miss Baker and Mr. Houseman and wrote Mike a long letter, telling him not to fear, that this was our country's system, that Eisenhower, whatever sort of president he might prove to be, was himself a good and decent man, that not all Republicans were bad presidents. It reminded me of my early childhood and my fearful questioning of my mother one day, after listening to her berating the capitalist system.

"Mama, isn't there even *one* good capitalist?"

But of course I went straight back to work and what I at last turned in was a 100-page hybrid, half treatment, half actual screenplay. Mr. Houseman liked it, and my contract was extended after my return to New York for a few weeks' more work on the screenplay itself, to be known on the screen not by Miss Baker's title, thanks be, nor even *Miss Baker's Dozen,* an interim title, but *Her Twelve Men.*

When at last I saw the picture itself I hardly recognized it—and I hated it, never told any of my friends about it in later years when it began to show itself on the "Late, Late Show," and never saw it again myself. The "card" indicated a collaboration.

Screenplay
by
William Roberts
and
Laura Z. Hobson

I had always thought a joint author's credit for a play or film meant two people working together throughout, like Russel Crouse and Howard Lindsay, or Oscar Hammerstein and Richard Rodgers. I could visualize them pacing around, tossing ideas at each other, trying bits of action or dialogue, playing gin rummy when they needed a break.

But William Roberts and I had never even met, not once; we had never talked by telephone; we had never written each other a memo, a letter or sent a telegram. We were total strangers.

The explanation slayed me, in good old Hollywood parlance. The front office, John Houseman explained, had thought my script too "intellectual." It needed more high comedy, even the lowbrow kind; it needed more action, the boys ought to do things like putting toads in the teacher's bed, you know, real human stuff to get laughs. *That* was good box-office.

I didn't throw up as I listened to the explanation, but never once since that day have I looked at a screen credit for two or more writers without wondering if they had ever even been in the same room together.

At last eight weeks went by and I was home again, with both boys home for Thanksgiving, each thrilled beyond bearing with my home-coming gifts of a portable typewriter for each of them, taking them, together with Jill Whedon, also Mike's age, to "21" for their first fashionable dinner, complete with weak cocktails and openly smoked cigarettes. For Chris there was a pink nonalcoholic concoction called a "Shirley Temple," the subteen's delight.

Watching them, being with them, gave me a pleasure unrelated to all the pleasant times spent in Hollywood's great restaurants with Hollywood's great stars. Getting back to my own manuscript again, to the unfinished *Reward,* was like coming back to myself again—even though it still had to wait out those extra weeks I was required to put in on John Houseman's script.

Before spring had begun, *The Reward* was at page 115, and I sent it off on its rounds a second time. But something inside me began that sharp little nibble once more. One evening, in a kind of doodling on my typewriter, idly writing notes to myself, I wrote a strange sentence, and then sat and stared at it.

> If only I could do what I did with *The Trespassers:* just tell the story of one family trying to do one thing—but what family and what thing?

The Reward came back to me from Lee and Dick and Edith with much encouragement, and I was happy. Yet a few days later, in clear dark writing that told of a tightly gripped pencil, I wrote in my log,

Decided *The Reward* is *not* a novel—told Edith to offer it as a 2-part magazine serial.

Whereupon my mind went blank, and then a few weeks later, in that same month of April, 1953, I suddenly knew what family, though it would be a long time before I could decide, doing what thing.

The entries in my log for the next twenty days were succinct and sure.

> *My* materials, p.1,2,3
> Rewrote nightmare scene
> Maybe start novel with house itself—
> black bunting—*slow it down,* new
>   p.1,2,3
> Sure about going ahead on novel about
>   Pa, Ma, my childhood in a "radical"
>   background.

And once again I had the blessed feeling of being "placed." This was to become *First Papers,* my longest novel, and what certain critics were to call my best novel.

How could I imagine that ten years of living, of joy and fear and shock and sorrow, would go by before I would reach those two incomparable words, "The End," and turn it over to a publisher?

In a serious novel coincidence is usually frowned upon by critics, by readers and even, with luck, by the author—and thus avoided. But even before I had completed the first chapter of that new book a real-life coincidence occurred that set me back on my heels. It came in the form of a request I could not overlook nor ignore, but it raised the problem of age, my age, a problem already locked into the opening pages of my book.

The editors of *Twentieth Century Authors* were planning to include me in their First Supplement, and would I please write a thousand-word piece about myself for it? The First Supplement would include about "seven hundred authors who have come to prominence since 1942." Their letter ended with a bit of delicate duress: "It is gratifying to note the large proportion of living authors who responded favorably to our invitation to write their own sketches."

Any such official sketch would have to start with the date of my birth. Yet that very question of revealing my age for all the world to see, was holding me up on my novel. If it opened with the Triangle Fire early in 1911, when I was nearly eleven, every reader would know exactly how old I was.

In a few weeks I would be fifty-three; when the book was published I would be fifty-five.

I had never lied about my age, had never made the customary five-year deduction from it, though from my middle twenties onward I had hated the two white wings flying through the dark brown of my hair, and by the time the white wings had widened and taken general command I had at last caved in to the persistent coaxing of advertisers and had gone in for my first "rinse."

That was only three years before, and I was still having rinses, not to my original dark brown but to what hairdressers named "ash blonde," and what I was forever after to call "middle-age beige." (Until, some twenty years later, I decided that Mother Nature knows best, and abandoned all rinses.)

But way back there in '53 I was still preoccupied with the question of age, and the overlapping of that sketch and my book doubled my dilemma. Should I say 1905 in the sketch, the way many women would?

But that would make the little girl in my novel, Fee, who would clearly be me, a child of six at the Triangle Fire; it would be unbelievable that she—that I—could have such feelings about that black bunting; it would force me to omit so much of my actual childhood; such a step would falsify everything that was to follow.

I set the novel aside and concentrated on the sketch. But I let everything possible distract me from it. I would do a spurt of research for my book; Good Housekeeping's editor, Herb Mayes, bought *The Reward* as a one-shot, which meant hours of cutting it, about ten thousand words' worth; Norman Cousins asked me to write Saturday Review's "Trade Winds" again, this time for three full months, and I began interviewing part-time researchers for the legwork.

Several weeks went by before I finally sent in my sketch to *Twentieth Century Authors,* no more than four typed pages, but pages headed by that horrendous phrase, June 18, 1900.

At last I returned full-time to my novel, making Fee an unadulterated nearly-eleven. But even beyond that hurdle of age, I found it hard going. I planned to have my book go from the Triangle Fire to the middle of the twenties, taking in the war, the Palmer Raids and the Red Scare, the Sacco-Vanzetti case, up to the resurgence of the Ku Klux Klan.

But what story line was there to hang my novel on? I was not one of those novelists who felt they could just write a kind of reverie or reminiscence and call it a novel. I needed some string of tension, a plot, however tenuous, that might take the reader's attention and hold it through its development and unfolding to the end.

I couldn't find it. I began to feel emptied of all inventiveness, and the mountain of research I saw ahead intensified my feeling that I couldn't manage this particular book. I began to think I should set it aside for a while, and write some other book instead, but I knew I could not get free of this one until I had done it.

It was the same inner compulsion I had had about *Gentleman's Agreement*; I had longed for it and here it was again, yet this time the dynamo to propel me seemed to have lost its power.

I had heard of writer's block, but had no belief in it; it was an alibi, one I would never use. Writer's block was laziness or lack of will power. I was not lazy; I *had* will power; surely I had proved that. This was not a block; it was a temporary aridity that would soon pass.

One night I read the opening scenes to Eric, telling him I was, for the first time, going to write about my own childhood. In my log is a sentence that was to plague me through many a dry, defeated siege at my desk.

"Will be your your best, your most important book." E—Plaza.

Not long afterward, I asked Lee Wright up for lunch, first sending her the opening twenty-five pages. The moment she said hello, I began to feel dejected. My log for that day said, "Judiciously pleased? Not deeply moved?" Any writer alive can feel that aloofness. All my doubts reared up around me, bristling and hostile.

If Lee was lukewarm about it, surely Dick Simon would be too. I sent him the same pages, and he was.

By now I knew that a novel mattered to him not *as* a novel; he was most attracted by its potential for smashing promotion and great big sales. Like most publishers, S&S pulled back hard on advertising books that were not sure best-sellers. I had seen the swift decrease in ads for *The Other Father* and *The Celebrity* when it became clear they were stuck in the bottom spots of the best-seller lists. What if *this* difficult book never made it even that far?

I was human enough to begin gazing at the greener grass in other meadows. But a different publisher meant a different editor, and that took me into yet other green meadows of supposing. Suppose there were some editor, a Maxwell Perkins kind of editor, who might be peculiarly receptive to this new venture of mine, even especially knowledgeable about it?

I wrote to Eric, wondering about the ethics of changing editors and publishers, and about my continuing trouble with my manuscript. Maybe there was such a thing as writer's block? He was off on assignment for Fortune, which by now he was calling "That magazine," preliminary to giving it up forever. I still have his answer.

> I happen to feel about my own writing, capacity for, possible rewards therefrom, future of, etc. . . . just as you felt about yours when you wrote . . . don't kid yourself that I am a stranger to these blocks, sticks and stymies; I know them intimately.
>
> But if you were to haul off and take a long look at yourself as others see you, I am sure you would emerge . . . with a new pleasure in yourself. You have written a lot—practically all of it has been promptly, eagerly published. Among your works is one in particular . . .

He then wrote at length about *Gentleman's Agreement*, and though his whole letter was as serious as mine had been, there came one paragraph about it that made me laugh.

> This was a flash in the pan, I suppose? An ape in the British Museum just happened to guide your fingers into the precise combination of a billion ideographs that made up *G's.A.*? Uh-huh.

He insisted that all good writers had "their downs as the price and penalty they pay for their ups . . . it is a pretty tough price to pay while actually at the cashier's cage . . ."

> I think you are paying *in advance* for what you are to accomplish next—and I think it is going to be pretty fine.

Eric himself had left his own private cashier's cage not too long before, paying his own penalties for a "down" that had been far more serious than mine. He had had some sort of emotional collapse that had

146

led him to a stay at the Payne Whitney Psychiatric Clinic, part of New York Hospital. He had been reluctant to talk to me about it, and I am now not clear about the reasons he did give me when he was out and apparently well again.

But what I was to accomplish next still refused to get accomplished. Despite Eric's faith in me, I remained stuck. I would write a page and then stop. I would rewrite it and stop again. The days dragged; the weeks passed. The aridity remained; there fell no sweet rain of renewed creativity.

My security contract had been activated when I had begun my book; with the initial three thousand dollars on signing, and five monthly thousands since, I had already received eight thousand—and I was nowhere. Each arrival of the monthly check had tightened the pressure on my nerves. I began to think of tearing up that magnificent document just to breathe free once more.

I also kept thinking of that different publisher, that Maxwell Perkins kind of editor who would be especially receptive to this idea of mine.

I had met one such, only casually, and had heard about him from people in the Authors Guild. He was perhaps a decade older than I, and would have been a young man during those years before the war when I was still a child; surely he would have vivid primary memories of that period, which might help me flesh out material I would be gathering from research in old newspapers and magazines. He was a nephew of "Red Emma" Goldman, the most famous anarchist in the nation, whose exploits and beliefs out-radicaled all the radicalism of my own law-abiding socialist parents.

His name was Saxe Commins and he was with Random House. He had been editor to such luminaries as Theodore Dreiser and Eugene O'Neill in his earlier years and was now editor of William Faulkner, Adlai Stevenson, John O'Hara, Irwin Shaw.

Every bout at my halting typewriter made me think of him again. Every time I turned away from it, I knew I had to search for some solution or go mad.

I cannot remember how I finally discussed this with Dick, but I do remember asking whether one publisher could ever approach an editor in another house, with the suggestion of a possible freelance arrangement on one special book. Nothing came of that preposterous idea, of course, but Dick was generous about telling me to go ahead and talk to Saxe Commins or anybody else I thought might help me through this difficult period.

147

I not only talked with Saxe Commins; I left forty-seven pages with him and then waited out the long hours that had to pass before I heard from him. And when he called, it was to invite himself up to my apartment for "a couple of hours with no phone calls," for a long editorial session. My log recreates that day for me.

> Saxe Commins here—12:30. I think deeply impressed with characters, theme. I'm going to have to work with him as editor.

The double underlining revealed the first firmness I had had for a long time. Saxe lent me his autographed volumes of his aunt Emma Goldman's autobiography, *Living My Life,* and I saw it would be full of background material. I talked with him by phone and even those brief talks spurred me on.

Another major entry shows that I did give up the security that had once seemed so wondrous.

> Leaving S&S; tearing up $50,000 guarantee! Going Random House with Saxe Commins as my editor.
>
> (They repay S&S $8,000 already paid me, and will pay me $1,000 a month for 18 mos—through Dec. '54, total advance of $26,000.)

Between those two entries had come further big talks with Dick and with Lee. Lee was none too gracious about it, but Dick gave me his blessings, and meant them.

We remained tight friends for the too-brief seven years that remained before his untimely death in 1960. He never read another page of what was to be my first novel not published by him.

EIGHT

THAT WAS IN JULY, 1953. In August, one month later, Saxe had a severe heart attack and when at last he was able to work again, it was not with me, but with authors whose books were close to publication. I perfectly understood why I could not see him.

For a while I kept on at my recovered pace, adding another chapter or two. But then I began to falter, and by the end of summer my writer's block was back, as intractable as ever.

I cut off the Random House advance at the $10,000 mark. The thought of even one more check when I was not writing sent me again into a spin of tension.

No longer did I ascribe writer's block to temporary aridity or laziness or lack of will power. I was not lazy; I did have will power. But the moment I turned to my manuscript, I found only that empty deadness in me. It was as if a part of me, the writing part of me, were paralyzed.

Many years later, for my press portfolio of *First Papers,* I arduously drew up a handwritten recapitulation, heaven knows why, of all the starts and stumbles and stops and recoveries that went into its writing. It shows that at the end of 1953, it was at page 150. At the end of 1954, it was at 150; at the end of 1955, it was at 150.

In the fall of that year, I wrote in my log, "Read mss. of my abandoned novel." Abandoned. Not neglected, not delayed, but abandoned. It hurt. It frightened me. Was I really through as a novelist? Was I never going to have a book published again?

Three days later, another entry: "Phoned Saxe Commins about starting on novel again." He invited me out to Princeton for a working weekend with him and his wife. For three weeks I edited, cut, rewrote those 150 pages, and sent them out ahead of me. It was two and a half years since he had seen one word beyond page 41.

It was a tremendous weekend—he still believed in it and in me. I made notes of his suggestions; we discussed problems; I went home filled once more with a fire of determination to get back to extended work.

But each time I went to my typewriter, there was nothing. By the end of 1956, I was at page 150; at the end of '57, 150; by the end of '58, that same 150.

Looking back now, I think that some part of that paralysis must have been due to Saxe's heart attack that cut short the immediate help and guidance I had so eagerly sought.

But something else had also returned just about then, the long-absent worry about money. Nineteen fifty-three was the seventh year since *Gentleman's Agreement;* the splitting-up of my royalties over that seven-year period had run its course. There was nothing further due me from the next two books. Were the proverbial seven lean years now upon me? With no royalties and no advances due, I was back in the precarious world of the freelance writer.

A long time ago Dr. Gosselin had joked about the "Thirty Years' War between the Zametkin conscience and the Hobson budget," and now I saw I might lose the battle for fair. My fees to my tax expert, my retainer to my attorney, my eternal ten percent to my agents, my taxes—I made a swift calculation one day and thought, My God, thirty thousand dollars a year going out before I buy a single sandwich for the kids or me.

I instantly cut back on legal service, tax advice, everything cuttable. I also began a search for new ways to make a decent living, writer's block or no.

"Trade Winds" pointed the way. People liked my columns about books and writers; what about the same sort of column for one of the radio shows, or better yet, as part of the new television morning programs? What about it for one of the big national magazines? I had no writer's block for other kinds of writing.

My log exploded with energy and doggedness.

August 13, 1953: Wrote Ted Cott of NBC about doing radio "column" on books.

August 20: Ted Cott; 3 PM. Maybe!

August 22: Wrote Frank Stanton, CBS, about radio program on books.

September 14: Phoned Herb Mayes about bk. col. for Good Housekeeping.

September 17: Lunch Herb Mayes at G.H. about book col; also humor column, "Back Talk."

September 21: Wrote "Back Talk" for trial.

September 25: Wrote Book Col. for Herb Mayes

September 28: Mayes wants "Back Talk," several months try.

September 29: Lester Gottlieb, CBS—possible radio on books.

October 1: Mayes signs for 9 months on 2 cols.
$750 for book/"Thumbing Through"
100 for research exp.
500 for "Back Talk—
$1350 per mo!

October 7: Seymour Berkson of INS about a daily column.

October 21: Going to start INS columns; 5 a week; 1 month vac; $20,000 a year; 400 papers.

These were not "over the transom" letters to people who would never read them, nor phone calls that never made it past a secretary. After I had resigned from my big promotion job for Time, Life and Fortune, I had for half a year written promotion for the Columbia Broadcasting System, and so I had met its president, Frank Stanton, Lester Gottlieb and others. Ted Cott I had met only recently, in Stamford, Connecticut, where I had taken a house for the summer.

But of them all, it was Herb Mayes who came through, not only with the two monthly columns for his magazine but with an introduction that turned me into that much envied creature, a syndicated newspaper writer with a daily column under my own byline.

INS, or International News Service, was a Hearst enterprise, which gave me some pause, but then so was Good Housekeeping, and that had never held me back from writing exactly what I wanted to write. Neither, I was promised, would INS.

Its managing editor, Seymour Berkson, and Herb Mayes were friends as well as colleagues, and Herb knew that Berkson was in pressing need for a new woman columnist to take over "Assignment America," which had long been written by Inez Robb, now transferring to the Scripps Howard chain.

Mayes recommended me as the perfect candidate; I had a meeting with Mr. Berkson; he asked if I could try a dry run of a column or two, then and there, "about anything at all."

"About anything but politics," I had said. "I'll never turn into Mrs. Political Pundit like Dorothy Thompson, and I don't even want to try."

And so I began to do a 750-word daily column for a string of papers, my weekly columns for "Trade Winds," my monthly "Thumbing Through" on books and publishing, and "Back Talk," which I signed with a pseudonym, the first since the Peter Field days of my marriage and the two westerns.

I called myself Felicia Quist, with a husband named Andrew. Felicia Quist's first appearance in print took place in January, 1954, in the same issue as Laura Z. Hobson's first "Thumbing Through."

The idea for it had come to me as I had read a few pages of a new series, "Man Talk," by Samuel Grafton, a serious columnist for the New York *Post*. These were subtitled, "The Intelligent Woman's Guide to a Reasonably Happy Marriage," written from the husband's point of view, and they were either so sentimental they made me sick, or so macho they made me mad.

"Back Talk" would appear on the facing page, subtitled, "My Personal Comment on the Intelligent Woman's Guide." Herewith the opposing openings of the twin pages, first from "Man Talk."

> You don't *both* have to get up early on Saturday and Sunday. Let your man have an extra hour in bed Saturday morning while you service the children. On Sunday let him reciprocate. A glass of orange juice and a vacuum bottle of hot coffee, left quietly at the bedside of the sleeping spouse, transform the morning into a vacation. Those who are deeply in love will find they enjoy both mornings, in different ways.

Right across from that, Felicia Quist had her say. She explained that she had luckily seen an advance proof of "Man Talk," and thought, Why, I'll try it out with Andy.

> I couldn't wait for my husband to get home from the office that day. . . . I said softly, "I have an idea I'd like us to try out. . . . about our weekends. . . .
> "You see, we don't both have to get up early on Saturday and

152

Sunday." [I didn't realize how accurately I was quoting Mr. Grafton.] "Suppose this weekend you stay in bed an extra hour Saturday morning, while I service the children, and then on Sunday you let *me* have an extra hour while *you* service them."

For a moment Andy didn't answer. His jaw fell and his eyes popped. "While I *what?*"

"Get Suzy and Joel and Johnny started," I said, beaming happily. "And maybe put a glass of orange juice and a vacuum bottle of hot coffee on the table beside my bed for me to find when I wake up."

"I work like a dog all week," he sputtered, "and on Sundays I'm supposed to tiptoe around bringing you juice and vacuum bottles? Oh, brother!"

Obviously, getting to see every month's "Man Talk" in advance was a niftly little setup for Felicia Quist and me, and why Sam Grafton stood still for it for nearly a year I never could understand, not even now. But when the inevitable, and legitimate, yawp finally came from him, Herb Mayes at last killed off "Back Talk" but I think its demise knocked off "Man Talk" too.

Laura Z. Hobson was luckier than Felicia Quist in the magazine world. My book column drew plenty of mail, my contract kept getting renewed, with suitable raises each year, and never once did I think I had to "write down" for this readership from the level that had become so usual for me to strive for in "Trade Winds." I never tired of it and was sure I could keep doing it forever.

It was a different story with my five-a-week pieces for "Assignment America." At first I reveled in my new status as a national columnist and enjoyed dashing off my daily offering, knowing it would "go out on the wire" and appear in print the next day, or be offered to the nonwire clients on a syndicated basis. When I told my friends of my new assignment, I would always name a few of the papers I liked that might use my column, but I felt honor-bound to add, "And the Hearst chain too." Then I would point out that my contract made it clear that any editor could dump a column he disagreed with or disliked, but if it ran he couldn't cut or edit or alter—it had to go stet.

A moment of keen discomfort greeted me on the very first day "Assignment America" appeared. The New York outlet was Hearst's *Journal-American,* and on the Op Ed page, right across from me, there was a political column by George Sokolsky, whom every civil libertarian in the country called a reactionary or worse.

That same day was the day for our regular meeting of the board of directors of the New York Civil Liberties Union, of which I was proud to be a member. It was a luncheon meeting, everybody easy at the start.

"That was a good column," one of the other members greeted me across the table. "But how does it feel being side-by-side with George Sokolsky?"

There was a ripple of laughter, and I could feel my face go hot.

"Guilt by association?" I asked the moment after, and turned the tables so promptly I could feel the whirr. Now the ripple washed over the civil libertarian who had seen fit to take that particular dig at me.

We talked then about whether it behooved writers to appear only in papers read by people of the same political bent. Wasn't that just "talking to yourself"? Might it not be a gain to address the unconverted? Though my main bailiwick was to be "human interest," I said I'd doubtless find lots of chances to speak up about things I deplored, and things I believed in.

And in the first two weeks, I proved that I could find those chances —and get them printed. My beginning columns avoided the controversial, true enough.

One was about the new "drunkometers" the police were testing on suspicious drivers, and I asked for "egometers," to measure the "brag impulse" in the fellow who had to beat you away from a red light.

Another was about the "Ford Popular" car in England at $770, and I predicted that the spoiled U.S. driver wouldn't look at it because of its dearth of chrome and gadgets.

In another I wrote of trouble at the Waldorf-Astoria when a couple arrived with fifteen trunks, and commiserated with city apartment-house dwellers like me, who lacked more than six inches of storage space.

I wrote a column about letters *not* to send to authors, another about idiot superstitions, and one about people still creative in their seventies, eighties, nineties—

But then came a little news item that offered me my chance to do something quite different. It was about a Mrs. Thomas J. White, of the State Textbook Commission in Indianapolis, who was said to advocate the banning of *Robin Hood* from school reading lists, "to get Communist writers out of the schools."

I had no trouble finding an opening line for my column that day.

> In all the wonderful wise-cracking hullaballoo about the 13th
> century character whom I shall hereafter always think of as
> "Comrade Robin Hood" . . .

I had my say on quite a few aspects of freedom of the press, on censorship, on book burning and its little brother, book banning.

In that same column I refrained from mentioning the banning of *Gentleman's Agreement* in the public high schools of New York for nearly two years, not because of any communist taint but because the Board of Education had deemed some passages "immoral." (Phil and Kathy had an affair, minus lush description, though they were not yet married.)

That column on "Comrade Robin Hood" was widely printed— even in the Hearst papers—and as time went on, I found many another chance to have my say on matters that were more than pleasant trivia.

Yet, fairly swiftly, it became clear that in the world of columns this was not even distantly related to "Thumbing Through" or "Trade Winds." There my material was eternally interesting to *me*, books, authors, writing, critics, publishers, material that came tumbling in to me with every delivery of the mailman or messenger boy. If it interested me, it seemed always to interest my readers.

At the beginning of my newspaper pieces, ideas had come popping effortlessly into my head, but by the third or fourth month that early celerity and felicity gave way to a deadly slow hunt for a topic I could use. I would wake up each morning instantly wondering, "What can I write about?" and day after day after day of that drudgery soon left both lobes of my poor brain full of nothing but sand and cactus.

There were welcome oases. I was sent to Washington for three days to cover Eisenhower's State of the Union address. I barely mentioned it, but wrote about my feelings at being seated in the Congress of the United States for the first time; I interviewed the young senator from Massachusetts, John F. Kennedy, not able to foresee Camelot or anything else, but finding the young senator delightful and appealing. It was during that trip that I saw Hubert Humphrey again, in his office, and also at lunch in the Senate restaurant, for that famous Senate navy bean soup.

But just beyond that Washington oasis there waited a long barren stretch in my own private life. Eric fell ill again, this time frighteningly so. He phoned me one afternoon, cryptically, and then disappeared into silence. I could not reach him at the University Club; I had no other number to try—he was no longer at Fortune.

At last a doctor I did not know called me. Eric was now in his care, had come through a very bad period and wanted me to know he would soon write me. My questions drew guarded responses from the doctor; I was not a "member of the family," he pointed out.

"I'm the most family he has," I wanted to shout, but I did not. Eric's son was now over twenty, but he didn't see much of him. By now he had lived apart from his wife for years; she lived in Sarasota and he went there only when school vacations were on to see his children, especially his little girl, more than a decade younger than his son.

I began to watch the mail with rising anxiety, and when the letter came, five sheets written in pencil, on University Club stationery, but headed, "Stony Lodge, Ossining, N.Y.," anxiety shifted to a deep foreboding.

> There is a good deal of havoc floating around in my life and in the lives of those who care for me, these days, but the first message I want to get to you is that as of today, for the first time, I am something that can be called *better*. Via Dr. K————, I know of the lovely—and characteristic—ways in which you showed your concern for me, and the first message I want to get across here is that though this may be a time for sadness, the time for worry is past. This is a most important change.
>
> After a terrible 36 hours, I cracked into a thousand pieces last Monday, and when I saw Dr. K. by emergency appointment at 8:30 Monday evening, he had no professional course but to get me, fast, into the first sanitarium that could be found. This turned out to be a true snake pit, and for five days I was a caged animal, longing for the strength to batter my brains out against a wall. Yesterday I was transferred here (Stony Lodge) which is no Ritz, but a kindly and human place, and now I am quiet; what is more, hope has come back to me—really strong hope, which you can share. . . .

At some length, yet elliptically, he went on to tell me what had happened. Dr. K., a psychiatrist Eric had never mentioned, believed this trouble had begun two years before, due to the fact that his doctor at the Payne Whitney clinic had suddenly left, without allowing sufficient time "to develop another relationship with another M.D., which I could have continued as an outpatient . . . and consolidate the

really enormous gains I had made. . . . As it was, the gains came unstuck
. . . I was left feeling . . . deprived by some huge capricious force
wholly beyond my control."

> Dr. K. is positive that the best years of my life are ahead of me;
> that I can come back, and keep whatever are the highest levels
> of peace and happiness I have known in the past.
>
> I am not going to get out of this without some cost. . . . I am
> waiting for transfer to Payne Whitney. . . . I will be facing a
> longer and harder course than the last time . . . I will be there
> for six months . . .
>
> All this, perforce, is about me. But I think of you constantly,
> constantly, constantly. . . .

In this letter there were more than his usual number of endearments,
which in ordinary times took the form of jocularities he knew I could
translate for myself. When Eric had belatedly congratulated me about
my new newspaper columns, sending flowers and an unsigned card, he
knew I would read his code at once.

Homage

from

An Admirer

(It's the third-day

reaction that counts.)

That was the healthy Eric, so when I found many departures from the
usual in this and other letters, I was able to deduce not the cliché phrase,
a cry for help, but the hope that I would believe in his ability to
recover fully and be himself as I knew and loved him.

Looking back now to that illness and the months that followed, I
think it must have been triggered by that simple little word, *slip,* used
by Eric when he had talked of Alcoholics Anonymous. He had told
me, and repeated it many times, that alcoholism was "a progressive,
irreversible and fatally terminating disease," and he had always added,
that even if he were to have an occasional "slip," he would never let
himself be fooled into thinking he could now manage his enemy
differently from the way he had done in the past.

But if this had been only a slip, it must have been a prolonged and
desperate one, which he had somehow managed to conceal from me

157

until his collapse. Even after he was well again, he could not make himself talk about that possibility, and I, obviously, had to refrain from digging at him about it.

So the next months, with him off at Payne Whitney, were indeed long and dreary; even my visits to him there were truncated and forlorn, not so much for me as for my poor unhappy Eric Hodgins.

In a sense I was newly grateful for the unflagging drive of my daily newspaper deadlines. In late spring another oasis appeared, a trip to Honolulu, with some forty well-knowns of press and television, as guests of United Airlines to publicize their new Dawn-to-Dusk flight from New York. It was glamor galore, with all the lush freebies, plus one mighty rare one: if a couple of us wanted to fly to another island, all it took was a phone call, and a small airplane, plus pilot, awaited your pleasure. It was like asking your doorman to hail you a taxi.

But there was nothing of the lush freebie about my next travel assignment, the best of them all. My employers were paying my expenses, but I was contributing twice what they did, because I wanted to take Mike and Chris along with me. It was *my* kind of trip, and their kind of trip, and though it lasted only a month, I was able to make columns out of it for most of the summer.

King of Prussia, PA.: Well, here we go again, my young sons and I and our car, touring the good old U.S.A. for the third time in five years.

We're less than 100 miles out of New York, . . . but the ties to home were cut the moment we slapped down the lid of the luggage compartment and headed west . . .

We don't know where we'll sleep tonight—and care less . . . "Tourists Welcome" will again become the greatest sign on earth, and "No Vacancy" the most discouraging.

The first time we embarked on such a tour (five years ago) my boys were 12 and 7, and many of my friends called me reckless and foolhardy to go off alone with them, to cross the country from coast to coast.

"Suppose they get sick . . . suppose the car breaks down . . . suppose you can't find a place to spend the night?"

Suppose, suppose—the little careful chorus went on sounding its thin note of warning, and finally I lay awake one night, assessing all the dangers and hazards ahead.

158

Suddenly a thought struck me: If I said I was driving the kids up to Albany, only 75 miles from home, nobody would have started supposing.

But the whole U.S.A. was just one 75-mile stretch after another 75-mile stretch. All I'd ever be attempting at any time was an easy 75 miles.

Is there any place in this land, I thought, where there aren't neighborly people within a 75-mile drive? Places to eat and sleep? Medical attention if a child runs a fever?

The questions carried their own answers, like bright flags of reassurance. The road was unknown and long, sure; it would take us through farmland and prairie, over great mountains and vast deserts to another ocean. But if one thought of it in small pieces, was there anything to fear?

I summarized that trip, and another two years later, as "getting to know the United States from the ground up."

Today we're off for the third time—how far and to where we don't yet know. Cities there will be for us, of course—but mostly it's the smaller places that draw us.

The smaller places and the biggest rivers and mountains. It's going to be free and spontaneous—except for one small silent hitchhiker I haven't yet mentioned—my portable typewriter, for my daily columns.

So long—I'll be writing.

For most of the summer my columns were again easy, natural, appealing to people who loved kids, people who loved this country, people who liked to see the names of small towns, perhaps their own small town, and the name of a neighbor, in their daily newspaper.

The datelines themselves, spacing out the names of major cities, gave me pleasure—Jessup, Maryland; Loogootee, Indiana; Sandoval, Illinois; Manhattan, Kansas; Granby, Colorado; Vernal, Utah; Bonneville, Oregon; Cannon Beach, Oregon . . . population 721, eight hundred miles north of San Francisco, a small place indeed.

We had come five thousand miles to reach this "other ocean," zigzagging our way across the top of the nation, me driving every mile, and here in a motel on a cliff high above the Pacific, we stayed for several days to rest, to get a bank of columns written before turning south and east and heading for home once more.

159

*　*　*

Home, and vacation for a month, and then all too soon I was again waking to that dragging query: What can I write about?

Eric was well again, or nearly so; for my birthday he gave me a cigarette lighter of sterling silver, the thinnest, most satiny silver I had ever seen. I loved it so, I took to smoking ten extra cigarettes a day.

Just about then, my closest friend Carroll Whedon telephoned me from Reno, Nevada. I had known she was divorcing John, whom I also loved, but I had not realized she would marry the very day she had her divorce in hand, marry a man in advertising she had met not too long before, a man I thought couldn't compare with John.

I tried to write John that night, and wept all over the letter, for the grief I knew he felt, for partings and endings, for pain and sorrow life so often held for all of us.

My eyes were red and swollen, my head was as thick as if I had a bad cold. In the morning, having breakfast in bed, I reached for my first cigarette and silver lighter. My routine morning cough started, more violent than usual; my lighter clicked but I could not steady it enough to meet my cigarette; my coffee cup sloshed a widening stain on my white blanket. The coughing went on.

I thought, Better wait till you're out of bed. It was the first time in years I had no cigarette with my coffee, but it gave me an idea: I'll wait until after lunch.

By noon I was thinking, It's ten hours since I smoked. I wonder if I could go until evening.

That was the day I quit smoking suddenly in one day, quit cold after some thirty years of two packs a day, three if I were playing poker till all hours or writing half the night away.

I had never even tried to quit; it was before the cancer scare—all I knew was my coughing had become incessant. I knew it had to be now or never, knew no gradual reduction would work. I kept thinking back to the time my father had quit smoking, when I was a little girl; I swore I wouldn't put Mike and Chris through the miserable times he had given all of us while he mastered his private demons.

My demons just about made me unable to earn a living; even when I had a good idea for the column, it took a full day's slogging to make it come alive.

I kept reaching for a cigarette, knowing it wasn't there; I kept chewing gum, hating the chomp-chomp of it; I drank quarts of coffee; I was filled with self-pity.

160

Once Chris stood near my desk, watching me tear out and destroy sheet after sheet of typing paper from my portable, and though all he probably felt was a thirteen-year-old sympathy for me, I suddenly shouted, "Stop staring at me like that!"—and knew I was being exactly the way my tormented father had been.

But not often; I think that was the one time I did let myself go, promptly labeling myself a monster as atonement. The lengthened labor of the columns reinforced my doubts about their future; I hadn't heard a word from Seymour Berkson about extending my contract with the built-in raise.

I asked for a meeting with him, and that night's log entry was pretty stark.

> about 100 papers; nix on option; nix on raise—30-day basis after
> Nov. 8

My first year ended November 8; the number of papers regularly taking "Assignment America" had declined; this didn't mean my columns weren't popular, some, of course, more than others. I could keep on indefinitely and Mr. Berkson hoped I would.

Nix, went something inside me. I had been in advertising and promotion for too long before I quit business to write; I knew what this meant. They too had misgivings about the future; for all I knew they were already interviewing other "women columnists." I was now on an interim basis; they could fire me at any time.

There was nothing for it but to resign and preempt that pink slip. Losing four hundred dollars a week, twenty thousand a year, unnerved me, but free of the daily columns, I'd have time to do novelettes again, and make up most of it.

I began a novelette at once. I wrote the columns for two full months more, but late in November I did resign as of the end of the year.

There is, in my log for the day after that resigning, an unexpected note. "Harry Luce—here; 5."

Usually one small jotted entry like that is enough to bring back an entire memory; my own memory being as acute as it seems to be, that small prod is all the switch necessary to open up the entire circuit between now and the past and back to now.

But this time it fails. I hadn't seen Harry or Clare for ages; the parties they went to were great affairs of state, not the parties I was still invited to, at the Cerfs', at Kitty and Moss Hart's and the like. The last time I'd seen Harry was when, to my surprise, he had attended a big luncheon at the Waldorf-Astoria for Adlai Stevenson's campaign, going not as a supporter but as a journalist and publisher. We had talked there, but even that was now two years in the past.

I must have written him asking if I might see him, indicating that it was about me and Time—he hated vagueness or obliqueness. Probably I expected nothing more than a session at his office, although, being Harry, so often doing the reverse of what other people in power would do, he might well have suggested that he come up to my apartment instead.

Clare had been appointed United States Ambassador to Italy, and though Harry was often in Rome with her, he was more often in New York, busy at Time Inc., living alone, inviting people to have dinner with him, almost as command performances; he was not a man who enjoyed evenings by himself.

The one thing that log entry does tell me is that I had begun to wonder about going back to the world of business, back to the old-time security I had had writing promotion for Time and Life and Fortune. Perhaps not going back full-time; I do not think that I was anywhere near the point where I had even begun to consider that, but probably doing some magazine promotion on a fee basis.

Nothing came of that visit from Harry, not in the immediate future, though his answer to the thank-you note I wrote him said, "It is great fun to talk publishing shop with you and I should like to do so again." But it must have been one of the component parts in my continuing concern about how best to adjust to the loss of my largest source of income, the daily columns.

For almost at once, after the last one was written and the last check had been received, the lean years did begin, and the first two of them were not very pleasant.

Writing a full novelette takes many weeks, even months, and by tax time, faced with big taxes for the year past, I showed part of *The Unfaithful* to Herb Mayes and asked for an advance on it so I could pay those taxes. He agreed, but it damaged me in some way; I had never had to ask for an advance, up till now advances had been offered *to* me.

A twenty-year-old story of mine, *City Doctor,* was remembered and exhumed from old files by William Dozier, a CBS producer, and made into a TV film starring Franchot Tone. The going rate for a one-hour show was still only a few hundred dollars, but I welcomed it. Occasionally I went on discussion shows on radio or television, mostly in the trial stages and soon canceled. My fee was sometimes as low as fifty dollars.

Soon I was falling behind on doctors' bills, dentists' bills, fees to my lawyers; I even began to be tardy with notices sent me by the bursars at my sons' schools. I borrowed money on my remaining shares of Time stock; I cut back on maid service, on new clothes. I still fell behind.

There was one course still open to me—subleasing our lovely big apartment, furnished, at a rental nearly double the basic $400 I paid, so we could move to some small place and live rent-free. But the idea appalled me.

We had lived there for five years. I had waited three years after the success of *Gentleman's Agreement* before I sought a much larger apartment, with a separate room for each boy and, for the first time, a study for me to work in. I had spent a good deal furnishing it; it was high up with glorious views of the city to the south and it was dear to me in ways that are analytically predictable: that little girl in Jamaica who had loathed the backward-rising staircase in the funny-looking house her father had designed, perched like a tubular bird high on a plot of rising ground—that little girl was always going to want an attractive place to live in.

Appalled or not, I knew I would rent it. In the fall Mike would be starting at Harvard—he was on the dean's honors list at Exeter, he had decided on Harvard long before, and nothing was going to make me keep him from college.

And Chris had again won the prize for composition for his grade at Riverdale—nothing would make me change him to another school to save fees. Because of further "behavior problems," he had been seeing a child analyst; after his first session he had come home saying, "Oh, a blissful day." Recently his headmaster had suggested that he was perhaps seeing too much of my friends and might better be living with boys his own age at the dormitory, going home only for weekends.

So I was living alone in my beautiful apartment, and at last I listed it for sublease with several good brokers. I wept at doing it; I thought back to what it must have been for my mother and father when the time came for them to put a white For Sale sign out in front of that house they had built and loved, and though I berated myself for this farfetched comparison, my own sense of loss remained painfully keen. Almost at once a subtenant appeared, the movie star Marie MacDonald,

"The Body," renting it for the spring and summer, and as I began packing our personal things I was forever finding myself crying.

I moved to a two-room suite at a small hotel, the Volney. Weekends Chris slept on a folding cot set up in the living room. There was no way we could have a place in the country for the summer, but Andrea Simon invited us to take over part of their big house in Riverdale while they went off to Martha's Vineyard.

It seemed a strange summer; we had no maid, we did our own housework and marketing and cooking. Mike got his first job, in the mailroom at S&S, at $37.50 a week. I began another novelette, *The Lovely Duckling,* and received an out-of-the-blue assignment from Redbook to go to Reno and do a piece on women and their six-week wait for their divorces. I tried not to let my deepening depression show. I took up bridge again, in a more serious way than I had ever done before, playing with better players, trying for a higher level of skill. When you had to keep track of how many trumps were out, how many spades or hearts or diamonds or clubs, you really found an escape hatch from more basic worries. I began to play often, and finally, at the urging of one of those better players, ventured to play in some of the city's bridge clubs, where "mama-papa" bridge was not condoned.

In the fall I rented a four-room apartment for us, prettily furnished, from a decorator friend of mine. The rent was high, but I had again subleased my big apartment, this time for a higher amount and for an entire year. We were still living rent-free. It helped.

There had been one other escape hatch for me not long before, a strange one, unexpected and touching, a formal proposal of marriage.

No, not Eric. Eric and I never talked about marriage, except for that one time over a decade before, during a visit to Dick and Andrea Simon—Dick was Eric's publisher too—when Eric had solemnly assured them both that he and I "would share our future together."

This time it was a proposal in the literal sense, in a direct manner, in a different setting. Christopher La Farge was one of the members of the Writers Board for World Government—in that long list of names to whom I had dedicated *The Celebrity* back in the early fifties, he was included as "Kipper." Back there we had tried collaborating on a short story, but never had he even asked me out for dinner until earlier in this spring of a growing crisis.

He was a member of a large, illustrious family of architects, painters and writers, and it meant a great deal to him that he was. His grandfather was the artist John La Farge, his father was architect of the Cathedral of St. John the Divine in New York, his uncle was for years editor-in-chief of the Jesuit weekly, America, and his brother Oliver was a noted anthropologist dealing mainly with the American Indian, author of many books, his novel *Laughing Boy* being the most famous.

Kipper was famous too, for his unusual novels in verse and for his first prose novel, *The Sudden Guest.* He was a little older than I, once happily married, then unhappily, and now divorced. He was very tall, very thin and devoted to his long-time home, his farm in Saunderstown, Rhode Island. He avoided New York—that may be one reason why I so rarely saw him except at meetings.

Even that one attempt at writing a story together was largely a matter of phone calls. I had told him of a wild-eyed political plot I had in mind, and he was instantly taken with it. This was during the time Senator McCarthy was accusing everybody of communism, holding up long lists of names of "subversives in the State Department."

Kipper never wrote a line for general magazines, and I always thought he felt a little superior to anybody who did. But this plot was nothing for popular magazines anyway, and he was positive that one of the "quality" magazines would publish it.

The story would be about a paradox character, a forger just out of prison, who is, apart from his criminal streak, a fairly fine fellow, well-read, intelligent, disgusted by the way freedom is being chipped away in this age of suspicion.

On the bus one day he finds an old wallet. It is empty except for one thing: an official card showing membership in the Communist Party of the United States.

In the newspapers that very morning is a story about a new group of people called down to Washington by subpoena, and as he stares at that official card, he gets a sudden idea, the notion of a great hoax.

He's going to use his one great talent to fight all the finger-pointers and accusers: he will forge a hundred cards, five hundred, showing membership in the Communist Party, in the names of prominent Americans in all walks of life, and send them to every newspaper and radio or TV station in the land. William Randolph Hearst's card would be sent, Congressman John Rankin, the Duponts, Nelson Rockefeller, Cary Grant, Frank Sinatra, Senator Taft, Henry Robinson Luce's—all "members in good standing of the C.P."

Before the hoax could be disproved, the scandal would have rocked the nation and perhaps induced a new wariness among decent people

165

and members of the government, before the next accusations could explode.

"I can't write it," I had told Kipper in the midst of his enthusiasm. "It needs so much technical research—I wouldn't even know how to start it. I've never even seen a party card."

"Neither have I. But I could find out—I have attorneys who would help me—I could write J. Edgar Hoover himself, right at the FBI."

And he had done so—I still have their exchange of letters, and J. Edgar's replies. . . . "Although I would like to be of service, I wish to advise that information in the FBI files is confidential and available for official use only."

I had even gone as far as writing a ten-page first draft of the story, called "The Plot." But in the end, I can no longer remember exactly why, we both realized there was too much danger of rejection, the fear of libel suits if actual names were used, and a kind of inertia must have set in.

Time passed and I didn't see much of Kipper until that spring, some three years later, when he asked me out for dinner. Several more times he asked me out; one weekend he had Mike and me up to his farm at Saunderstown while Chris was off on a school trip with his class to Florida. And then came the proposal of marriage, followed by two bottles of a fine white wine and a card, which I taped into a page of my log.

> This is a happy wine, for a happy occasion, no matter what may come from it. One does not have many such evenings.
> Drink, while you think!

He had signed it with a graceful phrase, the phrase of a poet.

I had not known what to think, not while Kipper was saying what he had to say about the prospect of marriage, nor in the days just after. He had been open about the mood he was in; he was in a period of some crisis himself, which he talked about as being "the drought" in his writing. I probably responded by telling him of my own writer's block—I can no longer be sure.

I *am* sure—and more than a little amazed that I could have been so thick-skinned or so vain—that I told Eric about Kipper and his proposal. For taped into that log, just a few pages further on, is another card, this one unsigned.

A Tribute to Perfection . . . or to Competition . . . or to both?
Anyway a Tribute.

But a day or two later came a very long letter from Kipper, a strange letter, again open, honest, loving— and appalling. He could have had no notion that it might be so, could not have seen that it might turn away any woman who had for years had to make her own decisions, any woman who was herself a writer.

> The more I have thought of what I did in suggesting we make a communal deal of life, the better I think of it . . . There seem to be only a few things that could make it a bad idea. . . .

He wrote of the doubts anybody might have about marriage, especially "as we are no longer young people, and have both suffered" the "doubt that verges close to fear." He talked of possible trouble that might arise if it seemed that he were "interfering with [my] career as a writer" . . .

> because of my absolute insistence (and it *is* an absolute) on using *this* place, from which everything must radiate. . . .
>   No matter what, or because of the difference in the sort of things we write, since both of us write as we must . . . I . . . would prefer to go down the financial drain rather than write what I dislike or even faintly disapprove, and the possible results of this could bring disaster . . .

In those days the vocabulary of feminism never entered my mind, but the implied ultimatum of his "absolute" made me draw back. I drew back even further from the implication of his incorruptibility. What did he think about anybody who wrote light fiction in times of need, or worked in a Hollywood studio, or wrote daily columns?

That letter didn't entirely finish me off; we spent a weekend in Atlantic City, we had several more weekends at his farm, he had me meet various members of his family. I recall vividly their general friendliness and warmth; I remember thinking, more than once, *Laura La Farge,* and remembering Madame De Farge and her knitting needles.

I remember as well a longing to be married again, wondering what it would mean for Mike and Chris to have a stepfather. Though

Kipper's farm was not a working farm, though it was rundown and meant a lot of housework and repairs—he had no maid—it did offer a profound change in a time when my own life was twisted with doubts. Might it not be that some sort of profound shift might set me back on that once happy path of real writing?

My manuscript was tucked away in a lower drawer of my desk under a stack of typing paper. It hurt even to come across it unexpectedly. Whenever I did see it, think about going back to it, that same sick sense of "nothing" returned.

Kipper and I continued to see each other throughout the spring— I was not seeing Eric—and in early June went off on a tour in my car, going Dutch on everything. Perhaps it was then that it became steadily clearer to me, and surely to Kipper, that this had been no more than an interlude for two troubled people in what we today would probably dub a "midlife crisis." But as that tour ended, we both realized we were drifting gently away from that consideration of marriage, until the quiet slippage of time transposed it into the past tense.

___ CHAPTER ___

NINE

THE SECOND OF MY two lean years suddenly turned leaner than ever. I had finished *The Lovely Duckling* and sent it in to Herb Mayes —only to have him turn it down. It had been years since anything I wrote had been turned down by any editor; it was the first time Herb Mayes had rejected a story I submitted to him. His only explanation was, "We're going to use less fiction."

And on the heels of this shock came another, also from Herb Mayes. With about five minutes' warning, and by letter, he killed "Thumbing Through," which had been running for three years and for which I was now being paid $1,400 a month. He was working on a new format for the magazine, a thirty-page service section of "Household How-To's."

Quite suddenly I had no income whatever.

I borrowed once more from my bank, with my several life-insurance policies as collateral; once I even dipped into Mike and Chris' small trust funds, which I'd been building up for them for years, borrowed to make payment to their separate schools; they both knew that those funds were untouchable until they were twenty-one years old, and they must have realized that I must be hard-pressed indeed to use my power of attorney to extract a few hundred dollars from each. Maybe it even frightened them.

Just about then Mike asked me if he might see Dr. Gosselin about something that was troubling him. Mike in trouble? Amiable, well-adjusted Mike? I assumed, of course, that he had fallen in love and was in that kind of trouble; I thought of some girl who was pregnant, or of some older woman he had been having an affair with and was unhappy about. He was nineteen; these things happened.

He saw Dr. Gosselin three times that week. He didn't tell me why, and of course Dr. Gosselin never offered one word either. It was to be many years before Mike himself at last told me why he had those three special sessions with Gosselin.

"I kept wondering if I ought to quit college and get a job," he told me. "Because we were so broke. But Gosselin said no. He said you would work it all out yourself, and it would be even worse for you if I quit."

I am glad I didn't know that at the time I found myself with not a dime coming in. I had gone into further debt, deep debt, with a ten-thousand-dollar loan—at four percent interest—from the Book-of-the-Month Club Schermans, my close friends who had been so ready to stake me years before so I could manage that pregnancy without fear. I was to pay it off in monthly instalments when the time came that I was earning money again. They knew I meant not to use it, that it was a sort of mental insurance against sudden disaster.

Once more my log exploded with job-seeking. I no longer tried for radio or TV shows about books; this time I was asking magazine editors for jobs as assistant fiction editor; I went to Bergdorf Goodman and many lesser stores seeking a job doing fashion promotion as I had done at Altman nearly twenty-five years before—at Russek's a Mr. Nemeroff wouldn't even look at my proof book; he had taken one glance at me and said, "We'll call you if anything comes up."

I knew what it meant. I was fifty-six years old; who needed a fifty-six-year-old in a store of high fashion?

For some reason I thought of Harry Luce and his courtesy when I asked if I could talk to him about something I cared about.

I called up Allen Grover, a vice-president at Time, and also a friend through many long years. I told him about seeing Harry and wondering about some sort of arrangement with Time, and let myself show him I was worried and tense. By now all my friends knew I was broke; I never went in for pretense—if I was broke all the people who knew me knew it.

There is an entry in my log I must have liked writing.

Al Grover called—"putting out feelers," nothing discouraging— Harry Luce back tomorrow—speeches till June 6—then Al will talk.

Still nothing happened. For the first time I asked Norman Cousins if I could do "Trade Winds"; always before he had asked me. He said yes and I was delighted. It meant $150 a week—for eleven weeks. Money coming in again!

I addressed my readers in my usual jovial fashion.

> Greetings, Salutations, Hello, Hi—and thanks be that Bennett Cerf picked on me again as his stand-in for dear old "Trade Winds."
>
> This will be, heaven help me, my fourth go as such. . . . [Since my first] I have written a grand total of 317 columns in newspapers and magazines, totaling roughly 250,000 words, which is plenty rough enough for me.

A quarter of a million words! Enough for fifty short stories, ten novelettes, two and a half full-length books. And never, in all those days and nights of writing those quarter of a million words, never even one word on my abandoned novel.

It was still at page 150.

One day I had an inspiration. I was with a woman I played poker with, who had become a friend apart from the card table. She had confided in me that she had once had an affair with Harry Luce, and still saw him fairly often. I didn't know how much credence to give to this—at that time I would have sworn that the last man in the world to have any affair would be Harry Luce.

But she knew all about my years at Time—knew, too, that I had talked to Harry and to Al Grover about some sort of promotion assignment, on a part-time fee basis, probably working at home.

"It's sixteen years since I worked for them," I said, "and they don't seem to think it's a crazy idea. But it could go on forever, hanging fire. Maybe the next time you see Harry, you could say something to expedite it."

"I might try."

"If you were my literary agent," I said, "trying to speed up some deal that was dragging along, you'd get ten percent. Why can't it be ten percent on this?"

She was a very sharp businesswoman, creative in various fields with a lot of ability and a lot of expensive tastes. My idea put a visible sparkle in her eye.

I was businesslike about it: I wrote a letter in triplicate about that "ten percent for one year" if she helped get me "a promotion job on any newspaper or magazine," and asked her to countersign all copies. I sent one to my regular agent, by then Phyllis Jackson of MCA (Music Corporation of America), stating that this concerned only a job in promotion, in no way altering their representation of me in any future fiction or books.

This was all accomplished before the day was out, and I began, jovially, to call her "my agent." She must have been persuasive. Soon she began to relay suggestions: write Nick Samstag, the present head of promotion at Time, drive up to his house in the country to see him and discuss the possibility, clearing things with him just in case so he won't think you're going over his head.

It was early summer. Again we had rented no country house but were staying in our four rooms in the city. Mike had a vacation job again, this time at Brentano's at $43 a week, and Chris was a volunteer typist, file clerk and office boy at Stevenson-for-President headquarters.

I wrote Nick and then drove up to see him. He seemed receptive; he made long distance calls, not to Harry, at my own request, but to James Linen, then the publisher of Time, a man who was not one of my many acquaintances and friends there, a man, I always thought, who had no personal interest in me at all but who had deep vested interests in running Time.

Finally there were dates for luncheon, the big one between Mr. Linen and Nick Samstag and me, when they said that for some time they had been interested in creating some new "prestige campaign" for Time but that the right one had eluded them. Maybe—

Again a happy entry appears in my log.

> H.R. Luce phoned in re job at Time. (1 year & 8 months since our last talk.)

Below that is another entry, on the same page.

> Nick Samstag—4 PM in re campaign; consultant @ $15,000 for 6 mos.—nix work at home.

Another week passed and the entry was even happier. It was August 6, 1956, a Monday.

Nick Samstag phoned. Had 2 more calls to Jim Linen at Bermuda re job at Time Inc (after HRL said, "Get her an office!") Will take job for 6 mo for $15,000—

$2500 per month!!!

$250 commission. "Consultant on special promotion projects." Starting Sept. 15—want short vacation with boys in Florida.

Just before we left, an airmail letter arrived from Rome, addressed by hand, containing an oversized picture postcard of the Spanish Steps. There was no letter, but there was a message written in a large sprawling familiar hand across the entire back of the card.

Dear Laura,

This seems to be the right means of communication—not only because I'm greeting you from across the seas in the old romantic world, but because the occasion is a festive one—Laura's return to Time!

I look forward to seeing you in NY—perhaps the very day you officially start work.

Cheers,
Harry

And so I was back at good old Time Ink, an ex-novelist, ex-author, ex-columnist, ex-everything, but once more an expert, at high pay, in magazine promotion.

Let me not pretend that I was unhappy at going back to the world of business, to the challenge, excitement, even the trouble of working with other people again. I was relieved, we were safe, my debts could be paid; I was exultant that at fifty-six I could get a job, not a measly little one but a great big job at the same thirty-thousand-a-year that I had had when I was forty.

Myself as an author of published books? The acceptance of that as a *given* had been fading away, and I was comfortably able to let it go right on fading.

During our vacation in Florida, a thrifty one in motels, I kept thinking about this change in my perceptions of myself, and I found an unexpected comfort in my own realism. I took a vow; I made a decision about me and writing: No more short stories, none, not even one in my spare time, no sudden articles, like the one in Reno, no more columns—nothing but my old trade of promotion. For the years ahead —I was sure that six-month trial would end up in a permanent job —my life would again be the life of a woman in business, with an office, and a secretary, and that big paycheck, until Mike and Chris were both out of college and on their own.

Buried below the solid earth of this decisiveness lay one small seed of possibility: maybe if I just let everything lie fallow for a good long while, maybe the other will grow again.

I never named that "other."

I never talked about it. I never mentioned my four books. If people did, mainly about *Gentleman's Agreement,* I was pleased but in a kind of reminiscent way, perhaps the way an actor feels years after playing his best-known role in a play when people identify with his name and mention it to him.

What I talked about was promotion. A prestige campaign is designed not to sell subscriptions, not to sell advertising space, not to do any obvious selling at all. The desideratum is to build good will toward a company—that thing priced at one dollar in annual statements. The company whose signature runs along the bottom of that prestige promotion often spends a great deal for that "one dollar" item.

Nobody rushed me. I spent the first weeks reviewing all the promotion ever run by Time, sitting in on meetings, lunching with Nick, with one or two editors, occasionally with Linen himself.

It soon occurred to me that the only time I ever sensed if not trouble, a kind of unwillingness, was when I was discussing promotion with Nick. He had been so amiable, even so willing, during all those preliminary moves about my returning to Time, but now that I was there, it was as if he had changed his mind. There is one quote from Nick in my log that shows I was not being oversensitive.

"You talk too much—let's face it—you talk too damn much."

Nick was not my boss. Though he was head of the department it had been made pretty clear that I was to report to Harry and Linen on the campaign itself; for some reason Nick chose not to ask me how, or if, it was getting on. It was as if he had forgotten what my real assignment was.

All the time, of course, my main preoccupation was with it, searching for some special idea, far away from the stereotypical. I was feeling sure of myself again; another magazine had finally bought *The Lovely*

Duckling; I had already returned the unused portion of the Schermans' big loan, plus another $5,233.40 to wind it up. At Time they paid you in advance. I could sleep again.

At the end of October, when Harry finally sent for me, I was ready. He asked me not to his office, but to dinner at his apartment. Clare was still in Rome; we were to be alone.

They lived then in a triplex apartment looking out on the East River, and I can still remember the two of us seated in a large, elegant dining room, at a table that could have seated twenty, Harry at the head of the table and me at his right, as if I were the guest of honor. During dinner, which he seemed not to notice, we talked of general things, with Harry doing most of the talking.

"Have you written anything yet," he asked as the coffee came in, "on the new campaign?"

"Not to show you, but I think I've found a great big area that might be the foundation for all of it."

"An area? What area?"

"A concept, sort of an underpinning." He looked puzzled, even irritated at this vagueness.

"It's a verb, Harry. One word everybody uses every day. I've got a picture of it."

"A picture of a verb?" His heavy eyebrows rose. "What does that mean, a picture of a verb?"

I spread my hands wide. "It's a photostat of pages seven forty-four, seven forty-five and seven forty-six of the *Oxford English Dictionary,* column after column about that one verb—the verb *to know.*"

"To know!"

"I'd like to write about the need to know, the deep human impulse to find out, to read, to learn, to *know*—not just Time, but newspapers, books, everything."

He leaned back into his chair. He never went in for words like *great, terrific, clever, super*—that sort of praise was foreign to him. But his eyes were alight with interest.

"The word *ken,*" he said suddenly. "Do you know that *ken* is the Scottish for *know?* It comes from the same root as *can.*"

"I never thought of that." I thought about *ken* and *can.* "It's nice, Harry. I like that."

I went home and settled down to hard persistent writing. Headlines had been shaping up for some time; now I was writing copy to go under them. I went to Young and Rubicam, Time's advertising agency, and began to suggest layout ideas—starting with those blown-up pages of the *Oxford English Dictionary*. The art director on the Time account, Ray Todd, and his supervisor were instantly responsive; when I stopped suggesting my own ideas for layouts they began to offer theirs, to show me photographs we might use, drawings, sketches. Not one was what anybody would expect.

Just after Thanksgiving I sent Jim Linen a note: "I have about six pieces of copy to show you and am yours to command." I was not surprised when I was sent for the next morning that it was in Harry's office that we met; it was clear that Linen himself felt that this was Harry's particular project.

I put the first layout down in front of them. There were my lovely columns of the verb *know*, blown up to occupy a whole newspaper page, and superimposed on them, in strong outline, the head and shoulders of a man leaning forward to read. The headline streaked across most of the definitions.

> KNOW . . . THE SAME ROOT AS CAN AND KEN
> *Know, knew, known, Cnawan, cnowe, cnoue, knaw, cneow, cneu, kneu, y-knowe, know*
> Down the ages, from Greek and Latin, through Old English, Middle English, closely related to counterparts in Italian and French and German and Scotch—
> Throughout the history of mankind, *know* has been one of the great verbs. "Well-established in all the main senses by 1200 . . . the verb has since had a vigorous life."
> People who *know* also have vigorous lives; they are the people with the instinct to master something, to enjoy it, perhaps to excel in it.
> I ken—I can. What a wonderful equation it is. I know—I am able.
> In the huge, various world of 1957, it is impossible to *know* more than one field really well. Which may be why so many people regard the trained researchers, writers and editors of Time as their indispensable allies for knowing something of many other fields as well.

Linen and Harry read it word for word, and then read it again. They looked at each other; they glanced, not at me, but at the other layouts I had turned face down on the floor beside my chair. I picked up the next layout and its copy, and laid them down before them.

This one was of a floor-to-ceiling bookcase in a living room; climbing from the floor up to the third shelf above was a five-year-old boy, reaching above him to a picture book he could barely tip out of its place. The headline was simpler.

The need to KNOW

It starts early, the impulse to find out, to look into, to KNOW everything.

We all have it, in our beginnings. And for some of us this instinct to know doesn't vanish with childhood; rather it reaches out as we grow older . . .

Again they read it twice, but this time Harry did look at me, nodding. I gave them the third layout. This was a picture of an old, foreign-looking man, his gnarled hand holding a steel pen over the lined pages of a child's exercise book, where he has been writing the letter *a* over and over, *a,a,a,a* . . .

Who wants to know?

Everybody. To some degree and about certain things, everybody alive.

The need to know, the hunger for knowing, varies from person to person, from topic to topic.

There were three more to show them, and each time they reacted as they had before. As far as the layouts went, these were only roughs, but my copy on each one was close to final. There must have been some suggestions of small changes, some queries about this phrase or the other, but I don't remember anything but a general euphoria, not only mine.

At last Harry spoke up as if to signal the end of the meeting. "It would appear," he said in his most positive tone, "that at last we do have a campaign."

Dear Harry,

Could I please see you for ten minutes today? It's an emergency. I've never been able to "report to teacher" on any of my large or small problems with the Know campaign. Nor am I able to now.

But on Thursday, my secretary told me that Nick's secretary had just said, "Laura's check next week is her last one, you know. She's only here for six months."

There had been no clues in the preceding ten weeks to signal me of impending drama. Since that euphoric meeting with Linen and Luce, it is true, there had been anything but enthusiasm from Nick about the Know campaign. "I don't believe it will ever run," he once said. "I haven't seen one final okay on any ad—you don't know this company as I know it," but friendly grapevines assured me that this was part of the Samstagian style and advised me to take it as standard operating procedure.

And things were moving along in acceptable fashion. Final artwork was ordered and submitted, sometimes sent back for revision, schedules were being drawn up on insertion dates in a number of leading newspapers, meetings were held to estimate costs of space, production —all perfectly normal preparation, complete with confusion and delays.

All this preparation fell under Nick's jurisdiction, and I paid little attention to anything beyond the copy and layouts and art. Every few days I would hear from, or have lunch with, one of Time's editors or executives to talk about the Know campaign, and each time I came away with an added fillip of gratification.

And then came that day in February when Nick's secretary told my secretary. I couldn't believe it; I couldn't bear it.

I called my "agent," but she was in Washington. I phoned Al Grover, saw him, told him, making no attempt to hide my dismay. He was furious, calling it an outrage, telling me to write Harry a letter at once. When I saw my "agent" late that same evening, the same thing occurred. Of course she would see Harry the moment she could, but the immediate course was for me to write him, to make it official, so that he might not take it to be some more of Nick's shenanigans.

I spent half the night writing Harry so I could take my letter to his office first thing in the morning. I put in specifics I thought essential, as reminders of needed background.

Six months was indeed the deal. Naturally, I regarded it the way I did years ago when you first hired me . . . "for a trial period —let's say six months." . . . the normal business finesse . . . so that if I failed to come up with anything first-rate, we could call everything off without awkwardness. . . .

But to have won your approval and Jim's, later Otto's and C.D.'s and Barney's and everybody else on this Know campaign —only to get the gate from Nick, is just too preposterous.

Which is why I ask whether I could possibly see you, briefly, some time today.

It was a bad night for me. To lose this job, to go back into debt? To return to that uncertainty about the boys and their schools, about bills and borrowing . . . I remember now with some astonishment at my weakness how ready I was to think that this was going to end my short happy return to Time.

Early the next morning Harry telephoned me himself, with no secretarial intermediary. He didn't announce himself; I knew his voice. "Well, we've started a process to work things out," he said, "so just keep very quiet for a day or two."

He barely gave me time to say thank you. He put up the receiver. That afternoon Al Grover asked me to meet him up on his floor, near the elevator, not in his office. He had heard from Harry, had read my letter. Then he looked at me importantly, as if waiting for my full attention. "But Laura, when Harry sends for you, you have to be careful. The one thing he can't stand is an emotional scene with a woman. You'll have to watch every word you say, control the way you act. I mean it—keep it absolutely calm."

A day went by before he sent for me. I did watch every word; as I recall it, I behaved like some uninvolved member of a dull business meeting. Harry seemed aloof, informing me only that the process he had mentioned was nearing completion. He didn't mention Nick, nor did I. When I left I kept my thanks to a slightly frosty matter-of-factness.

One day later Linen sent a formal memorandum, addressed to Nick and to me. I liked the first point.

The experimentation period is over. The Know campaign is now approved as Time's general newspaper effort for 1957 and hope-fully longer than that.

The next point said Nick would have jurisdiction of merchandising the campaign, proper placement and tempo, and the like, and the next point was another one I liked.

Laura Hobson will originate and write the advertisements . . .

Exactly one week later, in the New York *Times,* the Philadelphia *Bulletin,* and a dozen other leading papers throughout the country, the first ad of the series appeared. It was the *Oxford English Dictionary* page, and almost at once letters began to come in from English teachers, from headmasters, from people, even from the National Book Council, not noted for unsolicited testimonials.

> We think [it] has contributed a great deal toward the encourage-
> ment of lifetime reading habits—of Time, of every magazine, of
> books for profit, and books for fun.

The annual appropriation for the first year of the Know campaign was set at $500,000. After that first year, it won one of the Saturday Review's annual awards for Distinguished Advertising in the Public Interest.

It was to run, with me writing every word, for all the years I remained at Time.

The year 1958, which was to bring me to one of the most profound experiences of my whole existence, began amiably enough. Clare invited me to their house in Phoenix, Arizona, for a few days of vacation.

By now her ambassadorship had ended, she was not officially "in public life" and it may be that she was restless. A month before she had telephoned from Phoenix to ask me out for Christmas; I was astounded that she could think it possible that I would leave Mike and Chris alone at Christmas, no matter who invited me.

But this time I accepted with alacrity. I could stay a few days and then go on to California to my friends out there. I had heard about the stunning place the Luces had bought in Phoenix, complete with swimming pool; I had had no vacation since the ten-day trip to Florida before joining Time, and all during the past year I had continued to work at top speed, not only on the Know campaign, but on my new assignment overlapping it as official promotion consultant on Sports Illustrated, which at that time was still losing money in a big way. (One of Harry's rewards for "work well-done" was to load you with another great big assignment.)

"We'll have the travel department arrange your tickets," Harry's long-time secretary, Corinne Thrasher, told me the day I accepted.

"I'd appreciate that. I'll send up my check—"

"Oh; no, we always—whenever we invite anybody out there, we do the airplane tickets—"

"I can't explain it, Corinne, but I'd rather buy my own."

"Well, if you insist." She sounded disapproving. "There's one more thing. Mr. Luce does not like to sit next to anybody he knows when he's on a plane."

I laughed. "You tell me where he'll be sitting, and I'll be at the other end, a mile off."

And so it was. In those days, there was no nonstop to Phoenix; you changed at Chicago, with a half-hour wait, and of course I seated myself at the other end of the waiting room.

But Harry sought me out. Terra firma, it appeared, made a difference—he was in the mood to talk. I remember his holding forth first on the impossibility of giving up cigarettes, and I detected his irritation when I said I had quit. I wanted to add that by now it was three and a half years ago, but I thought I'd better not.

He was even more irked by the novel he had been reading during the flight from New York.

"I can't understand half the expressions in it," he said, exhibiting the offending book. "I suppose it's the new slang."

It was Max Shulman's *Rally Round the Flag, Boys,* a current best-seller.

"Should I read it and see if I can come up with some sort of glossary? I hear so much slang from my two boys."

He handed it to me, as if to rid himself of something noxious, and began to discuss politics.

Once more aloft, again properly removed from him, I opened to page one and almost immediately asked the stewardess if she could let me have a sheet of blank paper. Long before we reached the airport at Phoenix, I had a glossary that would either amuse Harry or vex him to death because it was indeed so young.

"We had this little rumble"; "It was the most" ("The most *what?*" I could hear Harry demand); "A series of assorted gropes" (I could explain that as necking); "An absolute gasser"; "Everybody went ape"; "My father—was he p.o'd!" (That one I would translate as "teed off."); "Hacking around," "yocking up a storm," "hot-rod Romeos," "Daddy-o," "Flake off"— All these would need not merely a single synonym from the slang of earlier decades, but a bit of explication. Easier would be "Weirdsville," "Dullsville," "Splitsville" and their little variations. At our weekly poker games, which I had at last resumed after those lean years of abstinence, we all said things like "Brokesville," "New Stacktime," "No Chipsville."

As we neared Phoenix, I left my delicious little task of glossary-making and went to the lavatory. I had to pass Harry's seat but knew I wouldn't even glance at him. Yet as I drew even with him, I suddenly stopped. Something about the way he was sitting caught my peripheral vision; he seemed slumped sideways in his seat. I did look directly at him—he was pale, waxy-looking. I knew something was very wrong; I knelt beside him, right there in the aisle.

"Harry, are you all right?" A stewardess came rushing up.

"Oxygen?" she said, but rushed off for aspirin and water.

I reached for his wrist, to try for his pulse, but he yanked his hand back. "It's nothing," he said. "I'm all right."

But I stayed there, kneeling beside him; his color began to return; he sat back, straightening himself firmly; he did look more himself. But I was glad we were approaching the airport.

The Luce chauffeur met us; during the drive to their house, Harry remained silent and so did I. Clare noticed nothing unusual when we arrived, and he told her nothing of what had happened in the plane, at least not then.

There was another guest, Charles Goren, the bridge expert millions of bridge players had made their presiding genius and card-table god. He was contributing a weekly column on bridge to Sports Illustrated; I had talked to him by telephone a few times on some of our promotion about his column, and had even met and played bridge with him.

This unlikely event came about because Clare loved bridge and played whenever she could find time. In New York she had phoned me a couple of times at the office, asking me to make a fourth at a game she was arranging for that very evening, and nearly always I had accepted, knowing that she would have invited not just any old common-variety bridge players for the rest of the four but somebody like Charles Goren himself.

Once I arrived at her house to find that we were playing with Goren and another world-class player, Boris Koytchou, and playing for two cents. My usual stake was a tenth of a cent, so that if you lost a thousand points, or a "ten rubber," you owed a dollar. In this game if I lost a ten rubber I would owe twenty dollars.

But I was the big winner—every hand I picked up just sparkled with kings and queens, so I simply had to win. Goren and Koytchou both wrote "Congratulations" on the score card and signed their names. I kept it as a memento.

But out there in Phoenix, after their days of golf, which I didn't play, when we finished dinner and went to the bridge table, with Goren as the main attraction, the stakes were different. Harry had taken up bridge only recently and was still the novice, so Goren laid down the law: no high stakes. Harry and Clare both protested that stakes didn't matter, but Goren wouldn't budge. We played for a quarter-cent; if you lost a ten rubber you would owe $2.50. We played a lot of bridge that weekend.

Five days later, about when I was leaving for California, Harry came down with a severe cold that suddenly grew into something much worse. Alarmed, Clare sent for their doctor, Hayes Caldwell, and the doctor quickly summoned an ambulance.

Harry or Clare must have told him about what had happened in the airplane, for Dr. Caldwell began questioning me and barely stopped until the ambulance arrived.

Why had I knelt in the aisle? How exactly had he slumped in his seat? To what side? Did I get to feel his pulse before he pulled his hand away? Were his eyes open? What did I mean by "waxy-looking"?

He went through it with me again, and the ambulance alone put a stop to it. I can still vividly remember being outside in the garden when the stretcher came out carrying Harry, looking so ill, so unlike the powerful Henry Robinson Luce the whole world knew.

Clare went along with him in the ambulance to St. Joseph's Hospital, and I followed after in the car driven by Arthur Little, their chauffeur. When I found Clare she was talking to a nun and she came to me weeping, saying, "If anything happens to Harry my whole life would be over."

It was a pulmonary embolism, or so I was told some hours later. During the hours of waiting other doctors had me repeat my report of Harry in the plane, asking me the same questions, with the same interest in any detail I could dredge up from my mind.

Many years were to pass before I learned that more than the embolism had occured, that a coronary occlusion had followed it, and that Harry was to be on anticoagulant drugs for the rest of his life. The decision had been made there in the hospital, surely by Clare herself, that the full truth must be kept from the press, from the stockholders, from the stock market, where Time stock might plummet at any reports of heart attack. The papers in Phoenix next morning did not even mention pulmonary embolism; their diagnosis was a severe influenza that had brought on pneumonia. The New York press reported the same.

As evening came, Clare said I just couldn't go off to California, and leave her alone with the servants, and I said of course I'd stay as long as needed and do whatever was needed. She was staying overnight at the hospital; I was driven back to the house and spent the next hours on the telephone to New York. I couldn't reach Harry's sister Beth but did reach her husband, Maurice T. Moore, called Tex, an attorney with Time's own law firm. I had known Tex and Beth for a long time because of Harry, and could let myself go as I tried to tell Tex everything that had happened—limited, of course, to that embolism. Even that was enough to make him say he would fly out in the morning and bring Hank, Harry's son, with him.

I also called Al Grover that night so that he could notify whichever of Time's other executives he thought had to know. Then I phoned my own friends in California, saying only that I'd have to shift plans for a few days. I also carried out various instructions Clare had given me about their half-dozen servants. It was a favor to me, in fact, that I was kept so occupied.

It was to be three weeks before Harry left the hospital. One morning I was allowed a brief visit; I bought a book to give him—no glossary needed—but the visit did not go too well. I think he was unwilling to have anybody see him so ill and not in command; I myself was oddly ill at ease to see him there in bed in his pajamas, so shorn of his usual Harryness.

Tex and Hank stayed only a day or two, and again Clare asked me to stay on, and again I agreed. I think now that once the fear about Harry was gone, I was finding it very pleasant to remain in all that luxury as an appreciated guest: Clare was always so amusing and unexpected—we steered clear of politics, so we were free of problems. One night my old novelette, *The Reward*, was on television; we watched it together and then talked of what she was writing for the theater and about the book I had set aside. All I said about it was, "God knows if it will ever be finished."

As always with Clare, one thing happened that was later to become an anecdote I liked telling. One day she up and asked me to leave the house for the weekend—but to be sure to come back Sunday evening. She needed the main guest room for two nights. Long before, she had invited Vice-President Nixon and his wife Pat—and that was an invitation one could not withdraw. But she would never ask me to move into a smaller guestroom.

I laughed in her face. "And you can't imagine me in the same house with Dick Nixon anyway!"

TEN

IN RETROSPECT MY NINETEEN days in Phoenix soon began to seem like a period of high drama. I came home to difficulties at work and at home, and I was often depressed and lonely, in need again of those old escape hatches.

In my log for all of 1958 I see no "E's" at all, so we must have been in one of those periods Eric was to write about in his unfinished autobiography when he said "we were in and out of each other's lives —with some very long lapses, it is true." This was one of the long ones—I cannot now remember why. It had not been a quarrel—we never quarreled—and it could not have been illness again. Maybe it was because—well, we were getting older. Eric was nearly sixty.

I went out a lot, to the movies or the theater when the boys were at home on holiday, to concerts, to the great parties at the Cerfs' and other party-givers'; I played poker again once a week in nearly all-night games, and I became a member of the Regency, one of the best-known bridge clubs in the U.S. I began to leave the office early, to drop in at the club rather than go home to a silent apartment, and soon I could justly be dubbed a bridge addict, spending time with people I had little in common with as to books or politics or music or anything but bridge.

A submerged guilt kept nagging at me. Was I to be a "bridge fiend" and businesswoman from now on, for the rest of my life? I remembered the story about Somerset Maugham, who was said to go to the casino at Monaco every afternoon at five for a few rubbers of bridge.

One day one of his youthful admirers, a houseguest and nonbridge player, remonstrated with him. "Oh, Mr. Maugham, how is it that so great an author as you can like to spend time at a card table every afternoon?"

"Young man," Mr. Maugham is supposed to have replied in a flinty voice, "if *that* is your attitude, you are in for an exceedingly lonely old age."

I wanted to believe that, and yet the guilt persisted. Years were to go by before my sister Alice, after one of our long separations, put me at my ease in one brilliant stroke.

"If you were a chess fiend," she said, "that would be all right. Pa wouldn't allow cards or liquor in the house—they were 'opiates of the people.' But *chess?* Chess is for the *intelligentsia*—go ahead and play chess every night—that's okay."

I never felt guilty again about playing bridge.

But even several sessions a week of bridge, and even my continuing success at the office, could not prevent me from a recurring sadness about the turn my life had taken. I was still lying fallow as far as that other went; if an idea for a short story popped into my head, I let it lie there unattended. I seemed to have become a permanent exile from that "other," like an American expatriate in Paris in the twenties in the days of Hemingway and Scott Fitzgerald, part of a different culture, never missing home, remaining away for years and presumably content to do so.

And there were more serious reasons for my depression, which so often seemed just below the surface, only too ready to rise and claim me. Twice Chris had been suspended from school, only for a few days at a time, and never for any cause that I myself regarded as reprehensible, except in schoolmaster's terms. One of those times was because he had gone to the city one night, slipping out a dormitory window after lights out, and taking his departure for a few hours—to go to the Mozart Café.

To me that was something to be happy about—but I was no schoolmaster, only a mother who was delighted that he too loved good music. But there were other matters that no mother could be happy about—he was nearly seventeen, deep into adolescence, ready to rebel against any and every kind of thing he resisted, one of which, as with all adolescents, was parents. Perhaps when there is only one parent the rebellion can be more sharply focused. We seemed constantly at odds, to argue, to quarrel—I am certain I was as much at fault as any other bewildered parent in the world. But wherever the fault there were spells of deep misery whenever he left the dormitory and came home for the holidays; I arranged for renewed sessions for him with his child analyst, and then went further and asked Dr. Gosselin to see him.

Each visit ended with me hoping that things would go better between us, with me, at least, making resolutions about being more temperate the next time something went wrong—and I think with young Chris making resolutions as well.

But the next time came, and little had changed.

Another crisis lay just ahead at the office, and through most of the spring and summer I sensed its approach and wondered how I could manage it. This time it had nothing to do with Nick at all, or with anybody in the entire organization of Time Inc.

There was one thing I had done, nearly a year before, that I had often regretted, and had slowly come to be ashamed of. There are very few things in my life, in my own perception of my life, that strike me as a little shabby, but whenever I think back to that particular matter, an embarrassed something in me calls it names like shabby.

It had to do with my "agent."

As the first anniversary of my new job approached, she had begun to hint that our "arrangement" should continue.

"But we said it was for a year," I said. "We put it in that letter—you signed it and I did, and I sent it to Phyllis Jackson at MCA, my regular agent. I said, 'ten percent for one year.' "

"But nobody dreamed there'd be such troubles with Nick—and they'll go right on happening too."

Whenever she saw Harry, she told me, she made a point of keeping him informed of Nick's continuing animosity on a dozen fronts. He resisted the news that there was to be a magazine schedule for the Know campaign in Life, Time and the "quality group." He had insulted me in a meeting with others, saying, "You're not central to this company." He kept ridiculing the special "woman's panel" I had established for Sports Illustrated, consisting of four able women, specialists in several fields pertaining to women, who were paid $500 a month each to make suggestions and write reports on new ideas, and to meet regularly with me and the publisher of the magazine and occasionally with Linen and Luce as well in the hopes of widening its appeal so that it might attract more women readers and subscribers.

"You said you can't 'tell teacher,' " she reminded me. "But somebody has to, as your representative."

We were at her house that night, I find in a letter I wrote to her some time later, and two paragraphs tell me now that it was far from being an amiable discussion between us.

> We did not even discuss continuing the payments until the summer of 1957, when I assumed they were ending, and you told me, "Harry will be very angry," if I stopped paying you regularly.
>
> There was then such a storm, with flung objects as well as words, across the room, that I unwillingly said I would go on for one more year . . .

And that decision, however unwillingly made, is what evokes the self-accusation of "shabby." I did not call myself that at the time, of course. All I actually remember of that moment as I search back through my logs and old letters is that I was weak enough not to risk a falling-out with her, that I must have listened to some cowardly little yelp inside me, "Keep the status quo."

That is what I did, month after month, for another whole year. Each check I wrote bore the phrase "Management fee." I have all the checks, twenty-four of them, for a total of six thousand dollars, together with a small packet of letters when they ended.

The crisis that came the following summer arose because a third year at Time was about to start for me, and she had already indicated that she expected to go right on earning her "honest commission." I used a nasty word.

There had been a huge newspaper scandal at about that time, about some disc jockey on some radio show who was being paid under the table to promote certain popular songs; the word *payola* was heard a hundred times a day in connection with it and now, over the telephone, when she said, "honest commission," it sprang to my lips.

"You mean payola. Two years is enough. I'll send one more check."

I got the verbal drubbing I deserved for *payola* and remained glad I had actually spoken those three brief syllables. That was when I made a decision. I sent a brief note, handwritten, to Al Grover.

> Dear Al,
>
> Before I lose my courage may I see you in private about a scandalous secret I have kept for two years and can keep no longer.

Apparently I felt that I had to confess to somebody right there at Time Inc., needed to lay myself open to whatever scorn or punishment might be coming to me, could no longer keep behind that wall of silence I had built when I had got my "inspiration" in that frightened summer of the second lean year so long ago.

Grover saw me that same evening. I told him how it had all started, so simply, and how it had changed after that first year was over. I spread twenty-three checks before him, saying I had just mailed the final one. I quoted phrases she had used, spared myself nothing in telling my part of it.

"Harry never knew one damn thing about it," Al said. He was astounded and more angry than I had ever seen him. "Harry would never have stood for this deal she made; if he had known about even the first one of those checks he would never have talked to her again."

He reminded me that weeks before I'd even asked her to "expedite" things he and I had had a big lunch about my going back to Time, and that he had phoned me to say he had "put out feelers" to Harry, and that there was "nothing discouraging" about it. "You never needed to pay her one dime of commission."

I told him it would be all right with me if he told Harry everything I had done, or Jim Linen, or anybody else in the firm; he did not say whether he would or would not, and I was never to learn whether he ever did.

But I felt an enormous riddance of a burden that had been growing minute by minute for longer than I knew.

In the letter I sent my ex-agent with my final check I put into words what I had been so woefully tardy in recognizing.

One thing I never did insist on, and should have from the first, was that our whole commission deal should have been public, i.e., known at Time to Al Grover, Jim Linen, Bernard Barnes, and also known to our personal friends.

It is the secrecy of it that I loathe. No agent's deal need be a secret. No lecture bureau's or artist manager's. And it was the secrecy that made me feel ill when you threatened to "tell Harry" if I didn't put you on the Sports Illustrated panel at $500 a month, or even when you used to say over a gin rummy game, "Harry won't like it if he knows you beat me again."

I sent a carbon of that letter to Al Grover. Whether he himself ever felt that I had been weak or shabby not to have ended it all at the end

190

of the single year she and I had agreed on when we signed that letter in triplicate, I do not know. Whether he ever did tell Harry or Jim or anybody what I had at last told him, I do not know either. I do know we remained friends for all my following years at Time, and way beyond them as well.

And then, on a morning in October, there came a letter that was to change my life as deeply, as pivotally as any other single experience of my life.

It was from Chris.

It was written on five sheets of a narrow notepaper, and the first two sheets were, in their way, a warning to brace myself for what he was to tell me. To write it had been difficult; he wished there were some way that might allow him not to write it, but there was none at all.

An icy fist began to clench in the depths of my body. I read on, through his reminders of the increased fury of our quarrels in the past months, of his return to his analyst, of my delay about further therapy for him, and of his deepening conviction that I would end all delay once I knew his true reasons for wanting it.

Telling me face to face was something he couldn't bear; he loved me and wished he could spare me the horrible shock and pain . . .

And then, on the third page, there it was. He was a homosexual.

"She came to the end," I was to write in a novel that was to be published seventeen years later,

> and stood as if tranced, without tears, nothing as easy as tears, stood motionless in the sensation of being smashed through every organ, through every nerve, every reasoning cell.
>
> Love for him, pity for his suffering, pride for his courage in telling her, horror at *it,* at the monstrous unendurable *it*—a savagery of feeling crushed her, feelings mutually exclusive yet gripping each other in some hot ferocity or amalgam.
>
> She read the letter again. Then only did she begin to cry, but not the ordinary crying, not she the ordinary weeping woman; it was, rather, a roaring sobbing, of an animal gored.

That, of course, was me seventeen years earlier. I cannot believe that it would be me today, if it had happened in the world as we know it now, and to me as I am now. But it was nearly thirty years ago, when even decent and intelligent people, who never thought in terms of sin and degeneracy and abomination, still did hold homosexuality to be an illness, a psychosis, some aberration that needed treatment.

I have that letter of his before me now. For years I thought I had lost it; off and on I kept searching for it all over my house, among documents, in files, among manuscripts and other old letters, positive that I could never have thrown that one away, certain that I had unconsciously arranged to suppress its very existence, and thus had hidden it in some arcane place, where it kept itself from reawakening my long-ago agony.

Only when I began to write the first volume of this autobiography and had gone to the bank to empty out my safe deposit box of its old documentation of my early life, the divorce papers, the sale of our house in Jamaica, Thayer Hobson's letters to me and mine to him, the shares of worthless stock in Ingersoll's failed newspaper—only then did I find that five-page letter once more.

And now as I read it again, and read it a second time, all these decades later, I find myself weeping once again; it is so young, so honest, so wretched and so filled with courage—a youth of seventeen just approaching manhood, and already in an anguish for which there was no swift and soothing anodyne.

Across the bottom of its final page, in agitated writing, is a penciled message I sent the same day I received it. For Western Union, I had specified *Fast rate, personal delivery, do not phone.*

> CHRIS DEAR, I LOVE YOU AND ADMIRE YOU AND THANK YOU FOR WRITING ME. OF COURSE WE WILL GO AHEAD. YOU ARE WONDERFUL. DON'T BE WRETCHED NOW. LOVE, MOM.

Stress, that sly damager, raider of nerves and tendons and corpuscles, engendered a good deal of illness for me in the following weeks and months. In volume one of *Laura Z* I said that whenever I was too sorely depressed something went wrong with my body, and sure enough I soon went through three acute attacks of cystitis, and some time later recurring bouts of tachycardia, officially known as paroxysmal auricular fibrillation; my physician assured me that this was not any sort of heart attack and that neither illness was serious, but the antibiotics and other drugs prescribed for me, together with the sicknesses themselves, were enough to diminish me markedly in energy and purpose.

I had been further drained by the steady search for the best analyst for Chris, no longer a child analyst, and one of the highest professional caliber. Dr. Gosselin, of course, gave me several referrals—I had turned to Dr. Gosselin once again on my own behalf as well as Chris's—and the preliminary interviews I had with two or three possible analysts, the attempts to estimate compatability between doctor and patient, the fear of making an unfortunate choice—all of it was emotionally exhausting, and when Chris was finally launched into this so-important new relationship, I was all but spent.

At the office, despite every effort I made to conceal any signs of unusual tension, my depleted state must have shown. One day the publisher of Sports Illustrated, Art Murphy, one of my bosses and one of my friends, took it into his head to send me out to California on a business trip "to have a look at the new lines of swimsuits."

In reality it was a paid vacation, all expenses included, but I accepted it eagerly. Out there I did spend a few mornings and afternoons in the offices and showrooms of Cole of California, Rose-Marie Reid and other leading manufacturers in the field, taking notes for the report I would turn in on my return.

But then I went off for nine days of pure holiday, still by courtesy of Art Murphy and Sports Illustrated, to a resort in Palm Springs, Ocatillo Lodge. I swam, I lay in the sun, I sent off the usual batches of postcards, I phoned Mike and Chris. And I wrote one letter.

> And so you are sixty, my dear Eric, or will be on Monday when this gets to New York. (And I along with it.) I've been out here for a brief vacation after a rather virus-laden two months, and I got thinking of your birthday, and what a special one this is, and I had to send you my birthday congratulations and birthday best wishes and birthday love, which carries with it something of all the different kinds of love there ever were anywhere. And memory too, and great desires for your happiness and achievement yet to come.
>
> You probably won't even be in NYC on your birthday, but it may be nice to have this on your return. I hope you'll still be in a birthday mood though, so you may feel everything I want you to feel: that you will be happy . . . and that you are glad of all the things that ever made you happy or fulfilled.

I signed it, "Always, Laura," and a few days later I had Eric's answer, two pages, single-spaced, on that familiar University Club stationery which had been his for so many years.

Yes, L, I am sixty, and your letter was so dear I all but wept at its kindness and warmth. I was right here and feeling rather eightyish on Monday, so twenty years, if *no* more, slipped off my back after a number of rereadings.

All that you have said . . . to me I say back to you: once more, with feeling. But you will not be sixty for some long time still; all I can warn you about in advance is that it is, well,—odd. You say to yourself, "Who, *me?*" and some clear, flat voice answers right back, "Yes, *you.*" This ends the dialog, except for some obscure muttering, as from a sullen waiter who was undertipped.

. . . You used the word fulfilled in your letter . . . and the word made me reflect on the slow way in which hopes for self-fulfillment shift to hopes for the fulfillment of one's children. On this score I would say things look good.

He then told me at some length about his son and his daughter, and asked for news of my sons. He talked about himself and his work. "My ties with Time Inc all are cut, and we'll to the woods no more, so I have no listening posts at which I might pick up news of you by deflection."

Are you happy and fulfilled and/or also glad, as I am, for all the things that ever made you so? . . . Could you work up any enthusiasm for having dinner—with me, that is? . . . You could make any manifestation of interest as tepid as you wished to, provided it was at least perceptible to an old, old anxiety case. . . .

So when I send you my love, too, we will both know that some things are unalterable.

Those two letters tell me now that our "lapse" must have been the lengthiest one ever, and my log tells me that we did have an evening together not too long afterward. But I see that there were no succession of "E's" in the following months, and my own memory tells me that despite the temporary surcease given me by that brief resumption with Eric and my trip to California, it was soon followed by another sharp descent into depression about Chris, with the nightly need for sleeping pills, with new bouts of illness, with the inner sense of a diminishing, if not a vanishing, energy and purpose.

Which makes it all the more astonishing to me, as I look backward now, that a sudden note appears in my log for a day in late April, 1959.

194

Sent mss of "abandoned" novel to Phyllis Jackson of MCA

She had never seen a paragraph of it. She had become my agent after I had stopped writing it; she knew of its existence but she knew only that it was to be half autobiographical, about my own family, the "Ivarins," and half invented, about another family, Evander and Alida Paige and their son Garry, New England born, Protestants, and the Ivarins' counterpart when it came to the great political issues of free speech, the rights of labor, the hatred of militarism and the whole spectrum of liberal socialism.

Six days after I had sent her my manuscript I made another entry about it and her.

> Phyllis J—re mss—"You must finish it: it's a duty to yourself, to the public—so moving, so warm," etc.

Almost atop that entry a string of others began to race across the pages of my log.

> Began editing novel at page 1—for fast retyping; p. 1–20 incl. New Material at p. 3
>   Read research again; started new research
>   Wrote 5-p. outline, 1911–1921, of rest of the story.
>   Worked 10 P.M. to 3 A.M.—edit 95, 96, 97—up to 119 inclusive; new material at 120.

I never knew, I do not know now, so many years later, why or how that implacable boundary of "nothing" was so suddenly recrossed and left behind, if not permanently then at least for a while. It may be that in that period of pain and despair some tiny synaptic connection was made in my brain, in my spirit, that said to me the only true solace is in writing.

One particular entry about the five-page outline, with those two embracing dates, tells me now that in some mysterious space in my unconscious, during all those years when I was lying fallow, some element of growth must have been quietly proceeding, sprouting ideas, decisions. For in the very act of starting that outline I suddenly lopped off half a decade from my original scheme, realizing that I myself had erected an insuperable hurdle by planning to stretch my story from the Triangle Fire in 1911, through the Great War, through the Russian

195

revolution, through the Sacco-Vanzetti case to the resurgence of the Ku Klux Klan in the middle twenties—a span of a quarter century.

A novel like that would need thousands of pages, or else be the thin anemic parody of reality, dismissing great events in a few glib sentences.

And so, after a five-year gap, my beleaguered book had at least beaten back one potential enemy, and once again my log began to hold not only dates of office lunches, bridge sessions, poker games, splendid parties, but those long-absent jottings of page numbers, of inserts, of new scenes, of rewrites—the solid clock-ticks of a writer's life.

I worked on it only at night and over weekends, the way I used to write in my thirties and early forties, before *Gentleman's Agreement* set me free for seven blessed years of full-time writing.

At Time, I was busier than ever on extra work I may have invented out of my own need to be so preoccupied at the office that it would be impossible to think, for a few hours at a time, of anything more private.

This extra work was a self-imposed and risky assignment, something I had long had in mind, something that turned into a sixteen-page critique of Time, which, as I perfectly well knew, Harry would be bound to consider a sixteen-page critique of Harry Luce himself.

If any proof were wanted that I had no need of anybody to act as my representative with him, this two-month effort of mine, and its outcome, would have furnished the most positive QED of all time.

Years before, back in the thirties, during my first stint at Time, all the liberals on the staff, and most liberals in the world outside, had been enraged by some of Time's locutions, like "Jew Blum" for the premier of France, or "Franco and the Falangists," instead of fascists. I was one of the devoted followers of the leading dissidents, Archibald MacLeish, Russell Davenport, Ralph Ingersoll, Eric Hodgins and other major writers, editors or publishers of Time and Fortune. But back then I myself had felt no responsibility about Time's locutions or editorial slant; I talked about them, yes, at times even with Harry, but I never felt I ought to take any formal stand. I was not one of the editors who decided yea or nay on how a story should be written. I was on the "business side," and in any case, my own political stance had not yet developed sharply enough to make me care very much.

Time magazine had long since ended the use of such nasty locutions, but bias and slant were most certainly still present, and since my own stance had become very firm in the years since then, the technicality that I had nothing to do with the editorial side no longer could quiet my conscience.

The perfect timing for speaking out was fortuitous. It arose in early summer, during all the discussions we were having about possible new turns in the Know campaign, now in its third year, and about promotion in general. Time's number of advertising pages had slipped that year, less than one percent, but any decline in revenue, after the hitherto uninterrupted climb, was "unacceptable" to the heads of the organization.

So when I asked Jim Linen one day if I might write "something long" about Time, he readily agreed, and my self-imposed extra work began. Doubtless he expected nothing beyond a long memo on promotion. I think even a brief sampling will show how wrong he was.

I started by suggesting that Time's "troubles" were not only promotion troubles but "something much larger."

> I began to wonder whether Time itself might be "in trouble" . . . and whether it might be not little trouble, but big trouble, the kind of trouble that wouldn't go away all by itself.
>
> As Time's critics and Time's rivals reached new highs in decibels and pages this year, I at last decided, though I am using the phrase loosely, that Time *is* in trouble.
>
> . . . It isn't trouble with Newsweek and it isn't trouble with U.S. News and World Report; it isn't even trouble with advertisers *as* advertisers . . . nor with media men pure and simple . . .
>
> I think Time is in trouble with many people who like Time and will forgive any minor boner or fluff because of their abiding good will and affection toward it.
>
> I think it's in trouble with people who remain Time readers despite certain matters they regard as major flaws, not minor at all, but major and inherent and continuing.
>
> And, unhappily enough, I think Time is in trouble with plenty of people Time values and respects, but who do not value and respect Time . . .
>
> Some of them are teachers and professors, some are newspapermen, some are intellectuals. Others are college students, authors, TV panelists, ex-Time advertisers and (whisper) Democrats.
>
> Some of them, true enough, are Democrats. But about half the nation's electorate has always been Democratic, and Time

managed perfectly well all along, despite Democrats. Right through the New Deal, the Fair Deal, though Democrats may have yelled foul every day, Time grew every week, every month, every year.

Grew bigger, grew richer, grew more famous.

But did it grow *up?*

Did it grow up enough?

I suggest that Time did not.

Not enough to meet the new test waiting for it, the minute the New Deal and the Fair Deal were out of the way.

The test put to it—by Republicans.

I do mean that with the coming of the Republican administration a whole new yardstick reared up for Time to be measured by, by admirers and detractors alike.

Time was in love, and one's maturity often is reckoned by the way one handles love.

True, Republicans were in the White House during Time's first years, but Time was just an infant then, and if ever it were guilty of a tantrum or of puppy love, nobody paid much mind. Its editors were still "those brilliant young men from Yale," its most livid critics had not yet talked of "the Luce Empire" . . . and even one foreign edition was only a gleam in the corporate eye.

My memo then summarized Time's vast growth in the next thirty-five years to its current national influence, its world influence through its many foreign editions, and it then said that since the Eisenhower administration's first year, Time had been facing a challenge it had never had to face before.

The challenge of victory. The challenge of love.

There's plenty of data around to support the idea that Time's old trouble of "bias" or "slant" took on a new dimension then and there.

I think that Time's soft new tones about Republicans jangled out brassy reminders of Time's other voice to too many people in too many important places . . . [which] led too many people to think anew not only about fair journalism, but about mature journalism.

I then proceeded to pile up some of that data; I gathered my own examples from recent issues of the magazine, I quoted from newspaper reports of a World Press Congress; I summarized some college surveys, among students and faculty, and I quoted a vital passage from a series of pieces, "The Newsmagazines," by Ben H. Bagdikian, a winner of the Ogden Reid Foundation Fellowship for an earlier study of the press in England, France and Italy:

> Time did not exclude unpleasant fact completely. In the case of a man it condemned, Acheson, it buried 62 lines of his considerable achievements in an avalanche—477 lines—of emotionally loaded words that stained the image. In the case of a man it approved of, Dulles, it buried 26 lines of grave and fundamental criticism in an avalanche, 617 lines, of words that glowed with heroic praise.

I took on Harry Luce himself on one of his favorite themes, that objective reporting is a myth, that "the responsible journalist is 'partial' to that interpretation of the facts which seem to him to fit things as they are." I wrote of my intense belief that just as liberal newspapers and journals had every right to exist in the world of a free press, just as radical or communist newspapers and journals had that same right to exist, so too did I hold that conservative, even reactionary, newspapers and journals had that the same inalienable right. But . . .

> I'm not going to suggest that Time "go objective." But I am going to say that Time . . . as it searches its ground rules and concepts . . . might also take a good look into its psyche.
> For few people would deny that Time not only has a journalistic conscience, but a journalistic unconscious.

Only the last three pages of my sixteen dealt with the question of future promotion. If Time *were* to embark on a new policy where any bias or slant were taboo, where there was no more burying under avalanches—if Time entered a new era of maturity,

> an era of new respect from the world, from Republican and Democrat, from teacher and intellectual, from the colleges and city desks of all the U.S. and far beyond . . .

I was bold enough to promise that then I could offer "four, six, ten possible campaigns within the first three months of the start of it." Our prestige promotion, I thought, could talk about "a new and total excellence."

> Things change, the U.S. changes, the demands upon Time change,
> Time itself grows and changes.

With trepidation and confidence mixed in equal parts, I took up my sixteen pages myself, not even trusting my wonderful secretary, Evey Benjamin, to deliver them safely. She had made one copy for Jim Linen, another for Harry, each freshly typed on heavy bond paper, because Harry had long before made it known that he would not "use up his eyes" by reading flimsy onion-skin carbon copies of anything, and every other officer in the organization had followed his lead.

The moment I did so, I returned once more to my night-writing on my book. There had been other distractions during the past two months too, these welcome and pleasant, for it was commencement day for each of my two sons.

Mike was graduated from Harvard, again on the Dean's honors list, and with his first adult job already secured, in publishing with Little, Brown in their Boston home office at $65 a week, good pay then for beginners.

His job interviews had all been in Boston, for he had fallen in love with a Radcliffe girl some time before, a girl I met, toward whom I felt warm and affectionate from the start, and who seemed to feel warm and affectionate toward me. She was staying on for another year, to take her master's at Harvard, which of course made Boston the only possible city for Mike. I was proud that his first real job should be in publishing. Heredity was all very well, yes certainly, but it seemed clear that environment had its good uses and achievements too.

And Chris gave me that lift of pride too. In his final year at Riverdale he won a National Merit Scholarship, one of the most prestigious in the country. Some half-million boys and girls throughout the United States had taken the qualifying tests in the spring, and of those, only ten thousand had survived and gone on to the second round. In the third and last test only one thousand of the ten thousand won the award. Chris was the only student at his school to do it. Since he could not be said to be in need of financial help, it was an honor with no monetary value, but the National Merit Scholarship was held in high esteem in every academic circle in the land. He was also elected to the Cum Laude Society of Riverdale, a sort of Junior Phi Beta Kappa, and he was a student-elect at Harvard College, Class of '63. No wonder his mother was proud.

My older son a college graduate, my younger son a college entrant, my self-imposed assignment at the office finally behind me—at least there were these heartening threads of achievement weaving through my persisting self-doubt and readiness to assume guilt that "I must have done something wrong or Chris—"

Once again there was solace in writing on my novel. By late fall my rewritten manuscript, plus all the newly written inserts, plus many new scenes, was ready to be submitted to Random House, but not to Saxe Commins, the editor I had gone to years before as the one person I so much wanted to work with. Saxe had had another heart attack, this one fatal, but all the while since then there had been no cause for me even to wonder who might become my editor. Now it turned out to be Bob Loomis, who, I was told, was editor to William Styron and other good writers. I had met and talked with Loomis through one lengthy lunch; he seemed responsive to what he knew about my book, and I felt a ready confidence in him before that first edit-session was over.

My manuscript was no longer at page 150. I must have destroyed at least fifty or sixty of those original pages, but I had been "writing forward" as well as rewriting, and now it had reached what to me was a new, even impressive, bulk. It was at page 241.

My log for December 2 was a premature Christmas present.

> Bennett Cerf called: "Loomis says it's terrific—that he's dazzled
> by some parts; needs much work but it's tremendous stuff."

Bennett had known all along, directly from me in phone calls, at parties, in brief letters, about my writer's block, about my newspaper columns and novelettes, and finally about my return to Time and a regular income. He had known too about my bouts of wondering whether ever I would, or could, return to my own writing. He followed his phone call with a letter. He had read what I had sent in.

> I have never lost faith in you for a single moment. I knew you
> were going to get back to that book . . . and I know that when
> it is finished, it's going to be a novel we will be proud to publish.

ELEVEN

BUT THERE WAS STILL a long way to go before Bennett could test out that high moment.

It was the dawn of 1960 when his letter came—a new decade, the sixties, and in June it would be my turn to say, "Who, *me?*" as Eric had done a couple of years before. The same flat voice that had answered, "Yes, you," would be there for me, ending "the dialog except for some obscure muttering, as from a sullen waiter who was undertipped."

If it were up to me alone, I would now say that those early years of my sixties have become little more than a dreary blur, with a few highlights, it is true, but in the main a fogged-over misted time of ache and sadness, for my Chris, for myself, for our quarrels, for our inability to arrive at any peace or even truce with each other, as if we were in some hopeless undeclared war.

He was of course in his second year of "real" analysis with a highly regarded physician in Cambridge—those were still the days when psychoanalysis was considered the one and only procedure open to parents eager "to do anything" to help a child with what was still thought to be some sort of illness or neurosis.

During the truncated holiday periods when he came home from Harvard, everything touching on reality went wrong. The one subject we could not approach was the one subject that meant most to him —and to me. He apparently could not see the "me" part of that equation; whatever I tried to say, or tried to ask, struck him as an infringement of his privacy—"It's *my* life, damn it"—and whatever he did choose to tell me struck me as a shaft of anger and reprisal for some wrong I was guilty of but could not even name. We lived, each of us, encapsulated in some unpierceable shell of pain. I, no more than he, seemed unable to break free.

It was years before I began to make a real study of this whole area of life and living, years before I began to realize that analysis of the ordinary kind might be no help at all, might even prove damaging, since most analysts in that era were themselves so convinced that only heterosexuality was "normal."

But enlightenment does not come prematurely, no matter how inexplicable that may seem a quarter-century later, and so those years that I would so gladly pass over by some phrase about a dreary blur had their own inner blindnesses for me too.

But it is not up to me alone, what to say now about those early sixties. For right here staring at me is my private little Library of Congress, my logs, daring me to claim "blur" and leap ahead to publication day of my novel in 1964. Those little red books, so uniform in shape and size, changing only in the gold numerals on spine and cover, suddenly seem to say, "Hey, here's 1960 and 1961 and '62 and '63—are you just going to skip them?"

Well, at least the highlights. Some of them are fine, some are harrowing, but each of them is endowed, in its brief jottings, with that power to recreate my past.

Fine, certainly, about me and my job.

Jim Linen—1 P.M. Maude Chez Elle about reshaping my Time deal; "It would be silly of Time to let you go"—HRL

Apparently after the driving push of my sixteen-page piece about Time I had become restless. Unlikely as it seems to me now, there are entries of interviews I had with the famous Bill Bernbach, president of Doyle, Dane and Bernbach Advertising, me bold enough to consider a career change at the age of sixty! I had made this known, of course, to Linen and to Harry, and I think it must have seemed unlikely to them too. One thing was totally clear to me: I was committed to staying on a good big salary until June 1963, the day Chris would be out of Harvard, when both my sons would be officially on their own and earning their own livings.

I can no longer understand my restlessness. During the fall, Nick Samstag had left Time, for reasons unknown to me and unsought by me; the Know campaign was continuing steadily and my long essay about Time had met with obvious success—albeit in an unpredictable Lucean idiom. Never for a moment had I feared that Harry would fire me or castigate me for it—he was always a man to accept a challenge —but never did I think, either, that he would find his own way to manage me and it.

Silence, total, unbroken silence from Harry was my lot. I had been invited to a series of special lunches by various editors and officials of the company, to talk about my long piece; they told me Harry had directed that copies be distributed widely; they told me he had called it "impressive."

But from Harry himself, not one word, not ever, even when I spent an entire evening with him. It was a simple entry that evening: "H.R.L. here. Dinner. *Great!*"

I remember that it was Corinne Thrasher, the ever-faithful, who had put that little turn of "here" to the evening; while she had been telling me what restaurant to meet him at, for that discussion I had asked for about possible new assignments, she had remarked that he was "so tired of restaurants."

"Corinne, do you mean I should ask him up here?"

"He'd certainly rather."

"I don't have a cook."

"He never thinks about food."

Nor did he. Two major things I remember about that evening: one his look of astonishment that I should even consider leaving Time, and the other his sudden statement on world affairs to come.

"Laura, I have it from the Rand Corporation—there will be a nuclear war this year of 1960."

The Rand Corporation of California had made the pronouncement; vaguely I knew that the Rand Corporation was at the heart of the military-industrial complex and presumably authoritative.

"Oh, Harry, I can't believe that."

He was off; for most of the evening he talked politics as he saw politics; when he permitted an interruption, I disagreed as politely as I could without letting him begin to think I might agree with him— but he didn't permit many interruptions. I remember a hideous fear licking at my nerves—could the Rand Corporation know something the rest of humanity didn't? Could Harry be right?

Fortunately the talk about me and Time had come first; it must have been the main reason for that underlined *Great!* in my log. A few days later, this:

> Lunch—Linen. "Harry called me in Fla. Talked half hour; Time will guarantee you $30,000—I to be your procurer with Life, Fortune, S.I., Arch. Forum etc. Everything better now that Nick is out of the way."

And the following day, just three words: "Stay at Time."

But *harrowing* was there too, tucked into those pleasant entries about my staying on at Time.

> Sent flowers to Eric; slight stroke Lenox Hill Hosp.

Again the news came to me from a stranger, not a doctor this time, but from a nurse. And again, when I telephoned Lenox Hill for a report, there was the usual hospital noncommittal reply, plus that maddening, "Are you a member of his family?" This time I could not even phone the University Club in the hope of a more meaningful report of what had happened, for Eric had at last taken the step he had been considering for years: he had moved out of the club and rented a small furnished apartment, with a part-time maid a couple of times a week, a maid I tried in vain to phone during the hours when she was supposedly at his flat.

So it was a full month after his stroke that I first heard of it, and before I knew that it was not a slight stroke, but one that had left his left side virtually paralyzed, that had slurred his speech, that would alter the physical aspects of his life for all the rest of whatever time he was to have. He would, of course, go in for strenuous and prolonged bouts of speech therapy and other treatment at the famous Howard A. Rusk Institute of Physical Medicine and Rehabilitation, but there would always be the residuals of his CVA, the cerebro-vascular accident.

"But you are still *Eric*," I used to tell him when I began to see him again. That would please him, but he would shake his head in denial. "The Eric part of you is still there; you'll see."

In a way I was right, and in a way he himself came to see it. Two years later he began to write a book about what it's like to have a stroke, what the fears, the melancholy, the anxieties, even the suicidal gloom that patients with a severe stroke are bound to be in for.

He called it *Episode,* and it appeared four years after his stroke. Subtitled *Report on the Accident Within My Skull,* it won immediate praise from critics and physicians alike. The American Heart Association awarded him the Howard W. Blakeslee Award for it, and it soon became one of the textbooks for medical students, for its correctness, for its insight, its honesty—and yes, its wit.

Rereading it now I find again and again lines that nobody but Eric Hodgins could ever have managed to put together. One example occurs during two acid pages about what a patient might have had to put up with even in a fine hospital, back there in the first month of 1960, before anything like a Bill of Patients' Rights had ever been contemplated.

> At 5:05 every morning, a low-flying airplane opens its bomb-bay doors and lets loose ten thousand freshly scoured stainless-steel bedpans, aimed straight at the highest pinnacles of the Tarpeian Rock. The incredible sound of this direct hit, which would have made Lazarus twitch on a Saturday before epiphany, announces the beginning of a new hospital day. . . .
>
> I have one more point to make. A fine and relatively new technical development has occasioned a giant retrogression in today's hospital patient care:
>
> In the old days, a patient "put on his light," to indicate he needed something, and a floor nurse would respond, to discover whether this something was Extreme Unction or a bedpan. . . .
>
> This was admittedly inefficient, and so now modern communications has changed it. Flush in modern hospital rooms is a handsomely designed grille, boasting several small telltale lights and a switch with a pullcord attached, its other end anchored to the bed sheet with a safety pin. (The longevity of the safety pin is one of the finest things about our affluent society; Walter Hunt took out the first U.S. patent on it in 1849.)

Who but Eric could have managed, while writing most seriously about a devastating illness, to link together Extreme Unction, bedpans, modern communications and the invention and patenting of the safety pin? Was it any wonder that I found him endlessly intriguing?

Once he was out of hospital and in his apartment again, with day-round nursing, we began to see each other a good deal, usually in the afternoons, and only for an hour. Once I asked him to tell me, if he could, what it felt like to have paralysis in his left arm and leg.

"There's no sense of 'whereness' left," he said. "Right now I do not know whether my left hand is on the sofa or on my knee—I have to look to find out." With his right hand he lifted his bad leg over his sound one, and looked away from it, over to me. "And if I didn't remember where I had placed it, I wouldn't know whether that leg was stretched out in front of me, or behaving like an ordinary man's leg, with foot on carpet."

He could no longer use a typewriter—his lifetime's basic tool for writing was no longer his, and I gathered that his return to pencils and pens was a psychic wound he had to fight off, as if he had been reduced to a schoolboy's status once more.

The assorted wounds and the deepening gloom were enough to send him back for the third time to the Payne Whitney psychiatric clinic, this time on the dread seventh floor, "the tightest floor in the hospital, where everyone is regarded, among other things, as a suicidal risk and treated accordingly."

It happened in early June, and he spent all his summer there. During the fall months we saw each other probably once a week—always at my house, always in the afternoon. I began to think he was improving, emotionally as well as physically; at other times I found myself filled with a premonition that something awful lay just ahead.

And then it happened. It was four nights before Christmas of that same 1960, and Eric invited me to the Oak Room at the Plaza Hotel, where we had so often been happy. He had a Christmas present for me, and I took along the one I had for him. But the moment we met, I knew he was having a "slip," and not a mild one. He was perfectly coherent, but there was that thick carefulness in his speech that proclaimed it. By the time we taxied back to my apartment, presents still not exchanged, I knew he was too "ill" to go off by himself. I asked if I might call his doctor; he flatly refused. He barely made it through my door.

Chris was already home from Cambridge; Mike was doing his six months in the Army Reserve and would be home only for Christmas Eve and Christmas. So there we were, the three of us, with Eric no longer pretending not to drink. Each time his glass emptied, he managed to get to the bar and the bottle of gin.

It turned into a four-day stretch young Chris was never to forget. Like all their school and college friends, my sons had seen plenty of heavy "social" drinking, but neither of them had ever lived with an alcoholic. Chris knew why I said we couldn't let Eric go off alone; we waited for the moment when we could help get him up the curving stairway of our small duplex apartment to the bedroom floor above. There were still two beds in the boys' bedroom; Eric would sleep in Mike's. He slumped onto it, fully dressed.

Now I did call Eric's doctor, for directions, help, advice. "There's a sort of circular stairway here," I told him. "I just know that every time Eric wakes up during the night, he'll go downstairs to the bar. He could fall and break his neck."

"You must not risk it. You'd better set a chair or table right next his bed. Put the bottle of gin right there beside him. I'll phone first thing in the morning."

But Eric would not permit a visit from his doctor. Day passed day, night followed night, Christmas came, Mike arrived, Christmas passed and Mike left. My log lists the presents we gave each other—I can remember nothing of joy or gaiety for anybody.

In the middle of that fourth night, Chris knocked sharply on my door.

"Eric's head is all bloody. He fell and put a gash in it."

Chris tells me now that he was not as stunned and frightened as I seem to remember him being; it must be that I transferred some of my own horror to my nineteen-year-old son. But the sight of Eric on the bathroom floor, with that copious rush of blood any forehead wound can produce, did shock me to near panic. At last I ignored all his assertions that he didn't need his doctor. In ten minutes an ambulance arrived, and I stood there with Chris, watching poor Eric being carried off on a stretcher to still another hospital, a small one, the Gracie Square.

The juxtapositions in one's life! Low point and high point, pain and pleasure can follow each other without a semblance of logic. A letter, a phone call, a telegram—and a metamorphosis can occur in your mood, in outlook, even in your own estimation of self-worth.

Out of the blue, you think, and yet, of course, it is never out of any blue, but out of one's past, one's work, one's beliefs, one's attempts. . . .

One such moment for me came in a telegram from Eleanor Roosevelt. I had met her just once, years before, on a receiving line at some reception, just after I had adopted my son Mike; somebody had told her of it, and she spoke warmly about it, wishing me, and him godspeed. She had been in the forefront of a nationwide effort to change the adoption laws of all the states so that birth certificates for adopted babies would no longer bear the possibly hurtful word *adopted*. Already several of the states had made the change, including Illinois, where I had gone to The Cradle Society in Evanston way back in 1937. So I had felt beholden to her and had told her so.

The telegram she sent came more than twenty years later. Perhaps it came not only because of generalities about my past but more specifically because I had, the summer before, put in weeks of volunteer work for the Kennedy presidential campaign, writing full-page promotion, working mainly on the religious issue of Kennedy and Catholicism, working specifically through Arthur M. Schlesinger, Jr., and more generally through Kennedy Headquarters in New York and Washington, as well as with the Saltonstall National Committee in Massachusetts.

Over twenty pages of my log are nearly illegible for that period before the election, minutely covered with names of people I had appealed to for money, names and places of meetings, headlines read aloud, copy submitted for approval, signatures granted. . . .

Whatever the reason, the telegram finally came.

I HOPE YOU WILL JOIN A SMALL OFF-THE-RECORD GROUP OF WRITERS AT DINNER AT MY HOME. . . . WE SHALL BE DISCUSSING IMMEDIATE PLANS FOR CONSTRUCTIVELY MEETING CURRENT OUTBURSTS AGAINST THE UNITED NATIONS. NO FUNDRAISING. WE ARE ANXIOUS TO HAVE YOUR HELP AND TALENTS IN GUIDING US.

Time, date, address, all the necessaries were there, and signed Mrs. Franklin D. Roosevelt, Chairman, Board of Directors, American Association for the United Nations.

I lived less than two blocks away from her house, and as I walked around and around, ten minutes too early, I was as eager and flustered as a youngster receiving his first praise from one of his lifelong heroes.

I had no idea who the other writers would be, and perhaps I felt flattered that I was the only woman among them. John Hersey was there; John Mason Brown, Book-of-the-Month Club judge and book critic; John Crosby, the newspaper columnist; Paddy Chayefsky; Clark

M. Eichelberger, lecturer and author, and executive director of the association; and some others.

And there was Eleanor Roosevelt.

My throat tightened. She was so like all the thousand pictures I had seen of her down the years, so like the endless images in the papers and newsreels and television programs—and even in the anti-Eleanor cartoons. She was taller and a little heavier than I had expected, but for the rest, there she was, old, and homely, and caring, and beautiful.

This was at a time when there were plenty of "outbursts" against the U.N. from plenty of outbursters, and the attempt to save the U.N. from weakness or extinction was one of the things to which Eleanor Roosevelt would give the remaining years of her life.

Only faintly do I remember what each of us writers said or suggested that night, nor what contributions any of us were actually to make to the cause later on. I do remember all the photographs, of FDR and their children, of Adlai Stevenson and of Nehru, all the books and the general air of crowded old-fashioned elegance of her drawing room. But what I can not forget at all was the long dinner table, with Eleanor Roosevelt presiding at one end.

It was a charming dinner, served excellently, no doubt, by two maids, from soup to salad. All that, too, is rather faint. What is sharp and clear and wonderful happened at dessert. For then the maids set down a big layer cake and a large bowl of ice cream at the head of the table, laid down a special cake knife, oversized serving spoons, a stack of dishes, and took their leave.

And Eleanor Roosevelt proceeded to portion out dessert for us herself, and pass it to us, one by one down the table, as if we were all her children.

And then again, low point—the first of two major operations, both within a span of eighteen months, that were to turn my whole life back, away from the security and big pay of business, back to the uncertainties and marvels of being an author again, a full-time writer once more, with an unfinished novel, by now at page 500 and still only at the halfway mark, and a publisher who still believed it was a book he would one day be proud to publish.

During one of my recurring bouts of night-writing in the past years, I had at last found something I had been searching for almost from the start, the fulcrum for the whole story, that hinge of plot that would move my two families, the foreign-born Ivarins and the native-born

Paiges, into tight conjunction, not merely as friends and neighbors but as people suddenly caught up in a cause that is central to both their lives—free speech and civil liberties.

It came to me one day when I was at my desk at the office, not even thinking of my book, but it was something I had first known about seven years before, reading an account of it in Emma Goldman's two-volume *Living My Life,* which Saxe Commins had loaned me for research on that period. It was an actual case of vigilante bestiality out in San Diego against Goldman's lover and manager, Ben Reitman.

Why it came to me then I shall never know; suddenly I was dredging it up out of my mind, suddenly realizing that as a novelist I could put Evan Paige right into the middle of that scene of torture and brutality, have him out there on some of his civil liberties work, and then have him turn to the best writer he knew to make the whole nation conscious of what was possible in that red-hunting era in pre-war America.

That would be Stefan Ivarin, writing pieces first for his own newspaper, the *Jewish News,* and then having his pieces translated into English for all the liberal or socialist press in the land.

I saw too, perhaps not just then, perhaps only in the aftermath of that first excitement at finding my solution, that the joint activity of these two men would lead inevitably to the thought that was central to my entire book. It is expressed by Ivarin, not aloud, only to himself, and from it came the title for my novel.

The two men and their wives are in an East Side restaurant discussing the series of articles they would do together. Paige, in his impatience, has gone down to meet the Ivarins at the *Jewish News.*

The smells of Europe's food were there—spiced meats, herring, dill pickles, cabbage soup, the rind of lemon, the sweet freshness of cherries, the baked sugar and honey of small cakes.

It all spoke to him [Ivarin] of his own beginnings, a memory, a recognition of a promise made long ago, to whom he did not remember, for what he could not say. He looked at the somber face of the man before him, born in New England, grown in the unflurried sureness of an American youth, educated to a profession of justice. And he loved him as he had never yet known he could love another man.

Various, but one. He himself the American born in another land and become an American by choice, by law, by document;

Evander Paige the American by birth, his first papers issued to him with his first breath—yet each knowing that a lifetime might go toward validating those papers and being worthy of them.

Again that old question by my readers: how much of it is true, how much made up? Out in Jamaica in my childhood, my parents did have friendly neighbors, Giles and Winonah Ford, whom I perhaps would not even remember except that they had a beach place out at Point Lookout on Long Island, and had invited my mother and Alice and me out there for a weekend.

But the Evander Paige of my *First Papers* was my own invention, as was his son Garry, the conscientious objector to war who would go to prison for his beliefs in 1917. Paige was patterned in part on one of the founders of the civil liberties movement in this country, Roger Baldwin, a man I had not yet met when I first wrote to him, introducing myself as a member of the board of the New York Civil Liberties Union.

I had explained the general purpose of my novel and asked his help in devising a solid reading course for me about the early days of what was first called the American Civil Liberties Bureau. Not only did he respond with all sorts of valuable suggestions, but it was the beginning of what was to turn into a cherished relationship in my life—and for my novel.

Nine years had passed since that letter, nine years since I had begun to write my book, three of them since Bennett had sent me his premature Christmas present, proclaiming his continuing faith in it and in me. By then it was late 1962, and I was going through a slow hard recovery from the second of those two major surgeries, this one an emergency operation for acute diverticulitis, with resections of various inner organs, and far more dangerous than the the first, for gall-bladder removal. Each time I had been out of the office for two solid months.

What profundities had occupied my thoughts during this year and a half, what speculations, what weighing of values were going through my two minds, my conscious one and that more powerful one, the unconscious, I can only speculate about now. One page of my log during that period has the single word, "Sabbatical?"—I must have been considering possibles. And I do know that there did come the day, while I was still in hospital the second time, when I picked up the telephone and called the office to say thanks for the flowers and good wishes. Harry Luce had sent some, and so had Jim Linen.

But I found that what I wanted to say could not be said directly to Harry—he was my friend. Jim Linen still had no affection for me that I could ever detect, except for his pleasure at the way I wrote promotion.

"Even though I am a real agnostic, Jim," I heard myself saying to him, "I think maybe God is trying to tell me something about my unfinished novel. Two major operations in a year and a half might be code for some message."

How he took this I have no idea but he did agree to a meeting as soon as I was able to return to the office. Then I think I surprised him.

"I have no horror about words like 'age sixty-five' or 'mandatory retirement,' " I began. "There they are, three years off. But I've begun to wonder if maybe I ought to retire right away and write my book, and wonder if Time Ink could help me do it now."

I had never asked for a raise, I told him, had never asked for a bonus; back in 1940, when I had left because of all the awkwardness of my being engaged to "Time Enemy" Ingersoll, Time had seen fit to give me a year's severance pay. Maybe if Time could again manage something or other financial to make me offer to resign years ahead of those three remaining years, I could turn to that unfinished novel of mine. . . .

And so it all worked out—less the two months' salary I had received during my second stay in the hospital. Before that $25,000 was used up, Chris would indeed be out of Harvard and on his own.

And thus began the year 1963, the year *First Papers* was at long last to reach its final page, page 970, a year when my log shows that I had only seven evening dates, the year when I made certain entries in my log on the penultimate day of the year.

> I finished—6 p.—to 970
> Mike and I to celebrate
> Cabled Chris
> Wired Bennett

The day before my log said, "31 p. this week." Elsewhere it said, "Half the book this one year."

And in those phrases and numbers, in that record of a whole year sans social life, without big splendid parties, that year minus evening clothes and entertaining, there lies a certain change in my whole attitude toward my life as it had been, in my life as it would be, in, perhaps, my secret plan for the old age that lay ahead of me and what I intended in my deepest being to make of it.

In an oblique way, an exchange of letters between me and Moss Hart gives me the most realistic clue I have to that slowly evolving change.

In the two-drawer file that stands near my desk is one folder labeled *Friends*. It is nothing like the thirty-or-so other folders in the file, for those are filled with material about agents, taxes, leases, letters to publishers, to and from editors, and all the rest of the paraphernalia of working and living.

Searching through this file just now for something else, I came upon a letter from Moss, dated during the very period when I thought I was writing nothing but my sixteen-page critique of Time. It was his answer to what I'd written him when I was halfway through *Act One*, not another one of his plays, but his first published book, his autobiography, also coming from Random House.

He had sent me an inscribed copy far in advance of its publication day, and I knew he'd been in more than the usual prepub anxiety about it, just as he knew I'd been on a distressing roller-coaster about my own book.

Three years before, he had had a staggering success as director of *My Fair Lady* on Broadway, but more recently he had had a miserable flop with his latest original play. Perhaps that was why I obeyed my impulse to write him in praise of *Act One* before I had even finished it. His answer came in a rush.

> What a wonderful letter to wake up to in the morning! . . . It is, as you know, my first venture into prose—it may forgive some of my avidity for praise, and my excitement when I receive it from a fellow-writer. Your words meant a great deal to me —please be my "commercial," and tell all your book-buying friends.
>
> And you *will* be unblocked, dear Laura. You have only to ask Our Publisher to learn how I suffered over the latter half of the book. . . . You . . . know nothing really matters but what emerges on Publication Day.
>
> It would be lovely if you would write and tell me how you liked the rest of it . . . We leave for Europe August 1st, but what a nice homecoming present it would be!
>
> Always,
> Moss

Who could resist such an open plea for further praise? My next letter, after I had finished reading his whole book through, was three solid pages of single-spaced type.

> All right, sit down, because this may take the rest of the summer
> . . . I finished it at 4 A.M., with my eyeballs hanging out on strings.
> I thought, Everybody in America who knows and cares about the
> theater *knows* Moss, but now they'll also love him. God, this kid
> who never finished grade school, who worked for a wholesale
> furrier and stank of wet furs, who wrote six plays while he was
> still a snob about comedy . . . and then sat there on the sand
> . . . had part of an idea . . . and wrote a title down, *Once In A
> Lifetime. . . .*

I put in all the details any writer is avid to hear, what scenes I liked best, which part put a knot in my throat, what lines made me laugh. I told him I had persuaded Random House to sell me an advance copy as a gift for a friend of mine who was in hospital, and quoted her praise for two whole paragraphs. And I even sent along the invoice marked Paid—the first private sale. I had no fear that such minutiae would seem tedious to him.

> I'd been afraid my own admiration for it was because I knew you,
> because at one point . . . you were terribly important to me and
> my life—(before you write about *Gentleman's Agreement* in *Act
> Two*, ask me about some mss I have that I wrote for you in 1947
> in the desert)—

His answer was pages long too, and if mine had been emotional, so was his response.

> I read it thru breathlessly, then once more with some degree of
> composure and finally quietly and soberly. . . . You made it come
> alive. Suddenly it was being read by another human being, not
> a stranger, God knows, but someone who was giving it a life of
> its own. It is a lovely moment when this happens.
>   I had begun it as an exercise in discipline. I had just written
> and produced a most hurtful failure, *The Climate of Eden*, and I
> was at loose ends creatively. I knew it was folly to write another
> play in a spirit of revenge . . . or to wipe out . . . the memory
> of that failure.

He ended with a pert postscript. "It *was* the very first sale! I shall frame it!"

Not long afterward we had a strangely somber talk about "hurtful failures," and without any transition I can remember, I found myself telling him all about that public-relations spree I had let myself in for on board ship with Alfred Hitchcock a decade before, ending at the Dorchester in London where a foul-up in logistics had landed me in a valet's or chauffeur's cubicle instead of the spacious VIP domain I had been led to take for granted.

And I told him, too, of my God-given burst of delighted laughter at that image of a tiny pin approaching a balloon of hot air.

"Moss, maybe writers as successful as you need to think back, way, way back, to the way things were that led up to all the success—I don't mean that you have to go live in a tenement in the Bronx and work for a wholesale furrier and stink of wet furs . . ."

We both laughed, and I am not sure Moss ever gave it another thought. He was never to write *Act Two* or *Act Three;* two years later he died of a heart attack. He was only fifty-seven.

But what I had said to him then must have been been forming itself in its way in my own mind—and must have gone on forming for a long time, for ultimately it changed somehow from vague embryo to live being. What about my own choices about being a "successful writer?"

Not once had I ever considered staying away from those black-tie parties at Moss and Kitty's, nor the more frequent ones at Bennett and Phyllis Cerf's. True enough I had written a whole novel, *The Celebrity,* trying to satirize that world where the great desire was not so much to *do* something as to *be* somebody, and of course I had absolved myself from any such vulgar aim.

But what was making me keep right on going to all those gatherings of the famous, the stars of stage and screen, more than lesser-known people, like the friends I used to have before I married Thayer the publisher and got to know the Luces and the Ingersolls and Cerfs and the Harts and all the others?

I cannot put a firm date to any resolution of my growing doubt, but I do know that somewhere along in the next years, one thing happened that serves as a kind of milestone for me.

It was at one of the big evenings at the Cerfs', with the usual crowd of the famous there, and at one point I suddenly found myself saying, half aloud, "Oh, *no,* not *again.*"

This ardent plea was directed at the world-famous playwright,

Robert E. Sherwood, author of such hits as *Idiot's Delight, The Petrified Forest, Abe Lincoln in Illinois.* He was very tall, very thin, very gifted, and, sooner or later at any party, very drunk. When that point arrived, Sherwood inevitably took the floor for his one and only song-and-dance act.

This would be a sort of stiff strutting dance across the carpet, his long legs extended like stilts before him, as he sang his own accompaniment:

> When the red, red robin, Goes bob, bob, bobbin' Along, *along* . . .

The first time I saw the celebrated Robert E. Sherwood do this routine I laughed at his chirping dance, as everybody else did. I laughed the second time, and the third, at other parties, and maybe the fourth or fifth. But then came that ardent plea, and I began at last to consider what I really deemed so splendid about these splendid parties.

The same thing had happened as I continued to hear Ethel Merman yielding to requests from guests and getting up to oblige with a roaring rendition of "Anything You Can Do I Can Do Better," or Mary Martin obligingly rinsing that man right out of her hair. Most of the guests, indeed, were famed on Broadway or Hollywood; there were a few writers, true. One was Edna Ferber, usually too acerbic to be awfully pleasing and another was young Truman Capote, when he was still the gifted writer in his young twenties, before he let himself become the darling of society ladies, the host of chic balls for five hundred "intimate friends" at the Plaza Hotel, and finally a kind of sad little clown on endless talk shows on TV.

But by and large the authors and publishers were the minority at the black-tie evenings I had so long enjoyed, and the time at last did arrive when I was able to stand off, in my mind, and look at the whole business of my social life. So much of it was connected to the neon lights of Broadway or the Klieg lights of Hollywood, instead of to people involved with my real interests.

Rather often I found myself wondering whether I ought to put an end to some of the neon and Klieg parties—or perhaps just stay away from a lot of them.

Then one day I found myself saying to Phyllis Cerf on the telephone something I had had no firm plan to say. She had just invited me to another big evening, dinner for twenty-four and the works. I know I meant to be tactful, but I also know that very often when I mean to be tactful, I end up by blundering into clumsiness, tactlessness incarnate.

"If you don't mind," I began, "I think I'll give it a miss." Why I couldn't have said I had another engagement, I'll never know; I'll leave that to the Freudians. What I did actually say at the moment, was filled with purpose, with decision, with turn-down. Of course she demanded to know why I was going to "give it a miss."

So I went blundering ahead, as I miserably recall, and told her I had begun to wonder about all the glamour in my life, in the life of anybody who ought to be thinking of writing, not of black-tie evenings with the beautiful people, et cetera. I must have made a total holier-than-thou ass of myself.

But I am not sorry. I do not think I ever was sorry. I believe now that deeply inside me I had at last come to recognize that as one grows older, there are choices to be made about what one does with one's energies, what one does with one's hours, and that by the time I uttered those uneasy words to Phyllis Cerf the choices had been readying themselves for some long time and the decisions, the good decisions, had let themselves be made.

And that was how it was possible for me, in the twelve months of the year 1963, the tenth year after I had first thought of writing a novel about my radical childhood, about that backward staircase and the black bunting on the house in Jamaica—that was how I was able to write nearly 500 pages in one year, with only seven evenings out, and most of those at concerts.

I did play some afternoon bridge, perhaps once a week, as a sort of coffee break for a couple of hours, between my daytime session at the typewriter, and the nighttime one that often ran on well past midnight. And there were two memorable trips out of the city as well, though each lasted only one night.

The first was to Cambridge to see Chris graduated from Harvard; he had had his first poem published by Harper's magazine when he was twenty, and his second about a year later. Now he had a summa on his senior thesis and a cum laude on his diploma. I was also to bid him farewell for the entire summer; he was off to teach young Africans in what was then still Tanganyika, at Dar es Salaam. This was not for the Peace Corps, though it was similar to it; this was a special Harvard project organized by the Phillips Brooks House, and Chris was one of the nineteen students who had signed up for it. I was proud of him on many counts.

The other overnight trip came in August, to Washington, and nothing could have made me miss it. It was officially called the March on Washington for Jobs and Freedom, and unofficially, forever after, the Civil Rights March on Washington, or the Martin Luther King March, the "I have a dream" March that drew a quarter million people to the Capitol.

On the plane an official of the NAACP, named Hill, who slightly knew me, invited me to sit with the other special guests—Lena Horne and others—high on the marble steps above the huge crowds. But I declined; something made me want to just march along with the anonymous others who were there to "bear witness." . . .

So those two overnight trips and those seven evening dates made the sum total of my social life in 1963. I did see Phyllis Cerf up at commencement day at Harvard; her son was being graduated too. She seemed pleasantly distant; we were a bit constrained at the airport.

And in the twenty-some years since then I was never again to be invited to a party at her house—with one great exception, when she and Bennett gave the ritual publication-day party for *First Papers*. But even that invitation came with its own backhand twist.

That ritual dinner took place on Monday evening, November 2, 1964. The Literary Guild had made *First Papers* its main choice for December; Bennett had made a solid paperback deal for it with Fawcett Crest Publications; my British publishers, William Heinemann, had taken it, with an advance ten times larger than any advance I had ever before received for any foreign edition anywhere, including all those for *Gentleman's Agreement*.

This novel was the first of mine that did not make the best-seller list in the *Times*, but it was a financial success before publication and a critical success after.

One of the quotes used most often and most widely in the months to come was from the main review in Life magazine.

> Her most autobiographical and therefore best novel. . . . Stefan is the storm center of the brightest and warmest family to appear in a book in years.

When Phyllis Cerf phoned me about the dinner party they would of course give in its honor—and in mine—she included one unusual sentence.

"We'll send out the invitations," she said, "but since you don't like the people we ask to our parties, we'll let you draw up your own guest list."

I suppose I should have demurred. Instead, I instantly said, "Great. For *my* guest of honor I'd like to have Roger Baldwin."

Baldwin was then in his early eighties, still active, not only in the civil-liberties world, not only with lectures and meetings, but physically—winters, he still went skiing. I had been in touch with him several times since that "can you guide me?" letter back in 1953, and he had shown an increasing interest in what my book was trying to do, and in the period it was covering, so that I was finally emboldened to ask him if he might find time to read it through in manuscript form before it went to the printers to catch any errors of fact or interpretation of that formative period in the civil liberties movement. He said he would make time.

> What a momentous job you have undertaken. But the subject is worth it and I would be honored.

Three months later I did indeed send him my still-uncut 970 pages, and he must have dropped many demands on his time to read all of it as quickly as he did. He disclaimed any ability to judge novels as novels.

> It stands up factually, and it is both gripping and persuasive. . . . Your references to me and the war and the civil liberties bureau are all quite accurate . . . you have caught perfectly the atmosphere of those hectic years.

In the margin of this letter is a note of my own.

> On phone he said, "I lived it all again—second half better than first—read on and on into the night."

By the time I told Phyllis Cerf with such alacrity that my own guest of honor for the dinner would be Roger Baldwin, he had become one of the legendary heroes of my life, on a par with Norman Thomas, whom I had also interviewed for my novel. A one-line entry in my log says, "Roger Baldwin here—book," so he must have followed that letter of his with a willingness to spend some time in an edit session, despite his disclaimers. The same entry notes, "Made changes R.B. suggests."

Those were not the only changes: I had set to work on a severe cutting job; about 100 pages were stripped away, roughly thirty thousand words, and the final manuscript was pared to a mere 870. And after all the cuts and all the revisions and all the work throughout the years—all had ended by giving me a deep sense of rightness about the whole.

Even the final paragraphs on the final page of my novel, where young Fee, now seventeen years old, watches her father's stricken reaction to the news that the first Russian revolution, in February of 1917, the moderate Menshevik one under the Kerensky government, had in October been crushed by the Bolsheviks—for me, even those last paragraphs held that rightness.

Fee had seen Ivarin weep with elation and joy at the first news of the moderate revolution; now she listens to him as he cries out to her mother about the second.

> "And now we'll see a terrorism . . . the whole world will see such a terrorism as the czars never dreamed of."
>
> "Perhaps it will fail too. Maybe Trotsky and Lenin . . ."
>
> "There is no 'perhaps.' There is no 'somehow.' " He suddenly put his head down, covering his face with his hands, right over his glasses. His shoulders were tight and high and they were shaking.
>
> He spoke again, and this time his voice broke. "My poor Russia," he said. "My poor Russia."

Apart from Roger Baldwin's, the other names I gave Phyllis Cerf were those of people who had been closest to me all my life, and also some good friends I knew professionally; virtually every one was a person whose own life dealt with writing or publishing books.

Mike and Chris, of course, were there (in rented dinner jackets); Harry and Bernardine Scherman; Andrea Simon, now a widow; John Wharton and his second wife Betty; John Hersey and his second wife, Barbara; Ann Petry, a novelist, and her husband; Marshall Best of Viking Press; my editor Bob Loomis and his wife; Charles and Rhoda Jackson of *The Lost Weekend*; and my best friend for thirty years and more, Carroll Whedon, who was now Carroll Elliott, and her second husband. I had invited Eric, but though he was greatly recovered from the worst of his stroke, he had thought it best to stay away.

We were twenty-four all told, and the Cerfs' elegant dinner was as lovely as usual, the roomy dining room given over to three large round tables, each seating eight.

When the brandy and coffee arrived at the close, Roger Baldwin rose to address us all. "I *know* the Ivarins," he began. "I knew them fifty years ago. Meaning, of course, that I knew the Zametkins, though I never met them until I met their daughter Laura, through this book . . ."

I don't know whether any other throats went tight at his words, nor whether any other eyes began to sting. I had dedicated my book "to the memory of my parents, Adella Kean Zametkin and Michael Zametkin," and for a moment a fierce longing swept me, that they might have lived long enough to know that I would become a writer of books and especially of this book, this novel that had so defied me, evaded me, that had sent me back in despair to the life of a clever businesswoman writing promotion, with a plushy office and fat salary —that had, in the end, brought me back to the incomparable life of somebody who can say, "What do I do? I write books."

——— CHAPTER ———
TWELVE

ALL THROUGH THE YEARS I had known that the time would come when I would sit down with Mike and Chris and at last tell them that I had given birth to Chris before adopting him.

From the very beginning I had thought that this one moment of revelation should come on Christopher's twenty-first birthday, in 1962, with Mike already a man of twenty-six. Whatever shock or trauma there might be for them would surely be handled better in maturity, rather than in adolescence.

I had discussed that intention a dozen times over with Dr. Gosselin, not only during my pregnancy but in many refresher courses since as my boys were growing up; I had also consulted the Sterbas, not only Richard, but Dr. Editha Sterba, herself a child analyst. And there was general concurrence that my plan was a sound one.

It meant keeping my secret for at least twenty-one years, from everybody on earth except my doctors, Eric, the Schermans, and those few others who had been in on it from the start.

And keep it I did. I had trained myself, and rigorously, that before answering even the most casual remark or question about adopting children, trained myself to check swiftly over my tiny list of "those who know" before answering the remark or question. In the twelve years since I had first been listed in *Who's Who In America* there was always the line, "Children—Michael and Christopher (adopted)." Every time I corrected proofs for another edition, I would read that phrase and think, Well, after I tell Mike and Chris, I'll decide what to do about that.

Chris turned twenty-one only weeks after that second operation, and my physician sternly directed me to avoid any possible emotional upheaval. I promised to wait for one more birthday.

One year later, though, Chris was still in Africa. In the fall he had returned to England, en route home after his scheduled summer of teaching, but then he had called me from London, in what I could hear was real distress. Could I possibly help him fly back to Tanganyika to round out a full year?

"Otherwise," he said, "I'll always feel I just did it for a summer vacation," and again I was very proud of him. At Harvard he had become an integral part of major student groups protesting nuclear armament, marching in peace marches, writing position papers; from Dar his frequent letters to me reflected his emotions about injustice there; he had cabled me after the army revolt that had British troops landing in Dar es Salaam. Even on the telephone I heard the depth of his feelings and commitment.

I owed him his graduation present; we had delayed it because he was leaving for Africa right from Harvard; now I remembered that I'd spent a few hundred dollars on an imported moped for Mike's graduation gift, so I called this Chris' graduation present and cabled him four hundred dollars for airfare back to Dar. That was why my log entry about finishing my novel included the words, "Cabled Chris." . . .

And so it was not until the night of his twenty-third birthday, at the end of 1964, that I sat facing my two grown sons, who knew only that I had "something important, and I think wonderful, to tell you."

I had planned it a thousand times, wondering how to put it, testing out sentences in my mind, altering phrases, rejecting them, trying out others.

I knew it would be hard, for me and for them. It is never easy for young people to think about their own parents in connection with any aspect of sex; in theory they accept the biological fact and immediately relegate it to so far distant a past that it has no reality in their private present.

Perhaps it was even hard for me because my children were men; I remember wondering if it might have seemed easier if they had been two daughters, now in their twenties and women, though now, so many years later, as I set down that vague subjunctive, I am uneasily aware that it contains a kind of feminist chauvinism, as if I were granting all daughters, all women, a readier empathy, a deeper insight.

In any case, back then, I could only think in terms of Mike and Chris. I knew I would not blast them with my news; I wanted to take them back into their mother's life, to try to make them see the developing circumstances that had finally led to so large an event.

I began way back, when I myself was in my twenties and living with Tom Mount—they had known, in surface outlines, all the main facts of my past, but now I told them of the two abortions that had then seemed so inescapable and that had so damaged my ability to have children. I went on to my marriage and those years of visits to sterility specialists in the always defeated efforts to have a baby. I told them, briefly, but told them, about Ingersoll and that heartbreaking miscarriage, "my last chance."

And at last I came to that Memorial Day weekend in 1941, when I suddenly knew that, after all, it hadn't been "my last chance"—that once again, just short of my forty-first birthday, I was pregnant. I did tell them who Hugh was, that we had already parted amicably nearly three months before and that not for a moment did I consider digging Hugh up from the past and telling him. And I also told them that I was blessedly free of conflict or doubt or dilemma about what I was going to do. This time there was nobody on earth who could let me down or give me days and nights of a destroying anguish. This time it was me alone, and I knew I could rely on me.

"So I went ahead," I said, "and had my baby. And that was you, Chris."

They had both sat there in silence, nearly motionless, each in unwavering absorption. I think my voice thickened on my last words, "And that was you, Chris," and I know that Chris was staring at me as I spoke them. But it was Mike who spoke first.

"Gosh, mother, it's beautiful."

Strangely—surely it is strange—I do not remember one word that Chris said, only the intent look on his face, as if he were sitting upright, in a concentration of hearing. I can feel again the inner sureness that swept me, that he was pleased, even gratified at this sudden added dimension to his own life.

We talked on and on; I told them that Hugh had long since married and had children, and asked them never to reveal his real name. But I added that apart from that one point, this was no longer only my private secret; it had become theirs, and if it was something they wished to tell their friends, they need not even wonder what I would feel at their doing it. I said, however, that for a long time I myself would keep on with my own silence about it—in a way I felt that they had

225

"inherited" the right to speak or say nothing—they would need time, perhaps, to know what would feel right to them.

At one point that evening I opened up a small packet of documents and checks that had been locked away in my safe-deposit box at the bank for nearly a quarter century, all containing my assumed name of Ruth Laura Mills that had served me during the months while I was "in hiding." It jolted me to come across once more my checks to the Harkness Pavilion at Columbia-Presbyterian Hospital, where Chris was born. Even sharper were my emotions as I saw again that original birth certificate, signed by Dr. Virgil S. Damon, issued to the infant Charles Andrew Mills, Jr., and together with it, the final birth certificate for Christopher Zametkin Hobson.

For me it was one of the momentous evenings of my sixty-four years of life. In that courtroom at Evanston, Illinois, twenty-eight years before, I had sworn to "shelter, educate and protect" my adopted son until he "should attain his majority," and then, five years later, I had repeated that oath in the courtroom of a surrogate justice right in New York City.

And now, sitting there talking with Mike and Chris, telling them at last, a circle that had been open quietly closed.

Momentous. I don't think I can be faulted for using that word for such an evening, but I am often at a loss about how to characterize other times that prove to have a lasting import but which slip by unremarked at the time, unrecognized, probably never to be recalled.

One such occurred in blazing tropical sunshine a few months before that evening with Mike and Chris while I was off on the first vacation I had allowed myself in more than two years.

I was on the beach reading a new novel, *To An Early Grave,* by Wallace Markfield, a reportedly humorous story about "Jewish intellectuals," and I was disliking it without pausing to analyze why.

This was at Marietta Tree's luxury hotel, the Sandy Lane, in Barbados, and soon a young couple near me were asking me what I thought about the book. This was just after the Literary Guild had announced its choice of *First Papers,* and they had read Random House's notices about its coming appearance and were apparently drawn to a "real live author."

They were in bathing suits, as I was, but each of them wore a gold cross on a gold chain, as if they could not appear anywhere without that symbol, even in bra and bikini, even in the briefest of swimming trunks. But we talked about books, and when they asked the inevitable, "What does the Z stand for?" I gave my usual reply.

"It's for Zametkin, my maiden name—it's Russian and it's Jewish." I thought they both stiffened, as if I had somehow rebuked them, and soon enough they went back into the water and we parted forever.

I don't suppose I would have any memory at all of those two with their golden chains and crosses, nor of that book I found displeasing, if something in the juxtaposition of the two had not merged into a discomfort that kept on preoccupying me after I returned to my cabin and sat on its deck looking out at the soft Caribbean blue of the sea.

If I carried my little red logs with me when I traveled, I might have jotted down a line or two and forgotten it. But my log was at home on my desk, thousands of miles away, so I felt muted and frustrated. I kept thinking off and on about Jews who converted, about Jews who wrote novels making fun of other Jews, about myself and my family, Jewish and agnostic. . . .

Sooner or later I was bound to feel my old unchanging need to write it down, and on a large lined sheet of paper from a loose-leaf notebook, writing in ink, I began what I thought would be a brief note.

Barbados, B.W.I. 7/17/64

Notes—on a novel?

To write about the assimilated Jew . . . and the "Jewish Jew" . . . about the implied accusation that to be assimilated is somehow a treason to Jewishness or "Jewry," that group-word I dislike, whether it's used by Jews to describe "their community" or by gentiles to isolate Jews in a community unlike the gentile community outside it. (Nobody ever speaks of "gentilery"; the connotations of Christianity are different, the opposite number of Judaism) . . .

The Jew who is an agnostic, I mean, whose family has been assimilated into a small-town world for 2 or 3 generations, who is perhaps married to a gentile—also agnostic?—and who says, "I am a Jew" because anti-Semitism exists. Whose children feel the same, who feel odd among "Jewish Jews," and wonder whether that oddness is analogous to anti-Semitism or something less wrong and guilty: a kind of xenophobia, though, at best. . . .

What about the woman with the cropped black hair here? The gold cross she wears; the gold cross her husband Alfred wears?

They are [the Christian equivalent of] "Jewish Jews" who did not assimilate; yet they are driven by some devil of need or shame. . . .

(Remember the article I began in Calif. 1951 about ASSIMI-LATION—*the dirtiest 12-letter word in the language.*) Many liberal Jews, who are all for the Negro's integration into the culture of the U.S., will think "coward" or "traitor" about the Jew who *is* integrated. . . .

The "brief note" went on to nearly all the other side of the page as I speculated about some of my friends, Christians and liberals all, who *had* enjoyed *To An Early Grave.*

Take . . . their delight in the "Jewish Intellectuals" . . . [finding them] hilariously funny. . . . their "true-to-life" conversations the exact counterpart of many Jewish critics, editors, writers, TV people they know. . . .

I didn't find them hilarious; I found them the stereotyped Jews of the anti-Semite, and offensive . . . Can it be that [those friends] unconsciously pounce with delight on the "Jewish Jew"—because it's such a belly-warming relief to get away from what they feel toward (assimilated) Jews like me? And back to Jews they can feel superior to, "legitimately"?

When I did get back home to my log, the only note I made about my Barbados stay was, "Switched to St. Thomas—too posh." Were it not for the handwritten page of notes, that whole double-episode of beach and book would probably have been lost to active memory forever; indeed I never even remembered that loose-leaf page for twelve full years. It remained safely tucked away in a file labeled, IDEAS, STORIES, ARTICLES, perhaps glanced at once in a while as I was thumbing through other papers, but not once a living presence until some time *after*—and I underline the after—after I had started my eighth novel those twelve years later, on what I truly felt was a new idea I had just developed: to write about a family in deep conflict, about agnostics, assimilation, changing feelings about Israel, and "what-do-I-mean-I'm-Jewish?"

It must be true that to a writer nothing is ever lost, nothing ever just a cipher in his or her experience. Yet people always ask authors, "Where did you get the idea for it?" As if the author himself or herself always knew the real reply.

Something else happened that year that could never have slipped by unremarked: the thirteen-year separation from my twin sister Alice was finally ended. Again it was I who made the effort at reconciliation.

"I just finished a novel," I wrote her, "about Ma and Pa and our childhood in Jamaica." I said I'd spent ten years, off and on, doing it, and ended, "If the Soviet Union and the United States now believe in 'peaceful coexistence,' why can't we try it once more?"

This time she answered me; I remember one phrase of hers, about "not expecting to see you again in this vale of tears," and we spent a five-hour afternoon together, trying to sum up all that had happened since that luncheon when I had told her about my visit from the FBI, though we scrupulously refrained from mentioning it or the interpretation she had put upon it. I am sure that we were equally determined to stay a million miles away from all thorny subjects, meaning politics.

After that we began to spend time together and even managed to joke away some of our unspoken feelings about that long estrangement: "If you don't make a fourth at bridge, I won't speak to you for another thirteen years." She had a weekly bridge game and invited me to act as teacher to help her and a couple of her friends lift their "mama-papa" game to the more skillful level of club bridge.

Once when she was weak and ill because of severe nosebleeds—she had always had high blood pressure—her son brought her over to my house one evening rather than let her stay at home alone; I made her stay with me for several days, taking care of her, taking trays up to her in the extra bedroom, talking about our children. Unexpectedly, a little later, she bought me a copy of Arnold Bennett's *Old Wives' Tale,* that story of a lifelong separation of two sisters, born in one of Bennett's famous Five Towns, one of whom remains there while the other goes off to a life in Paris. *The Reader's Encyclopedia*'s summary of the plot ends, "In her old age, she returns to Bursley to live—and die—with her widowed sister."

The fact that Alice wanted me to reread that long forgotten story told me much; we talked of it, guardedly, yet it told me, I felt, a good deal of what had made her, also a widow, accept this latest effort of mine at reconciliation.

It was lovely to have a sister again—until one night when she invited me to a meeting at Town Hall. It was called, "The Black Revolution and the White Backlash," sponsored by people known to us all, actors, playwrights, writers, journalists, poets, black and white. This was less than a year after the famous march on Washington, and I gladly went along with Alice, certain that if ever there was a subject

229

that would not prove thorny for my sister and me, civil rights had to be it.

Almost with the first speaker I was appalled. This was my first face-to-face encounter with what was to be the vast new movement for Black Power, and within minutes I felt myself assailed as that hated creature, a "white liberal." I was not being oversensitive; it went on and on, and by intermission I knew I could not just sit there meekly and take the rest of it; I murmured to my sister that I hoped she would understand that It was impossible for me to remain and be attacked as an obnoxious being, as Enemy Number One, and I left.

When I was at home again, alone and still agitated, I opened my log to make my customary brief entry of who, what, when, where. But this time the line or two at the bottom of the page spilled over for most of the next.

> Town Hall—with Alice—"Black Rev. and White Backlash." I left at intermission. They sneer at Gandhi & applaud Paul Robeson!!! . . . the hatred of the white liberal, the scorn of the nonviolence of Martin Luther King, the jeers at anyone who believes in the Civil Rights Bill now before Cong.—all sicken me. If these speakers for violence [I named them in the privacy of my log, but will not do so here]—believe that only Communism is the solution, why do they not say so? They say they are ready to spill blood—why not risk prison to tell the truth? They sound as if the enemy is not the white racist, but the anti-Communist.
>
> Good God! Can't there be common ground even here, to end bigotry?

Between those two shocked pages of my log are two old newspaper clippings, yellowed and fragile, like some faded gardenias preserved by a young girl as a memento of her first prom. They are columns written on two successive days by the widely known journalist, James A. Wechsler, who had agreed to be one of the sponsors of that meeting, not dreaming how it would turn out. Wechsler did name names—most of which belong to people still alive and prominent today. Even now it is good to reread those old columns;* when I think about all-black dormitories at most universities and colleges, which came into being at the insistence of black students themselves, when I think of

*See New York *Evening Post,* June 22, 23 1964.

230

any other black-arranged segregation of races, of black anti-Semitism—

Even a few of the sentences I underlined as I read those two columns should show what made me want to preserve those Wechsler "gardenias."

> The underlying thrust of almost everything said by the Negro panelists . . . was that the time had come to repudiate the spirit and strategy of the non-violence movement. . . . It was time, in short, for Negro militants to take matters into their own hands; if any whites chose to ride quietly in the back of the new bus, they might be accommodated, but let them not try to get near the wheel. . . .
> More than three-fourths of the audience was white, and it was from white throats that one heard the most passionate, sometimes semihysterical assaults on the white liberal corrupters.

One of those white throats was my sister Alice's. No wonder I found it impossible to sit next her and listen. And of course, when next we met, we had one of our old bitter fights—right back to good old square one!

That whole year was a jumble of activities, but I was writing all through the jumble—all manner of writing. For one thing, I was again feeling sharp money pressures; after all, we had been living for more than a year on that farewell bonus from Time.

So one sort of writing I turned to was my old trade of promotion. I suddenly remembered a big bold idea I had had ten years before, during that panicky time when I was so sure my newspaper columns were soon to end. It was an advertising campaign about smoking— that had been long before the first warnings about smoking and cancer, but there were plenty of people who kept trying to cut down on cigarettes or give them up for good.

All cigarette campaigns were addressed to smokers, urging this brand over that, but I thought it would make a stir to run ads addressed to people who had already quit. I had speedily written six ads at that time, admiring my headlines and copy as I wrote—but as far as I can remember, I never submitted any of them to anybody.

Now I dug them out, admired them all over again, knew they would make a hot campaign, though now that there was growing agitation about smoking and cancer, I did some rewriting to take that into account.

Then I telephoned George Gribben, president of Young and Rubicam, and asked for a meeting. Y&R was the official agency handling Time's Know campaign for all the years I'd been doing it, so Gribben knew me.

I can still remember some of my headlines and copy. The first was of a frantic man at his office desk, a large empty ashtray at his right hand.

> I *did* quit—and just about wrecked my whole life. I quit cigarettes—and in a week, my secretary left me, my kids were scared of me, and my wife and I were forever *at* each other.

Another was of a jowly-faced, stomach-bulging middle-aged man, disgustedly getting off a bathroom scale.

> I *did* quit—and I gained thirty pounds!

My original copy had then urged a switch to some low-tar brand, but now I rewrote that part to extol the pleasures of a good cigar, pointing out that no normal person inhaled the smoke of a fine cigar.

As George Gribben began to read my ads, glancing at my brief suggestions for artwork, I could tell that he was pleased. Nor was I surprised when he asked what fee I would want for the ads—perhaps $5,000 for the set? I had not made it clear why I wanted an appointment with him—had merely said it was about a "consultant idea."

"There's no fee for them," I now told him. "They're my calling card. What I'm here for is to see whether we might set up some sort of part-time deal while I'm waiting for my new book to come out next fall."

"A copy deal?"

"If you thought I might come up with some ideas for some campaign you've been having trouble with. Maybe for a few months' trial —that's how things started at Time for the Know campaign. These ads might be considered my first assignment."

I was pretty sure Gribben would never submit any campaign that was negative about smoking to any tobacco company in the world, but might he not want to take out some insurance against the chance of some other agency getting hold of it?

And that was how we arrived at a one-day-a-week job for me at a thousand a month. It was to be retroactive for a couple of months, so my "calling card" officially became their property.

I had done no promotion for over two years; this was like a return to a familiar and easier world. I really enjoyed my interim deal, and it lasted for sixteen months in all. Though I put in so little time at the office, I did work hard at home on my various assignments, came up with a number of campaign ideas that Y&R did submit to clients like General Foods and other large corporations, and sometimes went along on the actual presentation of copy and layouts.

Nearly always there was high enthusiasm, much rosy talk—and then some equivalent of, "We'll get back to you as soon as we've touched all bases on it."

Looking back now, I believe that none of my campaign suggestions ever came close to being accepted, acted upon and run in the newspapers or magazines. In those giant corporations I never saw any Harry Luces, never met one executive who would have spent half a million the first year on anything so unorthodox as the Know campaign, and then gone ahead with it for seven years. I say seven because the final proof in my Time Inc. portfolio bears the headline, "You can't *know* 1964 unless you *know* 1963."

But during those sixteen months I most certainly didn't limit myself to the Young and Rubicam kind of writing. I wrote, and sold, a novelette, *Woman Boss,* and wrote something I had long meant to do: one more storybook for children to balance off the one I had done twenty years before and dedicated "For Mikey."

This second one was to say "For Chris," and I suppose it's lucky that I didn't have a total of five or six children or I might have turned into a habitual writer of what the trade calls juveniles.

I enjoyed writing it, as I had enjoyed writing *A Dog Of His Own* all those years earlier, and I wrote it almost as swiftly. This one had a title that required quotation marks around it, for it was an account of the last weeks of a pregnancy, told in the first person by none other than a six-year-old named Chris.

"I'm Going To Have A Baby!" has a large picture of an excited kid leaping into the air, face all alight as he makes this announcement, and the picture is not only on the soon-to-be-destroyed jacket, but right on the indestructible binding of the book itself.

Inside there's Chris turning handsprings, saying "I know I am—I just found out today." That's the entire text of page one. The next page shows him with his attractive young mother and father—mother seen only head and shoulders.

"My Mummy told me—and my Daddy said it was true."

That "Mummy" reminds me that for the first time one of my books originally appeared not in my native land but in a foreign edition abroad. Random House turned down *I'm Going To Have A Baby!* but one evening my British publisher, Heinemann's Charles Pick, was at my house, and I showed him the rough sketches and title of the book, reading the entire manuscript aloud to him in about fifteen minutes, each minute accompanied by his chortles and sounds of liking it. A handshake followed, and in proper sequence a contract, small advance, and submission of illustrations, by airmail since the artist he chose was British, living in London. Only later did an American edition appear, published by John Day, with no changes except one: "Mummy" became "Mommy."

But the central character in the book was never either Mummy or Mommy—it remained Chris, telling us all about a pregnancy, telling us in his own terms as he goes through his whole new experience of waiting for his first baby brother or sister, giving us all the explanations from his friends about the stork, the rosebush, the angels in heaven, until he finally demands of his parents, "Where's my baby coming from?"

By now Mummy is shown in full, large, advanced pregnancy. "Why, right from me, Chris darling," she says, and Daddy adds, "And you came right from Mummy, too, when you were born."

Chris leans down to his Mummy's stomach, to hear his baby's heartbeat—"Hi, baby, hey, baby, can you hear me?" And then come the tough questions, page after page. "How did my baby ever get in there?" and later his bewildered, "How will it ever get out?"

And Daddy and Mummy give him all the good straight answers a six-year-old can absorb, right up to the final page of the bassinet containing a brand new infant, sex unspecified.

"I just had a baby," he shouts. "I just had a baby!" "I JUST HAD A BABY!" *"I JUST HAD A BABY!!!"*

Never before or since did I have a book that was praised both by Dr. Benjamin Spock, the baby guru for so many generations, and the Catholic Library Association, if I am remembering the name correctly. It went very well, in terms of juvenile sales, and I felt that I had squared off whatever debt I had left unpaid to the second child in my small family.

There was something else in the way of work that I was enjoying, a sort of hobby, more than work: being the anonymous editor of my favorite time-consumer, the weekly Double Crostic in the Saturday Review.

"I'm so good at solving them," my friend Carroll Whedon had once told me, "it frightens me."

That was way back when I was still having trouble over the definitions and empty squares and dashes. In volume one I said that I was never what we today would call a workaholic, that even when I was in a rush of writing, I could always abandon my desk and read a just-arrived magazine without any guilt, or play with the kids for a while, or listen to a new record I'd bought, or waste a couple of hours on that week's new double crostic.

But the editorship had come about purely by accident. I was having lunch one day at the Algonquin with the editor of the Saturday Review, Norman Cousins. He valued such talks, he said, especially about the magazine.

"Doesn't anybody ever *edit* those DCs of yours" I asked.

"Why? Is anything wrong?"

"Cuzz, go back and do the one in this week's issue."

There was a clue, I went on, that he would just hate. "One of the definitions says something like, 'describing certain people in the south of the U.S.'" I could see him go tense. "And the three-word answer works out as 'blacks and tans.'"

I had never seen anybody blanch, but Norman Cousins blanched. This was in the late fifties when Negroes still called themselves Negroes, when *blacks* was a word used only in stories by Somerset Maugham and such about the British colonies, like, "the native blacks."

"L. H.," Norman finally said, "would you edit them for me?"

"I'd love it. I do them every week anyway."

"What fee would you think—?"

"Oh heavens, what fee?" I was still doing promotion at Time in those days, so it was easy to decide. "All I'd want would be the great big Webster's Unabridged Dictionary—and that mahogany stand that goes with it."

It was a delightful hobby. I would receive the puzzles in manuscript form, everything left blank, just as it would be when the reader faced them in the magazine. I would solve them, reach decisions about the propriety and fairness of the various clues or definitions, check them for accuracy, and then phone in any suggestions for changes to one of the magazine's real editors.

At Christmas Norman sent me a check for $500, a bonus. I was surprised and pleased. But on the following Christmas he made a bad mistake: the bonus check was for $600. I thought, Good heavens, that's a two-dollar-a-week raise. Come *on!* So I picked up the phone.

"Hey, Cuzz, it's time we talked about some sort of regular fee."

We did. It wasn't much of a fee, but it was a formal thing on their payroll. Being the anonymous editor of their DCs took on a little extra shine.

Twenty-six years later, in 1985, through many sales and resales of the Saturday Review, I was still the anonymous editor of their double crostics.

But what I would have enjoyed more than any of those other things was starting another novel. I was in no great inner rush about it, because I felt that after the long struggle for *First Papers* I truly had earned a long vacation from serious writing.

I treated myself to a month and a half of travel abroad. Yet in London, my first stop for the British publication of my book, I found myself one morning in my lovely room at the Connaught writing one of those notes to myself that now seem so revealing. Again it's hand-written, in ink, on ruled paper taken from a loose-leaf notebook, and the first of its five sheets is dated London, April 23, '65.

> Not to write is terrible for me, and it is now 8 or 9 months since I last wrote anything . . . I must get back to writing or succumb to depression and loneliness. . . .
>
> To travel alone when you are nearly 65 is no gay lark (though was it ever? Even at 26 when I went on my first trip anywhere by myself?). That was to Miami, in the spring, after the hurricanes of 1925 . . . all I really longed for was to be at peace with Tom, whom I loved, and who was, for the time, working (at Ayer in Phila) and who sent me, also for the time, money to live on. $30 a week it was, but enormously vital, because for once *he* was paying for me instead of the other way round.
>
> There could be . . . a story in such a relationship—perhaps even a novel—but by now it seems so commonplace, I wonder if I could make it seem anything else to a reader . . .
>
> I have *always* been depressed between books, always. It happened after *The Trespassers,* and I saw Dr. G. about it; then it happened after each book, and now it is happening again, and has been for some months, though I have really refused to admit it, even to myself.
>
> Even writing this page is good. When I am writing, I am

unaware of anything else; time flies; I suddenly feel "comfortable," as if something had stopped bothering or hurting.

So all that "enjoying" I have just been telling about, my Young and Rubicam deal, my second storybook for children, my hobby of editing the DCs—though all of it was true enough, there must have lain, in some subterranean stratum of my being all the while, this other blacker seam.

My note-taking lasted for just a few days, and then I was off to Aulla, in the Carrera Mountains of Northern Italy, to be a guest at a week-long house party at La Fortezza, an old stone castle, which my host and hostess, being British, spoke of as having been "hired" for the month of May. They were Francis and Bay Meynell, more formally Sir Francis and Lady Meynell, two illustrious and delightful people widely known in publishing and political circles in London, whom I had first met years before and remained good friends with for all the years to follow.

It was after dinner one night with the Meynells, when all the other guests were enjoying a sharp variation of table tennis, that I first noticed something wrong with my eyes . . . I didn't see the ball accurately as it came at me, and kept missing. Later in Rome, looking up in a tourist's awed rapture at the ceiling of the Sistine Chapel, I saw again that there was something wrong. The edges of all the great paintings seemed to blur or fade; my distance glasses certainly needed to be checked up when I got home.

But once home I did nothing, until one night when Mike was over for dinner. I kept flicking off a fly, wondering how it had got into the house despite the air conditioning, saying something about its size. I thought Mike looked a little puzzled, and when I finally said, "It must be a horsefly," he spoke the quiet sentence that was to send me to the doctor first thing in the morning.

"There isn't any fly, mother."

"There it goes again," I said, waving it off.

"There is no fly at all," he repeated. He looked upset.

My hand flew up to my eyes. I had heard of retinal detachment and the blindness that could follow. How would I write? How would I manage if I couldn't?

Dr. James C. Newton, now head of ophthalmological surgery at St. Luke's Hospital, had me lie flat on a medical table while he did the longest eye examination I had ever had. It was not a detachment.

"It's a small horseshoe tear at the edge of the retina," he then told me, "in the right eye. That big fly streaking across is a standard symptom."

He would operate in the morning, first trying to "fuse" the tear by what he called photocoagulant heat. If that failed he would resort to surgery.

Today, photocoagulant heat is called laser beam surgery, and I was one of the early patients to have a retinal tear mended by it. Three doctors from other hospitals were there to watch his technique; it was done without anesthesia and there was no pain except for the sensation of intense heat and blinding glare. To me the worst part was the dread aroused by my instructions to keep looking at one point in the ceiling, where the two walls made an angle.

"Do not move your eyes at all, Laura. You *must* keep them from moving even for a second."

One of the other doctors held my eyelids open, and my whole being concentrated at that one point above me. If that blasting ray were to penetrate to the optic nerve? Is that what he meant? I never moved my eyes a millimeter's distance.

"Excellent," Dr. Newton said at last. My eye was loosely bandaged and I stayed in the hospital only for one night. The streaking fly was gone, but Dr. Newton had told me that in all likelihood the horseshoe tear would appear sooner or later in my left eye. He also told me that there were "early cataract changes in both eyes."

A new kind of depression took me. I had had lots of illnesses, lots of surgery, but when they were over, I had always known they were over for good. This time the "over" was different. It was over only for the time being.

"Look ma, no hands"—on Peugeot bike in Central Park, 1972. *Photo credit: Robert Schwartz.*

With Editha Sterba, celebrating the Sterbas' fiftieth wedding anniversary, 1976.

The desk in the living room at 923 Fifth Avenue, where the author lived for her last thirty years.

Trying Grandma's type-
writer—Kate, age 6½, 1977.

During the filming of a television adaptation of *The Tenth
Month,* 1978; with stars Keith Michell and Carol Burnett,
Kate (front left) and Sarah.

"Literary Lions Dinner" held at the New York Public Library, 1983. Other lions included James Baldwin, Philip Roth, Ved Mehta, Jerzy Kosinski, William Styron, George Plimpton, Arthur Miller, Susan Sontag and Elizabeth Hardwick. *Photo credit: Anne Day.*

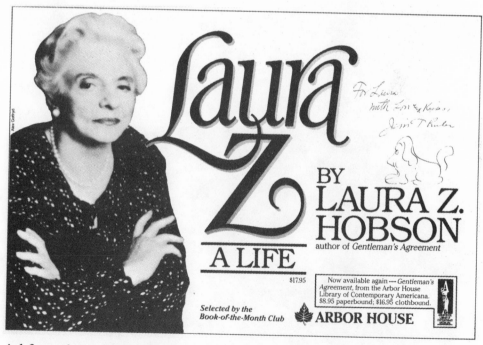

Ad for volume I of *Laura Z: A Life,* published in 1983. The photo *(credit: Alex Gotfryd)* was also used for *Over and Above* and *Untold Millions.*

Filming *Consenting Adult* in Vancouver,
September 1984, with Cheryl Downey...

...and with co-producer Ray Aghayan (center).

Thanksgiving 1984: with Sarah (left) and
Kate, age 16 and 14.

Chris on vacation, Cape Breton, Nova Scotia, 1985.

MEDIA AWARD

Presented to

CONSENTING ADULT

Starring MARLO THOMAS   MARTIN SHEEN   BARRY TUBB
Produced by RAY AGHAYAN and DAVID LAWRENCE
Supervising Producer DENNIS E. DOTY
Executive Producer MARTIN STARGER
Directed by GILBERT CATES
Based on the Novel by LAURA Z. HOBSON, Teleplay by JOHN McGREEVEY
A STARGER COMPANY PRESENTATION
in association with
DAVID LAWRENCE AND RAY AGHAYAN PRODUCTIONS
AN ABC THEATER PRESENTATION

for the responsible portrayal of gay and lesbian characters and issues
in the entertainment media

October 18, 1985

Alliance for Gay and Lesbian Artists
in the Entertainment Industry

The award won by the film of *Consenting Adult*.

The benefit showing of *Consenting Adult* film, January 1985, with Mike and his wife, Ann.

This postcard photo of Bette Davis was to accompany a section on old age. (See Afterword.) *Photo by Roddy McDowall ©1982 Harlequin Enterprises Ltd. © 1982 The American Postcard Co., Inc.*

"85 years old!! I don't believe it." June 19, 1985.

Birthday night, June 19, 1985, at Shea Stadium, with
Chris, Mike, Ann and Sarah (rear).

"Happy Birthday Laura
Hobson" on the big screen at
Shea Stadium.

Record of a lifetime: with some of the logbooks, summer of 1985. Slips of paper marked entries to be consulted in writing this volume. *Photo credit: Roddy McDowall.*

THIRTEEN

JUNE OF 1965 SAW my official induction into that obnoxiously termed section of society, senior citizens. To me the phrase was as coy as Ye Olde Sweete Shoppe.

"Are you called a junior citizen?" I demanded of my friend Carroll when she jeered at my indignation. "Why can't they be honest and just say, the old?"

"You're too good a copywriter," she retorted, "even to consider such a headline."

Despite the warning about a far-in-the-future cataract operation, I didn't feel old, or even very senior. The word *retirement* still held no terror for me, knowing as I did that I would be one of those who never retire.

It is true that I began to find new interest in newspaper articles about creativity and old age. Occasionally I would clip a paragraph or two and file it in another of my folders, this one marked HOBSON— MISC. EXCEPT AUTHORS AND BOOKS. So I know that Picasso was still painting at ninety-one, Grandma Moses at a hundred and one, and that Chagall was still at it at ninety-six. In one of my "Trade Winds" columns, written a decade earlier, while I was still a junior citizen, I had done a long item about a new contract Winston Churchill had just signed for a four-volume work, *A History of the English-Speaking Peoples;* he was in his middle seventies. And Toscanini was still conducting in his eighties, Georgia O'Keeffe turning out masterpieces though she was past ninety.

So the subject of age and aging obviously interested me as a general theme, and presumably my own age and aging as a particular part of it. My life had changed—assuredly it had in some important ways, but I seem to have accepted those changes with some signs of good sense. The inevitable experience of "the empty nest" had taken some toll, but as I look back now on that period I think I also found an unexpected ease in living alone.

Mike had long since become a New Yorker again; that first love which had kept him living in Cambridge and working for Little, Brown had finally come to a conclusion. He again had a job in publishing, had a place of his own, and a social life of his own. But he was one of those "good sons" who made time for his mother, for dinner together, for an occasional movie, a frequent concert, and even an entire weekend of nearly steady companionship during the days following the assassination of President Kennedy, when I, like everybody else I knew, kept a compulsive death watch at the television set.

And Chris was no longer at home either. Though I still find it sad to admit this to myself, his absence, in a way, put us on better terms. After Africa, he had taught in New York for a year; the bad times between us were unfortunately not a thing of the past—one entry in my log says, "Dr. Gosselin again—first time in three years."

The bad times, I am sure, had been just as bad for Chris. At times he had moved out, to stay at a friend's apartment, perhaps; then he applied for and received a scholarship at the University of Chicago and became a midwesterner, except for holiday seasons. He had always been a good letter-writer, and the tensions that were so quick to spring up between us when we were together remained quiescent or absent when we wrote or talked by phone.

And there was Eric. As I had predicted, the "Eric part" of him was still there, but his terrible illness had made for physical changes I was still so fortunately free of. He used a stout cane on the street, a rubber-tipped one that proclaimed to approaching people that this was not a fashionable stick, but a medical device for the disabled. He found it too difficult to ride the city buses or subways; he resisted taxis, and became in part a person who stayed at home because going forth took so much effort.

But we kept on seeing each other, less frequently, and always at my house. One thing that did induce Eric to go out was music—always "my treat," since I had season tickets for the Philharmonic. Once, shortly after his stroke, we'd been talking about the great new concert hall nearing completion over on the west side, wondering whether it would ever get to seem normal to hear music anywhere but at wonderful old Carnegie Hall.

"My one ambition," he said, "is to live long enough to hear at least one concert at this new Lincoln Center."

That he did; the auditorium for the Philharmonic had its first concert in 1962. Though I had never had aisle seats for concerts, I carefully arranged to get them for my new season tickets so he would never have to struggle past people's knees.

Since finishing *Episode,* Eric had done no prolonged writing, but an editor he knew kept suggesting that he write his autobiography.

"If I do it," he said, "it will be more as therapy than as literature."

Whatever it was, I wished he would do it.

I had done no prolonged writing either. I kept telling myself that there was no rush, that I needn't start to do any hard thinking, but you can never control the thoughts that go on while you are "not thinking," while you are taking a walk or a bath, while you are asleep.

I felt sure about one thing: I wanted *not* to try another book that was tightly based on some part of my own experience. I found myself thinking, even saying aloud, "I want to write about *them,* not about me."

I had written a short story I liked, "Custody," which was in part about a college boy converted to Black Power, and I had begun a novelette, *Ruthless,* that I didn't expect to like in the usual sense but thought would be interestingly different because it was indeed about *them.* It was about a woman, a *Social Register* type, cool, self-centered, ambitious, who sets her sights on a world-famous British actor, married though he be, and married though she is herself.

In one of my half-doodling notes to myself I had once written reproachfully, "I never write about scoundrels," and the possibilities in this story still held me. At one point, as I had done long ago with my novelette, *The Reward,* I began to wonder if it might not be a novel instead, and I began to work at it as if it were just that—whatever, there certainly was no resemblance between this kind of work and what there had been on *First Papers.*

It didn't go too well. I was forever rewriting or inserting new scenes. By the middle of summer, with greater alacrity than usual, I was welcoming chances to get away from home and manuscript. I had a delightful long weekend at the Cape, at Quisset Harbor in Falmouth, with Jane and Ben Spock, sailing on their twenty-three-foot sloop *Turtle,* going with them to my first old-fashioned New England clambake; I accepted other invitations for weekends, or, as was the case with Carroll, middle-of-the-week stretches at their summer place in Rhode Island. And never did I feel that guilty little nudge, You ought to be working.

Early fall brought distraction more welcome still. One afternoon Mike brought home a girl he wanted me to meet, a pretty, dark-eyed, dark-haired girl, Ann Gould. She was working at the paperback house of Fawcett Crest, and they had met at a publishing cocktail party. In a few weeks there was a note in my log.

> Mike told me about Ann
> Then later, Ann & Mike here
> They're engaged!

They were married a month later at the Church of St. Thomas More, known in the neighborhood as Jackie Kennedy's church. Ann had been born into a Lutheran family, but during her college years, had converted to Catholicism. In one of the early talks between the three of us, we somehow got around to the Church and birth control. Ann waved that off.

"They were wrong about Galileo too."

I liked that and was prepared to love my daughter-in-law from the start. I had always known that dire old-wives' jingle, "Your daughter's your daughter for all of your life; your son's your son till he gets him a wife." I didn't believe it for a minute, and was delighted with their delight at my idea for their wedding present: a two-week honeymoon trip to the Caribbean, in Jamaica.

Old wives' tales aside, after a son's wedding, it does take a good while to calm down, and when I did get back to *Ruthless* it was still slow going. I had begun to refer to it lightly as "my stylish novel," to my friends, my agent, even to my editor at Random House. Why I didn't realize that that was a pejorative phrase, why I didn't see that it revealed my own belittling of the whole idea, I was never able to answer to my own satisfaction. This was not another case of writer's block; it was just that I took so little pleasure in writing that I began to wonder if I were going stale.

And it was in that mood that I happened on a short television interview about going stale, a purely coincidental bit of timing that created not just another hobby but a major change in the daily routine of my life. And in time, at a meeting of the Authors League Council, I was virtually dragooned into writing something about it.

In the early fall a year later, at lunch, everybody was asking everybody about their summer vacations. There was talk of Europe, of California, of South America until it came to me.

"I rode a bike for twelve hundred miles," I said.

"Where to?" About six voices asked it.

"All in Central Park. Not just the summer—I started a year ago."

"Write me a short piece about it," said Herbert Mitgang, not only an author but one of the editors of the New York *Times.* "For my 'Topics' column."

"I never write short pieces," I said. "They're harder than long ones."

Two days later I got a letter on the best stationery of the *Times,* signed *Herbert Mitgang, Editorial Board.*

Dear Laura,

The title of your essay is "1200 Miles by Bike in Central Park."

Now all you need is 750 words below the title. Copy is due a month from now. We don't kid around here.

Regards,
Sincerely,
Herb

I laughed at the succinctness, meaning to ignore it, and set it aside for a polite refusal by phone. Then I found myself turning to my typewriter. In a way it *was* a good story. "Topics" appeared every Saturday morning, in the *Times,* across the top of the Letters columns. I always turned to it when I reached the editorial page.

One month later there I was. The footnote in italics said, "Mrs. Hobson, Central Park cyclist, is better known as an American novelist." The headline was just what he'd said it would be.

About a year ago the eminent cyclist and cardiologist Dr. Paul Dudley White looked straight at me from the TV screen and said, "Whenever anybody asks me if he's going stale or losing his creative ability, I feel the muscles of his legs."

Next day I rented a bike in the park—British-made, three-speed, hand brakes, $1.25 an hour. I had had a bike as a child but that was indecent decades ago, so I started where there were no witnesses.

Then I plodded around the special bike path, an oval tape of pavement 1.7 miles long, from 72nd to 59th and back, from east side to west. I dismounted just to breathe.

But my outraged muscles and I went out the next morning, and the next and the next. On the Sunday, with the roadway closed to cars, I had my first sight of a New York on bikes, on skates, skateboards, trainer-wheels, soapbox scooters, tricycles, tandems. It was a marvel, but all 500 rentable bikes were already gone. That week I bought my own, complete with speedometer, to measure whatever miles I might manage.

It took ten days to get to ten, then twenty, then thirty. I still did only the one orbit, still got off repeatedly to breathe. I had no ambitions about distance, no prescribed stint. I just liked it.

It was October, the golden time, and I began to look forward to the swish and brush of the leaves as my wheels slipped through them. I crossed forty, then fifty, and one morning I did the oval twice and knew a triumph. It grew colder, but I went right after breakfast.

I don't keep a journal or diary, but once I start writing a book, I do keep a work log. For Nov. 13 it says, "Page 90, 91, 92," and up above, "100 on bike, 5 wks." The next bike notation doesn't appear until Jan. 9. "First bike since big snow at Xmas. At 243."

Somewhere along in there I began to wonder for the first time how many miles you could do in a month once you were really fit and the weather really good. How many in six months? In a year?

And also somewhere in there came lawlessness, civic sin, at the very least, civil disobedience. I had never, not in four months, not in 300 miles, ever disobeyed the park ordinances that bound me to that 1.7 with its faded yellow stencils: Bicycle Path— Pedestrians Keep Off. Now the word treadmill would pop unwanted into my mind; I began to look about. Visible everywhere under the winter-bare trees were the pedestrian paths, all but abandoned in the morning hours, inviting, beckoning, unknown.

One morning I did it. Delight! Change and exploration. What graceful arcs and dips and rises those paths made, how charming each new vista. But their stencils sternly said: Pedestrian Walk —No Bikes.

A little research showed that Central Park has six miles of bridle paths, six and one-half of roadway for cars, only 1.7 for bikes. And it has 58 miles of pedestrian walks.

If only, I began to think, if only those 58 could be marked, Never on Sundays, Never on Saturdays, Never on any Afternoon, but Weekday Mornings—Bikes Welcome. Mayor Lindsay, Mr. Heckscher, retroactively Mr. Hoving—if only!

One day in April I did five miles without getting off once. From then on it was five every morning, often six or seven. I crossed 500, then 600 and wondered, 1,000 by Labor Day? (I made it four days ahead.)

My bike anniversary came in October and fitness and work weren't the whole story. I had grown to know the park as I had never dreamed of knowing it, I, a born New Yorker, living only a few feet from it for years. I got to know every pond and lake and wading pool, every playground and playing field, every unexpected statue (would you believe Beethoven?).

I found out that squirrels will scamper aside at the ring of your bell but that a whole carpet of pigeons will scarcely riffle; what sends them is a sharply aspirated Wheeee. I saw the Mall marked off for kids' races and hopscotch, and smelled new-cut grass again, and clover. I got to know which puddles would dry an hour after rain and which needed a full day, when ponds froze over in winter and when they thawed in spring.

I had grown up in a small town in Queens; this, in Central Park, was the feeling once more. It was an urban Walden, lying out there green and gray in cloudy weather, green and bright in the sun, bronze in fall, white in winter, but always there. I never knew before that I loved it.

Herb Mitgang sent me an acceptance note, also on the dignified stationery of the New York *Times,* but this time scrawled in pencil. "You are awarded the *Croix de Bike* for a lovely article in every way—facts and attitude. Take a day off." Later he told me it would be included in an anthology of one hundred years of the best pieces in the *Times'* "Topics" for which I would be paid an honorarium of $40. The *Times'* fee was $100.

But I also received on the official stationery of the City of New York, signed by Parks Commissioner August Heckscher, "a very special permit which you may use if you should be stopped on a pedestrian path within the morning hours."

I was sixty-six when I took that first ride on a bike in Central Park. As I write this now, I am just eighty-five, and every one of those intervening years saw me ride a thousand miles, making a note in my log as I crossed each new hundred. There were a few lapses, after hospitals or surgery, but eighteen years later, on the first day of my

1985 log, it says: "Bike total is 17,233." And on every one of those miles I carried that special permit with me. I never forgot to shift it from one jacket to another.

Nor did I ever worry again about going stale.

The muscles of my legs were not the only sign that my new bike regimen was good for me. Just about the time I was well into it, I reread my whole first draft of "my stylish novel" and then asked my agent, and by now my good friend, Phyllis Jackson, to read it and see if she could tell me why my vague dissatisfactions kept right on coming at me. She called me a few days later. It couldn't have been an easy call for her to make.

"You don't feel good about it," she said quietly, "because it really isn't very good."

She went on with her own kind of phrasing, about it not being "your kind of novel," about my own doubts persisting because my own instinct was the only judge that should ever matter to me, and my instinct was going thumbs down.

It wasn't easy listening for me either, but listen I did, and told her I admired her for staying away from easy talk and that infuriating, "Something doesn't quite come off" or "It's good but it won't play," that I have occasionally heard from a cowardly agent or Hollywood producer. Then we set up a sandwich lunch date at her office so we could talk.

There I told her there was one novel I wished I *could* write. "For years, I couldn't even consider doing it—it would be based on something I've kept secret for about twenty-five years. But now—"

And then I told her about my pregnancy and the birth and adoption of Chris. I saw her expression change, I saw her lean toward me, I could feel her inner conviction that no matter how much I invented to change the story, *this* would make a novel that was "my kind of novel."

That same night I went to my typewriter and began it. I hardly paused for the way to open it. All I knew was that I was not going to write about *them*—it never amounted to anything when I did. I was not a calm observer of others; I was somebody who needed to dig material out of my own being, had to write, in my books at least, about what I knew was true, and then try for that mysterious amalgam of fact and invention that might make a novel I would be glad I had written.

I was like a paleontologist, I thought, on a dig. He finds one or two bones and then reconstructs a whole dinosaur out of it; an archeologist finds a few artifacts and reconstructs an entire ancient civilization. What I've always done is take a chunk of my own life, yes, but how much I then had to create and construct out of my imagination or talent or whatever it is, to make a whole novel out of it.

I wrote only a single page that night, page one, a page that was never to be rewritten or undergo any change except for some minor pencil editing of a few words or phrases.

> The moment was to stand out forever in her memory. There she stood, alone and naked, thinking of nothing except the minutiae of the bath, toweling herself dry, gazing idly about the warm steamy room, then at her image in the long panel of mirror in the closed door.
>
> Her breasts looked fuller. She had gained no weight, but her breasts, always small, looked fuller.
>
> A shaft of hope struck through her and she looked at herself entire. Below her navel there was the faintest globe of fullness too.
>
> Had the years of longing fused into some betraying lens of illusion? . . .
>
> Oh God, let it be true.

That night I slept the untroubled sleep of sureness. I had only one consideration to take care of before I could go ahead, but first thing in the morning I wrote Chris.

> This is a very large question I put to you, and I hope you will be very clear about how you feel before you answer me, for it involves my life and yours.

I told him about the book I wanted to write, told him of some of the "inventions" I already knew of that I would put in, and said, "But that would be a problem of technique and story, not the problem I pose to you here."

> Which is, May I? It is your secret too, as much as mine . . . I write you this now because I . . . am abandoning . . . my "stylish novel." It never did develop; it remains a fraudulent piece of smart nothing . . . the relief of not having to work on something I have no liking for is already enormous. Two years down the drain—but a painful two years, with self-doubt all the way.

This novel I would be proud to write. May I try it? It would be, I hope, real, not phony, warm, not stylish smart . . . I was going to phone you, but decided it would be better to give you enough time to think about your "share" in the matter.

I love you.
Mama

He seemed to need very little time to be very clear about how he felt; he called me the same day he got the letter. It would be fine for me to go ahead; he would be "sort of proud."

And it was fine for me to go ahead. Within days a note in my log says, "God, a different feeling—to write something that *matters* to me."

There were other reasons that made me want to lose myself in work —early in the year I had lived through my dearest friend's struggle with cancer. "Can't really work well because of Carroll," my January pages had said. "Took Carroll to hosp. for radiation treatment." Soon there was a note of higher urgency: "Will take C. every day at 11:30."

Her daughter Jill had a two-year-old toddler and couldn't take part in this arduous routine, and her son, I think, was doing a TV writing job in California. Carroll's husband was chairman of a public relations firm, part of a very large advertising agency; I dare say no big busy executive could leave his office every day to take care of his wife, especially when the marriage, now thirteen years old, had been developing a good deal of stress and distance. Carroll never went in for detailed confidences, but I could see that she was often available in the evenings for a concert or a game of Scrabble, and she did let me know that Bob was often absent on weekends on business trips to Washington. I had thought unhappily, "Business trips over weekends?" and I saw myself that she was drinking and smoking more than was usual with her. I could guess that she was not in the frame of mind that denotes contentment, much less happiness.

She lived only five blocks from my apartment; I would walk over there every morning, then get a taxi and tell the driver to "throw the clock" while I went upstairs for a "terribly sick friend, to take her to the hospital." Some drivers just drove off, but usually they heard the urgency in my voice and waited.

By early February Carroll was almost too weak to go out; the visits were reduced to three a week. She knew what her illness was, but she never spoke the word cancer to me. It had started just before Christmas; she had telephoned me one day from Lenox Hill Hospital to say she

248

had a lesion in the esophagus, and Chris and I had gone over on Christmas day to see her. I don't know whether it was she or her husband who later told me that she had had a small operation under local anaesthetic just below the collar bone, and that after the immediate biopsy, they had simply sutured the wound and prescribed chemotherapy and radiation. I am sure she knew, as I did, that they were informing her that her disease was too far gone to merit any major surgery.

The time came when she could no longer live at home and became a patient at Memorial. One day, visiting her, I learned that her husband had sent up the company limousine so that I might take her for a grand tour of Central Park, which she loved. It was a bitterly cold winter day, but sunny and bright under a glistening blue sky, and she leaned her head back against the velvet seat and looked at everything we passed, scarcely speaking. I think she knew she was saying farewell to the park and to life itself.

The last time I went to the hospital to see her, I asked if she needed some new things to read and she shook her head for no. "I'm just waiting for what's going to happen to happen."

She died at four-thirty that night. The newspaper obits were brief, telling of her various copy jobs and editorial positions on McCall's and other magazines, and of her being a trustee of Vassar College. She was just fifty-seven.

It was the first death, since my mother's, that tore me to the core. At times, after I had entered my sixties, I would tell her jokingly that I was jealous of her because she was nearly a decade younger than I; here I sit now, the grateful possessor of twenty-eight more years of life than she was ever to have, twenty-eight years more of work and gratification, of pain and joy, of memory and experience, the twenty-eight years of living that my dearest friend was denied. As I write of her now, remembering what she was, I weep for her all over again.

Five days later, Harry Luce died. I was saddened and shocked to hear it, but there are many levels of grief, and for me this was warm and real but not of that same "core" intensity. I went to the memorial services, but planned to reach the church at the last minute because I wanted to take a seat in a rear pew, far removed from family members or any of the people I used to know and work with. Apart from Clare and the family, the church was nearly given over to Time, Life and Fortune editors and executives, and as the service ended, I slipped out quickly and alone.

I live only a block away, so I didn't need to wait around for a taxi.

I don't know why I was so sure I didn't want to talk to anybody just then. So many people I knew, or whom I read in liberal magazines, had always criticized everything about Harry Luce and his magazines. I wonder what they made of the fact that so many other people, liberal too, and disagreeing sharply with much of his political stance, kept right on admiring and loving him for his other virtues.

I wrote to Clare, whom I had not seen privately since that three-week visit to their house in Phoenix when Harry had had his first heart attack, which they told the world was influenza, and told me was a pulmonary embolism. She sent back the formal printed note I had expected, "Mrs. Henry R. Luce and the family acknowledge with grateful appreciation your expression of sympathy," but on the back of it was Clare's familiar handwriting.

> Dearest Laura,
>
> Thank you for your dear note . . . I feel so terribly lost without him. I do hope, one day, we can get together again. I expect I will return to New York soon, for Arizona is meaningless without him.
> With affection over the many years,
> Clare.
> We met at your house, 34 years ago. I heard from Thayer, who is living in New Mexico, I think.

Later in that same year, Thayer died. Then there was no grieving in me, merely a backward-looking at what so long ago he had meant to me and my life. I wondered whether I ought not write to his brother, the one member of Thayer's family who had always meant the most to me, whose signature had so often appeared, alphabetically just above mine, on full-page newspaper ads about civil rights and nuclear war.

I felt shy; he was the Right Reverend Bishop Henry Wise Hobson, and though he had once jocularly referred to himself, during a week-end visit to his house on Fisher's Island, as "Bishop of the Procter & Gamble diocese of Southern Ohio," that had been over thirty years ago, when all the world was young. By now he might well have become a far more formal person.

My own uncertainty irritated me, and I thought, It's not a matter of Emily Post's *Book of Etiquette*—if you have the impulse to do it, do it. I did write, and almost by return mail had his reply.

He welcomed my letter and was glad I had written. He told me of Thayer's last years of severe illness, "an increasing struggle . . . so I'm thankful he has found release."

> Yes, you and I have often been linked in supporting or protest-
> ing a variety of causes or movements. We've frequently felt
> and thought alike . . . Now that I'm 76 and retired, I keep pretty
> quiet. . . .
>   Monie joins me in all good wishes. We have always been
> thankful for your success and admire what you have done.
>
>   As ever,
>   Henry

I discovered that such letters help; perhaps my own letters had helped *them*. But I was moved most deeply by a few brief words from John Whedon, to whom Carroll had been married for most of her adult life and whom I secretly wished she had never left. John lived in California; several years after the divorce he too had remarried, but I had always known that he still had an abiding love for Carroll, and during her awful months of illness John and I had kept in touch by phone and by letter.

Two days after her death he sent me flowers with these few brief words.

> To a wonderful friend
> with love and great gratitude
> from John, Dorothy and
> from Carroll too.

So, intense work on a book I liked was a boon to me in many ways in that year of 1967. It was to be a prime example of that amalgam of fact and invention that I have talked about. In true life, on the very day I knew I was pregnant, I had told Eric, risking everything that had barely started between us, fearful that the telling would reawaken his old pain about his first wife's death in childbirth, offering to let him take a year's sabbatical from me until it was over, dreading that he might instead decide on a permanent departure. What he did was to stand by me and help me all the way.

But here came invention, basically changing the novel: Dori too has just met a man she cares for, but she can't bring herself to tell him her great news—"I'll tell him next time, not tonight." She puts it off, and then puts it off once more. She wants to give him time to know her better, she thinks, she wants him to know why she has never had children, what it means to her to go ahead. She falls in love so rarely, she can't endure the idea of a return to loneliness.

For nearly a third of the book she keeps silent, hating that silence, she a straightforward person now dealing in the deception of fear. "I'm big and brave when it comes to [my friend] Cele or [my brother] Gene," she excoriates herself, "but I run like a rabbit . . ."

When at last her changing body makes silence impossible, and she does tell him, there is first a leap of joy for him as he thinks it is *their* baby, then shock, consternation, jealousy, rage, separation—and thus the fusion of fact and invention took something I had lived through, and turned it into a creative work.

I wrote in volume one of *Laura Z* that only once did I give a frivolous answer to the inevitable question from readers, "How much of it is true?" And that was with this book, *The Tenth Month*. Many of my real friends asked it, and many of my not-so-real bridge friends at the Regency Club and elsewhere asked it, and to all I gave the same offhand reply.

"Oh, about ten weeks."

I was always to think of *The Tenth Month* as my "happiest" novel, but some pretty unhappy things happened to it, and to me, before it ever reached the light of pub day.

Random House turned it down. The rejection came just when the second half of my advance was due, came when my book was only a third written. I had had short stories turned down, had had a novelette turned down, Random House had even turned down my storybook for children, but never before, not once in my life, had I ever had a novel rejected by my own publisher.

More than that, Bennett Cerf demanded that I return the ten-thousand-dollar advance I had received when we signed the contract. It called for a twenty-thousand-dollar advance, but I had asked that it be spread to two payments. I had budgeted for this one now due, I was counting on it, I was doing nothing else to earn a living because I was giving all my time and energies to this book.

The rejection shocked me, but Bennett's demand shocked me even more. Phyllis Jackson protested, unofficially by phone and then officially in writing. The editorial sessions I had already had with Bob Loomis, she said, had gone well; I had always been amenable to an editor's suggestions for change or rewrite; this "sudden death" was a development neither she nor I could understand. What were his reasons for it?

She was never satisfied with his answers about "the doubts we have." It was just unsatisfactory. I told Phyllis that back in 1950, while the Cerfs and I were warm friends, with their eight-year-old son Chris and my son Chris together every day, planning their future publishing house, The Cerfson Company—that one day, driving to New York from Provincetown with Phyllis Cerf, I had had the impulse to add her to the small group of people who knew about Christopher's birth. I had assumed she would tell Bennett, as any wife would, and I was sure she had done so.

Did Phyllis Jackson think that could in some arcane way account for Bennett's abrupt action now? We speculated about it and decided, "He couldn't be that narrow." But an acidic note did appear in my log: "Bennett phoned . . . an evasive, small-minded talk." He even offered as one of his reasons the fact that the delivery date, January 2, 1969, specified in the contract written three years before, had expired four weeks ago.

It seemed incredible to me that this man who had never once showed displeasure or impatience because *First Papers* had gone ten years beyond the specified date, was now using this technicality to dismiss a work in progress as "unsatisfactory," was casting me out as a Random House author, and demanding repayment of an advance long since spent.

But Bennett was adamant. "You tell Laura that unless that advance is returned, no publisher in this country will ever even look at her manuscript—they'll all know there's a lawsuit hanging over it."

That phrase, "a lawsuit hanging over it," sent me into despair. Phyllis assured me she would find another publisher soon; Mike, who never read my work in unfinished form, read my 116 pages and kept telling me I would soon have another contract, but a stone of apprehension and self-doubt weighed heavier with each day of waiting, each night of tattered sleep.

Since that ritual dinner party four years earlier for *First Papers,* the Cerfs and I had barely seen each other, but I never had the slightest suspicion that the break in our social life, artistically arranged by me, might impinge on our publishing relations. Now I sensed something hidden in Bennett's iron demand for that repayment, Bennett a multimillionaire who knew perfectly well that I had no comfortable capital to fall back on for it.

Was my book really so unsatisfactory, so unpublishable? Maybe I should have defied him, maybe I should have said, "Okay, so sue me, hang the lawsuit over my manuscript." But as I have said, I am not the litigious type; I knew that if I flung the challenge at him, I would never write peacefully or confidently until the case was settled—and lawsuits could take years.

So I gave in. Maybe that should read "caved in."

Some fifteen years were to pass before I exultantly read in the *Times* that a federal court in New York had dismissed a lawsuit brought by Dell Publishing against a young author who had refused their demand that she return a $14,000 advance they had paid her for a novel they rejected as unsatisfactory.

And who should that young author be? Julia Whedon, whom I had known since her babyhood as Jill, Carroll's and John's daughter.

> "The court finds that Dell was under a good-faith obligation to give Whedon an opportunity to revise the manuscript to Dell's satisfaction, with Dell's editorial assistance," Judge Lombard declared. "Having failed to do so, Dell itself was in breach of contract, and Whedon was entitled to retain the advances paid to her."

With a sort of retroactive "Ya-a-a-h" at Bennett, I saved the clipping, admiring Jill's nerve or toughness or whatever it was. It went on to tell of her new contract with Doubleday for an advance of $15,000. "In accordance with Doubleday's editorial suggestions," said the *Times*, "Miss Whedon added two chapters and made line changes on the balance of the manuscript." Two or three years later *A Good Sport* was published.

I too, after what seemed an eternity, found another publisher. One day in April, Phyllis called me. "Jonathan Dolger says, 'Of course there's a book in it.' "

Jonathan Dolger was then an editor at Simon & Schuster. My log began to carry other entries about Jonathan and my old publishing house. Dick Simon was no longer there, but it was like a homecoming.

> Korda, now ed-in-chief of S&S—"We're very excited." $15,000 advance; 66⅔% of paperback; deliv. date, Oct. 1970

Of course ten thousand of that went to Random House and five hundred to my agent, who wouldn't repeat the commission of the first ten thousand, so what I had was forty-five hundred to see me through nearly two years of writing. But that paperback deal outweighed all money matters. Never before—or since—had I ever broken through the "unbreakable" practice of the entire publishing world, that on book club or paperback deals, it was fifty-fifty between author and publisher. Only a few authors had ever done better than fifty-fifty, and here, all unexpectedly, I had become one of them. I hadn't even known that Phyllis Jackson was going to try it, nor dreamed that she could persuade Simon & Schuster to agree to it.

A surge of new confidence sent me back to hard, steady "writing forward." *The Tenth Month* was turned in ahead of that contractual date, but S&S postponed pub day to January to accommodate Redbook, which had bought digest rights to it. It was taken by one of the Literary Guild's clubs, and on Thanksgiving Eve came a telephone call that dwarfed all the other good news. It was from Jonathan Dolger.

"Are you standing up or sitting down?" he began.

"Jonathan, *what?*"

"The paperback auction closed today. Three houses made offers, all of them over a hundred thousand."

"Over a—oh, Jonathan!"

I had known there was an auction scheduled for some time or other, but Jonathan had decided to keep silent about the exact date, to spare me the last hours of nail-biting suspense. No wonder the first part of my conversation with him that Thanksgiving Eve was limited to variations of "Oh, Jonathan."

When my book at last appeared there was a sprinkling of cool or cranky reviews, but virtually all the rest were wonderful. The one that was to be quoted in all the ads, and used on paperback jackets and on foreign editions, was by Edwin Fadiman, Jr. in the Saturday Review. "A celebration of life," he called it.

> In the tradition of *Gentleman's Agreement* [it] deals with prejudice, the prejudice of middle-class, neo-Puritan morality. Wise, witty, loving without being sentimental, sexual without being pornographic, *The Tenth Month* . . . has something important to say, and says it almost perfectly.

_____ CHAPTER _____

FOURTEEN

SOMETIMES I MARVEL AT the resilience I must have had to manage to continue writing during that difficult period of the abandoned "stylish novel," and then my abrupt departure from Random House.

As the first word of trouble came from Bennett, I was slowly recuperating from a severe pneumonia, not the usual viral type but a staphylococcus variety that, according to my physician and the specialist he summoned, was far more life-threatening.

I was at New York Hospital for ten days, and in an oxygen tent for nearly all of them; in those days hospitals had not yet come to the tiny tubes in your nostrils for oxygen; you were zipped into a large square tent of transparent plastic that extended over your upper body. I had been recovering from a nasty flu, but it suddenly got worse. I had been admitted at nearly midnight—taken by ambulance to the emergency room after my doctor, on the phone, heard that my breathing had become very shallow and constricted.

Though I was shifted to a private room the following morning, the only bed available that first night was in a semiprivate one so narrow that the two beds in it barely afforded passageway between them. And it was on that first night, when I was not yet feeling any relief from the oxygen being fed into my tent, that something happened that was later on to become one of the things I remembered most vividly about my whole hospital stay.

In the early hours of the morning a priest entered the room and made his way carefully to the woman in the bed opposite mine. I could see that she was very ill; a nurse had told me she had just had surgery, and that only a few days before her husband had died.

Through my transparent cubicle I could hear the priest murmuring prayers and words of comfort to her. I could have reached out and touched his black robes. After he made the final sign of the cross over the woman he had come to see, he turned toward my bed, leaning down toward me as if he would speak. I zipped open one corner of my oxygen tent.

"Are you a Catholic, madame?" he asked gently.

"No," I heard myself gasping, "but my daughter-in-law is."

That was enough for the good priest. He made the sign of the cross over me and murmured prayers, wishing me a complete and speedy recovery. When I thanked him, I really meant it.

Only much later did I begin to be amused by my own part in that little episode. During the war people used to say, "There are no atheists in foxholes." I don't think I surrendered my lifelong agnosticism even for an instant that night in the oxygen tent, but maybe some scared little voice inside me suddenly said, "Why pass up any chances?"

Nor do I believe I was really that scared, though it is true that I was absurdly upset when a student nurse, obviously a product of our celebrity culture, excitedly announced to me, "Tallulah Bankhead had the same staph pneumonia you have—she's in Roosevelt Hospital— she just died."

It is also true that when I finally made it through what is generally called "the crisis," I did ask my doctor if he had been at all worried about the outcome.

"Only about the long delay in getting you on oxygen."

I knew he meant possible brain damage. I was still in the oxygen tent, still too weak to do much reading. The Sunday *Times* was left unopened except for the book section, which I had asked a nurse to dig out for me.

Now I asked for the magazine section, a pencil and something to lean on, drawing them all into my plastic breathing box. I turned to the page with the big weekly crossword puzzle and the biweekly double crostic beneath it, ignored the crossword but went at the double crostic with a rush.

Half an hour later I made a telephone call to Bry Benjamin, my physician. His nurse, probably thinking something had gone wrong, put me through immediately.

"No brain damage," I told him. "I just solved the Sunday double crostic, one-two-three." . . .

On the first full day I was in the hospital, my sister Alice suddenly appeared. I was surprised, because once again we were estranged and had been for several months. I could scarcely remember why; I know we had argued hotly when she refused to sign a gun-control petition on the grounds that it was "just a pretext to disarm the blacks." There was also a set-to because she was convinced I had "made a play" for one of her daughter's beaus, a young playwright in his twenties, forty years my junior, though she knew I had always disliked dating any-body even five years younger. More serious still was her resentment because once, at a family weekend, I had said it was nice that her granddaughter was named Laura, despite her having told me on several different occasions that she had been angry at her son and his wife for the way they ignored her protests about the choice of that particular name.

The immediate cause of this latest separation was that one night the previous summer, during a bridge game where I was being teacher, I was short-tempered and irritable. In the days following I had phoned her twice, only to have her hang up, leaving me trembling with frustration and resentment. Then I had written her at some length, hoping to patch things up before they could harden into another brick wall. She never replied.

Now, seeing her come through my door at the hospital, I was sure Mike or my doctor had called her to say I was seriously ill. She stayed only a short while; I was too sick as yet to say much; she was restrained, and the oxygen tent was in itself an obstacle to any real conversation.

After I was well, the separation was resumed, and at last I had to accept it, as I had done years before. But as June 18, 1970 approached, I wrote to her once more.

Dear Alice,

And so we are seventy, and I at least can send you greetings and love left over from happier days, before you had to banish me to some Siberia (with one exception when I was in an oxygen tent—as if I were worth more consideration in an oxygen tent than out of it).

You have some insurmountable grievance against me, though

258

I doubt you could really explain it to any neutral listener. The first "exile" of thirteen years was based, you said, on your feeling that I meant to "turn Paul over to the FBI." This one can scarcely be because of a ten-second tiff at a bridge table two years ago, or even because I said it pleased me to have little Laura have the same name I had.

Perhaps the analysts could discover the hidden complexities that engender such dislike or hate, strong enough to make you hurt or insult me, rob me of the feeling of family, of Lizzie and Paul and their four children, of yourself, the only living member of the family who is my age and generation.

Perhaps the analysts know why I have never disliked or hated you in turn, and do not now. I mourn at times for my lost sister; at other times I grow furious at the way you killed me off without giving a reason, like *Red Channels* or Joe McCarthy; at still other times, I can laugh that though many people have some regard for me, my own sister cuts me dead, with all her friends and relations cutting me dead too.

But today we are seventy and life is nearing its close, and something in me is still strong enough to send you a word on this big birthday, and hope that the rest of it may go well for you.

Happy Birthday,

I could not know that this was to be the last letter I would ever write her. Nor that it would be nearly ten full years before I would ever see or speak to her again.

She could not know either. But this birthday letter of mine went unanswered too.

There were other sadnesses, other griefs, in my family life during those years—in what family is there none? But as I wrote further and further into this second part of my autobiography, inevitably approaching the question of how much I can write freely about, and how much I would need that reticence which I had earlier promised myself—

Let me take the liberty of setting down again those particular sentences, which now become more pertinent than ever.

I don't mean that I will permit myself no reticences, nor that I will feel obliged to weep in public over whatever griefs and

259

disappointments and sorrows there may have been along with the delights and joys. I simply promise that if it is written here, it will be true.

Those lines gained strength and meaning as I wrote further and further into my life, and somehow, in that undersea meadow where grow the small green shoots of conviction, there began to appear a line of demarcation, particularly about my sons and their lives.

When they were little, in school, in their teens, in their college years, even a little beyond, then they were my children, and I felt a total freedom to write them into my own story.

But later, when they left home, when they had lives of their own, when, in short, they became men, I could no longer feel that their lives were an intrinsic part of my account of *my* life. And so I slowly began to be consciously aware of that line of demarcation that had been growing greener and stronger without my knowing it.

At last I can claim it; at last I can put it into words: of anything painful between my grown sons and myself, I will claim that reticence I had instinctively written of, four years ago in the late summer of 1981. Somehow I will know when I can permit myself an exception, and that exception will arise only in case there be some vital, inescapable connection between my family life and my life's work of writing.

Perhaps such an inescapable connection began on a June day just before the woeful decade of the sixties had run its course. I did not recognize it as such at the time, however, though I did know at once that it held a kind of fierce magnetism that drew my entire attention and held it fast.

There was a small story in the newspapers about a street riot the night before in Sheridan Square down in Greenwich Village, a riot outside the Stonewall Inn, though its doors were padlocked and its windows boarded up.

The reports were brief and vague, partly burying the fact that Stonewall Inn was a gay bar. The trouble had started a day or two earlier, when the police had raided the place over its liquor license; there had been what the police termed "resistance," and thirteen people had been arrested.

But that was background; the night before an even larger crowd had gathered, a hundred or two hundred people. When the police cars arrived they stood their ground; there was none of the usual disappearing act, "to keep out of trouble" when cops arrived at gay bars. This time they fought back; they answered the flailing nightsticks with hurled stones and bottles and coins; they even uprooted a parking meter and used it as a battering ram to force open the padlocked door.

The papers didn't report all the details then; they did not know then —surely the participants themselves did not know then—that these Stonewall Riots were later to be called the birth of the gay movement in America, the Boston Tea Party of gay liberation.

I don't think I was perceptive enough as yet to realize that something like this was inevitable. The world of the sixties had been seething with uprising and protest, the civil rights movement, women's rights, sit-ins at college buildings and universities to protest investments in South Africa, and a year earlier, after the assassination of Martin Luther King, the riots in a hundred cities ablaze in rage, and above all, so potent a resistance to the war in Vietnam that President Lyndon Baines Johnson had to strike his name as a possible candidate for re-election in the fall.

But as I read about the Stonewall Riots I could not be objective enough to know that there was a blood kinship between this resistance and all the other resistances. The one thing I did know was that I was passionately held by every word I could read about it. From time to time I had already heard or read about gay clubs springing up on various campuses, groups of lesbians or gays forming their own groups, under names that included the word *gay* or *lesbian,* not old-fashioned societies with names that half concealed their identity, like the Mattachine Society or Daughters of Bilitis. These new gay groups were today's young who were, as the phrase went, "coming out of the closet," saying to their peers and to those in authority above them, "Yes, we are," each member saying, "Yes, I am gay."

Slowly it began to seep into my consciousness that what I was coming upon was not an occasional exception or bravery, but a *movement,* a surge of newness in the attitudes and emotions of people who were gay.

I did nothing active about it; I just read whatever I came across in the papers or magazines, and that was little enough. But I recognized that for me, anything to do with homosexuality anywhere now bore an invisible stamp, Top Priority, and after Stonewall Inn, I found myself beginning to go to the library for books that I had either read years ago, as far back as my twenties, or books I had never read at all but knew were connected with this major theme of my life.

261

They were all novels; it had not yet occurred to me to start any serious study of whatever had been published medically or psychoanalytically about homosexuality. I can not believe that at that time I had any solid notion that there might have been anything to study except old work by Krafft-Ebing, Havelock Ellis and, of course, Sigmund Freud. They were all nineteenth-century or early twentieth; I probably relegated them all to the archives of the past, though I remember a reservation in my mind about Freud, thinking I ought to look up some essays of his I vaguely knew about, not dealing with dreams or infantile sex, but sex in general.

Instead I read André Gide's *Corydon,* which I had never read, and *The Well of Loneliness,* by the English writer Radclyffe Hall, a story of two lesbian women that I had read just after college, when it was the sensation—and shock—of the publishing world on both sides of the Atlantic. I reread parts of Proust, especially those dealing with Albertine and the Baron Charlus. And I read some modern novels dealing with homosexuality, good ones and bad ones, *The City and The Pillar,* by the young Gore Vidal, *Giovanni's Room,* by James Baldwin, even some books I found distasteful because they went in for the specifics of sexual contact I always found in abominable taste, whether the specifics were homosexual or heterosexual.

I also read, with a delighted sense of discovery, Mary Renault's novels about ancient Greece, all of which I found beautifully imaginative and literate, *The Last of the Wine* and all the others.

I can't remember when I first began to notice that although all of the Mary Renault novels dealing with homosexual love in the Greece of Alexander the Great, of Plato, of Socrates and Theseus were joyous, even noble, the various modern novels I read about contemporary life among homosexuals always ended in pain and grief, a suicide in one, a betrayal in another, a murder, always a tragedy as an inevitable part of the story. This was true even in *The Charioteer,* by Mary Renault herself, a story about two men in an English hospital after World War Two, one wounded and the other slightly crippled.

I have always been a voracious reader, perhaps a compulsive reader, as far back as my childhood in Jamaica when I went to the public library every afternoon of the week to get a book to read that night when my homework was done. When half a century later I was in England for the publication of *First Papers,* that habit had not diminished, and so, when my publisher there, Charles Pick, discovered that I knew little of Trollope beyond one of the Barchester novels I had been bored to death with at Cornell, he presented me with a Trollope I had never even heard of.

"You'll not be bored with *The Way We Live Now*," he said, and after five pages I knew he was right. Thereafter I could not stop reading Anthony Trollope. In the next two years I bought no less than sixteen of his novels, the best-known ones and the lesser ones, and read every one of them in one continuing bout of enjoyment.

So I was by nature a reader, and when I found my interests turning to novels dealing with a theme that had become one of my own major themes, I once again "could not stop."

And imperceptibly a sense arose in me that there was some sort of lack in what I was reading, an absence of completeness, an omission I could not specify. Again and again I tried to dig down into that mystifying chasm, hoping to answer my own query about what it was I wanted that was not there.

I never could; always I came to the ending of a novel with the conviction that something else that ought to be there had been ignored. Each time I would think, Well, sometime or other I'll figure out why I feel so dissatisfied, even with the books I'm sure are good books.

I don't mean to imply that at that time my whole attention, my whole mood, was one continuum of feeling about the subject of homosexuality. Life rarely permits straight lines in anybody's development, at any age, and in my busy days there were the usual number of detours.

One of the most satisfying occured just about the time of the birthday that made me write that futile letter to my sister Alice: I had a special houseguest for the two full weeks spanning that birthday, one who was like no other houseguest in my entire seventy years. It was a two-and-a-half-year-old named Sarah, my granddaughter, my first grandchild.

Younger women, women in their forties or early fifties, often dreaded that turn of the wheel which made them grandmothers. But when Sarah was born I knew only delight that at long last I had achieved that status.

Everything that's said about doting grandmothers is probably true. Mike and Ann had been married for over two years before they had a baby, so I was more than qualified for any doting role. Now they were expecting their second child in the fall and wanted to get away on a vacation while they still could. So they were off to England and Sarah came to live with me, complete with her beloved cat, Pidgett.

The first day went without a hitch, but the first night brought back to me the all-but-forgotten sounds of a small child's heartbroken crying—"Where's my mommy, where's my daddy?"

Mike had installed Sarah's padded playpen in the extra bedroom; it was roomy and comfortable; she took her afternoon naps in it rather than in her crib, and we all were certain she would feel more at home in it than in a strange bed. When I prepared it for the night, with her own blanket and toys and pet animals, all was well while I sat beside her telling her a story—that too took me back to the long-ago era of storytelling at bedtime. Soon Sarah's eyes were closing.

But when I left the room, she was instantly awake and crying. "I want my mommy, I want my daddy." I told her that mommy and daddy would be shopping for wonderful new toys in England; it didn't help. Nothing could console her, no further storytelling, no glass of water, no sip of milk, *nothing*.

Should I let her sleep with me in my own bed? Some dim memory of Dr. Spock's tenets told me no.

Then I had an idea.

I went to my own room; there was a small armchair in one corner, old-fashioned French provincial in style, with upholstered arms, and in another corner a low circular chair, also upholstered and also with arms. I hauled them together, right near my own bed, face to face; luckily their seats were very nearly level with each other, and the arms made a protective ring around them, like the sides of a crib. I spread a folded sheet over the two seats and placed one of my down pillows at one end of this new arrangement. Then I went to fetch Sarah.

As I carried her into my room, she was still sobbing uncontrollably.

"Look, Sarah, it's a special Sarah bed. You're going to sleep right next to Grandma Laura all night long."

I put her down so that she faced me, and I stretched out on my own bed. I kept talking to her quietly about how nice it was to have a special Sarah bed, and soon there came the spasmodic gasping breaths to space out the halting sobbing. At last she fell asleep.

For half a month I again had the pleasure of watching a child I loved at the start of life, of seeing the tiny day-by-day accretions of learning —"What's that box for?" (my electric pencil sharpener); "Why do those birds stay on the ground?" (pigeons in Central Park); "Can I push them down?" (the keys of my typewriter).

And when Sarah's visit was over, I went back to the other extreme of watching someone I loved approaching the end of life. Eric had steadily grown more feeble in the last year. Now he was living in a small hotel on East Fiftieth Street in a two-room suite where he could have maid service, room service and, more importantly, immediate help in an emergency.

He did not come to my house any more for that hour or two in an afternoon; I went to visit him instead. He was working on his autobiography—therapy or literary effort, the sheets were piling up, though it was never to get much beyond his first years at Time Inc. in the middle thirties. So there would be nothing about his becoming a novelist and writing *Mr. Blandings Builds His Dream House,* and nothing about his reaching the strength to acknowledge that he was not just a social drinker but an alcoholic whose only hope lay in joining Alcoholics Anonymous and rigorously sticking to the vow, "I will not take a drink today."

But we couldn't know then that it would be cut off halfway. I longed to read some of his manuscript but he never offered it. "Not until it's finished," he would say, and I understood, for with the exception of reading the first scene of my first novel to Dick Simon and Andrea, and the further exception of asking Mike to read the rejected pages of *The Tenth Month* while I was so tense about finding another publisher, I had never been one of the authors who took it for granted that friends or family were eager to read work in progress. And Eric was doubly not one of them.

But I was glad to see his manuscript grow. Writing was one of the pleasures he could still count on. We still went to the Philharmonic, but only occasionally; it was still my treat, with a sadly necessary extra feature. I would always arrange for a car and driver for the evening, to pick me up first, then go for Eric at his hotel, then on to Lincoln Center. After the concert ended we let the audience file out before we took our own leave. The car was always waiting, and we then did the tour in reverse.

Music still meant surcease and release to Eric, but one day he did something that told me that music itself was closing down for him. I had gone for one of my brief visits to his hotel; by now he had a nurse for most of each day, and once, as I was leaving, she took me out to the elevator.

"Mr. Hodgins," she said, "always seems much better for a while *after.*"

On that particular visit, though, he didn't seem better at all. He had been listening to a record, and the nurse had switched off the power as I came in and returned the record to its dust jacket. On the coffee table in front of him there was a beautiful album of Mahler's nine symphonies, and he seemed to be staring at it until the nurse left the room. It was a big album, especially bound in heavy leather, a gift to him some years before from William S. Paley, president of CBS, whom Eric had worked with during President Truman's administration on the Paley Commission on natural resources in Washington.

He turned the album around on the table so that it was facing me. "I can no longer lift it," he said. "I want you to have it."

At that time I had not yet begun to understand Mahler's music as deeply as Eric did, nor to admire and love it the way he did. But after I went home, bearing that too-heavy album with me, my own Mahler education began as I kept playing Eric's records over, and over, and over.

But before that year of 1970 ended I received something else that was to stir me so fiercely that it marked the year for me. It was a letter from Chris.

Just as 1958 was always to be, for me, "the year I got Chris' letter telling me," so this letter marked 1970 as "the year Chris told me he had come out."

He was still a midwesterner, having finished his postgraduate days at the University of Chicago, living and working in Detroit. This was a four-page single-spaced letter full of all sorts of matters, some about politics, some about coming home for Christmas, some about his efforts to find the best secondhand car with the money I'd given him as a celebration over the big paperback deal on *The Tenth Month*.

But the part that had moved me so deeply came on the last page, just before the close, and he introduced it by saying he wanted to raise one more point—gay liberation.

He was sure, he said, that I had heard something about such a movement by this time, and then said he had been in it for a long while, first in Chicago and then in Detroit, where he was in a group of about thirty people. Every sort of politics, he said, could be found in the group "from radical to establishment to utopian," but that was for "another conversation."

The main thing it meant to all of them was the end of secretiveness, a determination to define their "problem" not as their own "deviation" but as society's persecution, whether by police and officialdom or in the form of psychological theories . . .

They would no longer accept any definition of themselves as "sick," he went on, nor would they be afraid to fight back, that they had already confronted employers, police, churches.

He ended his letter by saying that for all the reasons that made these things difficult to talk about in a family, he remained uneasy about telling me all this, but that he wanted to do it before coming home for the holidays.

As I read his words I had to keep brushing at my eyes so that I could see. The courage, I thought, the young courage, just as I had over that other letter when he was only seventeen. Now he was a man of twenty-nine, and he too had made the decision to reject the world's ancient judgments.

I remembered his babyhood, when he was a "head-banger," I remembered him as a toddler, the "no-I-won't" kid, and I remembered his school years when he was so often in rebellion against all authority.

And now I re-evaluated all those signs, seeing them perhaps as the early signs of independence, the seeds of this mature strength to say "No you won't" to a culture that would force him to live out a life of apology and deceit.

I telephoned him my admiration and approval and my love. I couldn't tell him that there was something different now in that love, a kind of obeisance to what he had become.

An end to secretiveness. I had hated it for years, hated it for him, hated it for myself. For twelve years his secret, of course, had been my secret, more closely guarded than that other secret I had kept from the world for twenty-three years. That other one I had longed to shout forth; this one I too wanted to guard, was even glad that I had no choice. In public I had laughed at jokes about homosexuals, fearful that angry protest might "give something away." When somebody would ask, "And your other son—is he married?" I would offhandedly say, "Still playing the field, I guess."

I could not even express my feelings when I read about the Stonewall Riots. Mike knew the secret, my sister Alice knew it, and I had told Carroll and Eric. But for any real revelation of my feelings, for any real discussion and probing, I was limited, once more, to refresher sessions with Dr. Raymond Gosselin.

And so, for me too, a new era began the day I read this letter from

267

Chris. I cannot remember how much time had to elapse after that first shock of relief and pleasure in reading it, and reading it again, and then reading it once more—I cannot even guess how long it was before it began to occur to me that Chris' life was not the only life that had changed by his decision.

But the time did come, with a kind of shock and pleasure of its own, when I found myself thinking, If he's come out of the closet, then surely I can come out too.

FIFTEEN

ONE MORNING, IN THE first week of the new year, a strange voice on the telephone asked, "May I speak to Mrs. Hobson?"

"This is she."

"This is Rod Hodgins. I wanted to call you before you read it in the newspapers."

"Oh, Rod."

"My father died last night, and I know he would have wanted—"

I can't remember what I said or how I thanked him for his thoughtfulness. I can't remember whether I wept when I hung up. All I do remember is that off and on all day, I kept thinking, Eric's gone, Eric's gone. But the page in my log for January 7, 1971, has two entries, each two words long, one high at the top, the other down at the bottom.

Eric died.
Concert, alone.

The obituaries were long and did honor to all his achievements—I still have the one from the *Times.* Memorial services were held a week later in the chapel of St. Bartholomew's Church on Park Avenue, and again I had the need to go in only at the last moment so that I could find a silent seat in an anonymous pew, far removed from all the Time and Fortune people who would be there.

I knew that Eric's wife and children were seated close to the altar, but something restrained me from more than a glance in their direction, mainly at his son and daughter. For some reason I kept hearing Eric's bitter words, nearly eleven years earlier, as he told me that at Lenox Hill Hospital, in the first hours of his stroke, when they talked of notifying his family, he had managed to inform his physician, mainly in vehement sign language and shakes of his head, that it would only be worse for him if they permitted his wife to come up from Florida to be with him.

And as I listened to the minister's beautifully rounded phrases of eulogy, I sat there imagining how delightedly and with what wit my Eric would have ridiculed all the pious and standardized clichés.

In that week between Roderic Hodgins' telephone call and the memorial services, publication day had arrived for *The Tenth Month*. I had sent Eric his copy some months before, one of the first ten copies I had received, and it had touched him in a highly personal sense, for through it, despite all the changes in the plot, he had relived that first year we had spent together so many years before, when we were still so young, so free of illness or darkness about the future.

So the year 1971 began for me in a deeply troubled way, not about my work, but about the totality of my life as I could estimate it, after Chris' letter, after Eric's death. On the surface I managed as well as one was expected to, just after publication of an already successful new book. I took a vacation at St. Maartens in the Netherlands West Indies; I busied myself on my return doing the required cutting job on a story McCall's had bought for a handsome price, one I had written a year or so before, again a serious story—I had long ago given up on light romantic love stories. This one I had called "Deep Rap" because it was, in part, about a member of the hippie generation, but McCall's changed that to "Lost Girl," making it the only thing about the printed story I regretted.

But for all these activities, I was never really free from my persisting preoccupations. I remember no specific time when I finally could identify what I had felt was missing from all the novels I had been reading about homosexuality, but apparently my unconscious had kept busily searching, for at last the answer presented itself to me. It was not like a sudden turning on of an electric light by clicking a switch; it must have been more like the gradual shift, at dawn, from night's blackness to a dim grayness and then on to the clearness of early morning.

But at last I saw that in all those books, one person was always missing—a parent. Every character in every book might have been an orphan, existing solo, without a mother, without a father. Even the authors whose work I read with pleasure, I now realized, managed that orphanhood in the pages of their novels.

I knew that in real life those authors might have concern for their parents: Do they guess about me? Do they know? Should I tell them? Ought I spare them the pain of actually knowing?

But in their work, they gave themselves over to the minute re-creation of their own feelings, their own quandaries, their anger or pain or desolation. I had never found any thought of their mothers' and fathers' feelings, of *their* quandaries or anger or pain or desolation because a beloved son or daughter was homosexual.

Why hadn't I? Why wasn't there a novel about those parents?

The question seized me; it would not let go; it kept appearing and dissolving and then appearing once more.

A few weeks after I came back from St. Maartens, I asked Jonathan Dolger, my editor at Simon & Schuster, if he could come up to my house to talk about what might be my next novel, my seventh. My preamble must have startled him.

"I may never let this book be published, Jonathan, and I won't know whether it's yes or no for a couple of years. But it always takes me two or three years to write any novel, and by the time it's finished I should know one way or the other."

Pledging him to secrecy until I did know, I then told him about Chris and his recent letter telling me he was "out."

"But I'd have to be sure that it's not just out in Detroit and Chicago," I went on, "not just among his own friends. Otherwise I could never turn the manuscript over to you or anybody else."

I told him of my voluminous reading in this special world, and of my conviction that one aspect of life in that world, always overlooked, might make a valid theme for a novel. I hadn't anything like a firm plot to offer him as I went on; all I knew was that my central character would be a parent or two parents. I was thinking of a story about two families, one that was intelligent and decent when their son told them he was gay, and the other who took the more usual reaction: Never Darken My Door Again.

No editor could have responded with a greater immediacy. "Go ahead," he urged, "start it, of course we'll keep it secret, but begin writing it." He talked about what he knew of people who were gay, of how he felt about the new gay movement, and the more we talked the surer I was that I could write that "overlooked" novel.

I began a different kind of reading, no longer just novels. My library was not one of the branches of the public library system; you pay annual dues of $60 a year at the New York Society Library, but you may take several reference books home at once, and keep them for weeks, even months if you become buried in some sort of continuing research.

I don't mean that I was an ignoramus about where modern psychiatry stood on the subject of homosexuality. Like most intelligent people, I knew the main points of the Kinsey Report that had so startled the world of the late forties, about the prevalence of homosexuality in every society in the world, in every culture, in every group, knew that ten percent of all males were homosexual, and a slightly lesser percent of all females.

But far more pressing was my interest in the less famous Wolfenden Report, a study ordered back in the fifties by the British government, about whether the state or the law should have any power in regard to homosexuals, or as its chairman, Sir John Wolfenden put it, to "consenting adults acting in private."

This Wolfenden Committee, I discovered, was no little group of liberal psychiatrists, but a large and illustrious gathering of judges of the High Court, sociologists, members of Parliament, professional women, attorneys, ministers meeting in more than sixty sessions over a period of years. Sir John himself was an educator and sociologist, chancellor of Reading University, and his report had been hailed as one of "the major social documents of the twentieth century."

In the next months, indeed in the next years, I was to read, to study, to take notes on many books by many modern psychiatrists. Many of them I bought to make into my own private library; some twenty are still in my possession. Writing now about that time, and about those books, I find myself turning to them again as if I were again beginning to do an essential kind of research, but soon I see that this turning backward is an escape mechanism, trying to delay writing about that long-ago storm of anxiety that had compelled me to read and study, read and study.

Once before in this volume, I let myself shift from the first person to the third, when I quoted from "a novel that was to be published seventeen years later." Perhaps I may yield again to that inner necessity for a surrogate and turn to a woman I called Tessa in that novel. She too was making a study of dozens of books by experts in the field.

And as [she] proceeded, she would marvel at the fluctuating opinions of the highest authorities. As surely as one psychiatrist wrote a paper pronouncing homosexuality an illness or disease, another would declare that there was nothing ill or diseased about it; as soon as one body of new research offered proof that homosexuals were neurotic or even psychotic, a counter body of new research would offer proof that tests of two scientifically controlled groups of men, one group heterosexual, the other homosexual, both groups matched for I.Q., environment, age, economic factors, parental influences—that these most scientific of tests revealed no differences between the two groups on any level of human behavior or character or potential or achievement, apart from the single level of sex.

Her overriding reaction to such manifold disparities of theory or opinion within the world of psychiatry or analysis had at first been a heightened confusion and a nearly plaintive impatience with all the warring points of view. Later, a good deal later, this gave way to a kind of thin hope. It was a new kind of hope ... unrelated to that long-ago hope for miracles that would turn homosexuals into heterosexuals. This was not only alien to that frantic earlier hope; it was on another plateau of thinking and feeling.

So little was yet sure. So little known. So many fine minds were out there in the world, in England, in this country, in Denmark and Sweden and France and everywhere else, thinking and theorizing and testing and formulating new approaches to the problem of homosexuality. From this sort of inquiry in other fields, this manifold, warring, contradictory inquiry, all knowledge had finally emerged; could it be that man was now at some new threshold about the age-old subject of the homosexual?

She had begun to wonder about that, and with the first tentative thought of such a possibility, her life seemed to move a notch from where it had always been. She hoped for nothing less than that threshold; she could feel it off there somewhere, waiting to be crossed, perhaps already crossed. . . .

She whose life had so unexpectedly become meshed with the thousand variables embraced by that single word, homosexual, with all the thousand questions of potential, stigma, acceptance, disability, persecution, she who cared so intensely within herself about the world's history of rejection, now could find in this very disparity of opinion among the various "experts" the first seeds of change for the future, change that might carry with it change for her son, change for all the other sons and daughters of all parents who had been unable as yet to move that single notch.

Thinking of them all, her heart filled.

My heart fills again as I copy out those words I wrote so painfully fifteen years ago. It brings back the intensity of that longing to learn, to know more than I ever had known about the once-taboo subject of homosexuality. And when I was well-launched on this new learning, I found myself increasingly committed to pursuing it, as if I had signed on for the most important seminar of my life.

And I knew that I would never cut a class, would never skimp on an assignment—and that there never would come a time when I would give myself a final grade and feel, "That's the end of it."

Sometimes one escapes serious concerns by shifting to light ones, but at other times the most effective escape is found in a switch to some other serious concern, though this may arise from a more impersonal quadrant of life, and even have some side effects of amusement and speedy satisfaction.

So it was with me in the spring and early summer of 1971, while I was still searching for ways to start my new novel, and it concerned, of all things, a new weekly television show that had just won the Emmy Award as best new comedy of the year, "All in the Family."

The first show I'd caught had been enough for me, all about the horrors of a black family moving into one's neighborhood, but now the Emmy and the huge promotion about being number one in the Nielsen ratings, made me wonder about this new phenomenon of bigotry-for-laughs, and I began to watch the reruns.

Week by week I grew more offended and more convinced that I'd never feel right if I just kept silent about this newest outpouring of racial and religious prejudice. Way back in the late thirties I had been impelled to write an exposé of the way some of New York's most prominent, most influential—and most conservative—people had managed to kill off an anti-Nazi project, Freedom Pavilion.

At that time I had no larger hope than to see it published in The Nation, with its limited circulation, a seven-page insert that in fact became possible only when a friend of mine put up the money to pay for the extra paper my piece required.

But now I thought I could count on being published in a newspaper known the world over, perhaps the New York *Times*. My first call was to Seymour Peck, then the editor of the Sunday Arts and Leisure section, a man I didn't know. I told him I wanted to "write a hostile piece" about "All in the Family" and wondered if he might be interested in seeing it. His immediate yes, with the proviso that I hold it to 1,500 words, started the process that was to take most of my working time for several months, meeting all kinds of people in the antidefamation and civil-liberties field, telephoning to arrange for meetings, interviewing their officers, doing other kinds of research.

Nor did I neglect CBS, the network so jubilant about its big new hit, again pointing out to the press department and others there that I was "writing a hostile piece" about it. I asked if I might see early reviews and even a couple of kinescopes of shows I had missed. A vice-president there, asking only to remain anonymous, saw to it that I had access to everything I asked for and answered every question I asked—with just one exception, on which I got nowhere. He'd call me back, he said, after calling Hollywood, where the show originated, but when he did call me back, it was still nowhere. It was as if my question was somehow unanswerable. Or indelicate.

It was late summer before I finally sent in my piece, "The Laughable Business of Bigotry," totalling not 1,500 words but about 10,000. The page in my log for August 27 makes me live again that first jolt of pleasure.

Seymour Peck phoned!! "It's staggering—I am staggered by it —not going to cut a line—going to try to put it on front-page of section, not on TV page—will run Sept. 12."

It appeared at the official start of the new TV season; not a line was cut, nothing changed except for the title, under a huge picture of Archie Bunker, a title no reader could ever skip.

As I Listened to
Archie Say, "Hebe" . . .

I have a most peculiar complaint about the bigotry in the hit TV comedy, "All in the Family." There's not enough of it.

Hebe, spade, spic, coon, Polack—these are words that its central character, Archie Bunker, is forever using, plus endless variations, like jungle bunnies, black beauties, the chosen people, yenta, gook, chink, spook and so on. Quite a splashing display of bigotry, but I repeat, nowhere near enough of it. . . . The Number One Nielsen, I'm told, means an audience of some 40 million families per week . . . 100 million people. Old people, young people, black, white, Protestant, Catholic, Jewish, well-educated, ill-educated, secure, insecure—100 million people every week.

The reviews, I said, had mostly been raves, though now and again, a critic called it "painfully offensive," or found it "crackling with racist remarks . . . crude and coarse," or spoke of "gratuitous insults," adding it was "irresponsible to air a show like this . . . when our nation is torn by racism."

But the majority of reviews were ecstatic, one of the most widely quoted being by Cleveland Amory, whom I dubbed "that crusader against cruelty to animals, the four-legged kind." He called it "Not just the best-written, best-directed and best-acted show on television, it is the best show on television."

A few phrases that kept popping up in many of the reviews pulled me up short: "an honest show" and "honest laughter" and a "lovable bigot." Norman Lear, writer of the show and one of its producers, was often quoted. "My father was what you might call a lovable bigot, as Archie is."

> A lovable bigot. Your friendly neighborhood bigot. This is an honest show. This is the way it really is . . . I had no less than 97 clippings from all over the country . . . and these bouquets cropped up again and again. . . .
>
> I began to be haunted by the notion that there was something I had to get hold of . . . something the critics weren't saying, not even the . . . experts I sought out in the field of race relations . . .

Most of them seemed not to have taken any position on "All in the Family." I talked to the top people at the Anti-Defamation League of B'nai B'rith, to the National Conference of Christians and Jews, to Dore Schary, Mayor Lindsay's then recently appointed commissioner of Cultural Affairs, to Roy Wilkins' secretary at the NAACP, who repeatedly managed not to let me reach Mr. Wilkins himself. I also talked to the heads of other organizations that resented bigotry, at the Catholic Archdiocese, the Italian American Civil Rights League, the public relations office of the Commonwealth of Puerto Rico—everywhere I met a sort of "no position taken" or "no comment," though at the same time I sensed an eagerness to see such a piece written, and a quick response to my point of view, and even to my awkward question.

. . . That question was tied into the special point I was trying to get hold of. Somewhere in there among all the phone calls and interviews, I began to go back to the night I first really tangled with "All in the Family" . . . It was the night of the Emmy Awards, and it involved the word Hebe.

Johnny Carson was the glamorous master of ceremonies that night, with a glamorous audience of TV professionals, actors, writers, directors, producers, the works—and beyond them the national audience looking on. Just after the announcement [of the winner] and, of course, in the spirit of the show, Johnny Carson wisecracked, "Norman Lear—a nice guy for a Hebe." The audience roared with laughter.

I suppose Norman Lear laughed too. Would he have laughed, I suddenly wondered, if Johnny Carson had said, "Norman Lear, a nice guy for a kike?"

Unthinkable. Johnny Carson would never never—

I know he wouldn't. Besides, it was never never used in the show. Hebe, yes; chosen people, yes; yenta, yes; yid, yes. But kike? Never.

I began to listen for it as I began my little study of the reruns. Never. And sheeny? Never.

Had Norman Lear never realized that what bigots really called Jews was kike or sheeny? That they didn't really go around talking about the chosen people or one of that tribe or yenta? That their own words, the words they actually used were kike and sheeny? Then why did Norman Lear, in this honest portrayal of the bigot next door, never use either?

And that other word. Where was that one, among the spades and coons and jungle bunnies and black beauties? I was listening to the shows regularly by then . . . jotting down the actual words Archie was so free with, and I never once heard it. But do the bigots of this world really talk about spades moving in next door, or not breaking bread with no jungle bunnies, or signing petitions to keep black beauties from ruining real estate values on the street?

You know the word they use. The one word, the hideous word.

Unthinkable too. Don't even print it. Nigger.

You know and I know and Mr. Lear knows and the anonymous vice-president of Press Relations at CBS knows that Archie Bunker in the flesh would be holding forth about niggers moving in next door, and not breaking bread with no niggers, and getting up a petition for keeping niggers from wrecking real estate values on the street.

Everybody knows it. Then why doesn't this honest show use the real words that real bigots always use?

Is there a little list of Forbidden Words floating around CBS? Is it a little list imposed by Mr. Lear himself? Or is it a little list imposed by the Program Practices Department, and the CBS executives in charge of that department?

That was my one big question. Instinctively I knew the answer, but tied into it was that other point: What was that list for? Were the honest producer and the responsible network trying to make bigotry more acceptable? Were they trying to clean it up, deodorize it, make millions of people more comfy about hearing it, indulging in it?

It strikes me that, unconsciously or consciously, that's just what they were doing. And of course it was the essential trick, to make this show laughable not only to the bigots out there, but also to the "bigotees," the very Hebes and coons and spics and Polacks themselves.

Do you think any of the nation's blacks would laugh if Archie Bunker constantly said nigger? Do you think many Jews would laugh if he said kike?

I gather that in the first show he did say yid, for nearly every one of the early reviews include that little word, but then something drastic must have happened, for yid was not once said in all the shows I saw myself.

Another missing word was Mafia, though I did catch one remark about a dago artist painting a ceiling in Rome. Missing also was any name-calling of Catholics. None of that "hotline to the Vatican" and "Pope in the White House" that was so rampant among bigots in the 1960 election, not even any micks and Irish micks.

Strange, all these omissions. But then there are some 20 to 35 million first- and second-generation Italian-Americans in this country, and some 13 million Irish-Americans, and, often overlapping, over 48 million Catholics, and if you got *them* good and sore, as well as nine million Spanish-speaking people and six million Jews and 23 million blacks, where would your Nielsen ratings be?

And there you have the basis for my peculiar complaint: there's nowhere near enough bigotry in "All in the Family," not by a long sight. How about showing the real thing for a while before accepting any more praise for honest shows and honest laughter? What about laying it on the line about bigots, and then see whether CBS switchboards light up with nothing but cheers?

But this is supposed to be a comedy! I know, but a network is supposed to care about the public interest . . .

To be among the first to teach impressionable children that they're not wanted in certain neighborhoods, that there's something that makes people laugh at them and look down on them and call them names, seems to me callous, even cruel. Indeed, to teach other children that it's quite all right to go around saying spade and Hebe and coon and spic—for of course kids always imitate what they see on TV—that seems to me pretty cruel too.

I went into a discussion then of laughter and cruel laughter, and the distinctions between them, of jokes that hurt and jokes that don't, of words that wound and words that do not. Of course CBS would never never use words that were *sure* to hurt or wound—and at once I was back at my indiscreet and awkward question—Was there a little list of Forbidden Words, that list nobody had ever yet acknowledged? Was my question doomed to get nowhere?

That tore it. I picked up the phone and at last made the one call I had been telling myself all along was futile—to California and Norman Lear. The anonymous vice-president had long since told him I might call him, had briefed him on the one question I most certainly would ask, had even given me the special number I was to use.

Mr. Lear was tied up on another line, his secretary said, and illogically enough, while I waited, I thought about network censors and censorship in general. I am unalterably opposed to all forms of censorship, not only the interior hidden kinds within an organization or government, but also to any external and public forms, such as pressure on sponsors and libraries and the press. Equally unalterably, I believe in a citizen's right to protest, in peaceful assembly, on lecture platforms, in books and plays and films, and in the newspapers.

Two or three times the secretary came back and apologized for the lengthening delay and finally she said that Mr. Lear . . . would have to call me back later on.

It was some hours before the call came and when it did, it was not Norman Lear out there in Hollywood, but his PR man, right here in town.

"Norman Lear," he began, "says if you would go out to California, he would be delighted to meet you, run some tapes for you, spend all the time you might want in a personal inter-

279

view about 'All in the Family,' but he feels that this is too sensitive a subject to discuss on the phone."

And that was that. One last time, nowhere.

Or was it?

The hullaballoo was beyond anything I could have imagined. My phone rang every minute throughout the Sunday, and it so happened that the monthly meeting of the Authors League came the very next day. Normally after a book of mine came out, my fellow authors would say, "Nice review," or "I'm going to read it right away," but this time there was a general rush toward me as I came through the door of our offices above Sardi's restaurant in New York, with slaps on the shoulder, hugs and even a few resounding kisses. "It's just what I've been feeling all along."

The third Sunday after it appeared, the *Times* ran a "TV Mailbag," with an oversized headline: *Archie, Lovable or Lamentable?* In a two-column italicized box, the *Times* explained.

On Sept. 12, Laura Z. Hobson, in an article "As I Listened to Archie say, "Hebe," criticized CBS for its TV series, "All in the Family." Here is a small sampling of the many letters received, which, by a 4–1 margin, agreed with Mrs. Hobson's views.

There followed about twenty letters, and the next Sunday another twenty, and the third Sunday another—until the *Times* at last sternly declared, "The TV Mailbag is now closed."

Of the infrequent minority letters, one was from John Rich, who identified himself as director of all the shows, and thus was hardly a disinterested or neutral party, and later one from Norman Lear himself, even less neutral and disinterested. Each letter indulged in some *ad hominem* remarks about me, including a reference by Mr. Lear to the fact that I was seventy-one years old. Messrs. Rich and Lear pooh-poohed the existence of any list of Forbidden Words, either at CBS, in Mr. Lear's head or anywhere else. Perhaps some readers felt that at last they had an answer to my indelicate question. Me, I simply felt, once again, nowhere.

Did my piece do any good? I don't think that's half as important as its opposite number: did "All in the Family" do any harm?

Look what happened to TV comedy right after Archie and that Emmy and those Nielsens, the burst of ethnicity all over the networks about junk-collecting poor blacks like "Sanford and Son," or rich, movin'-on-up successful blacks like "The Jeffersons," spluttering wise-cracks that were often cheap, salacious or just plain clownish. "Chico and the Man," covering the Puerto Rican front, was a little less distasteful but fully ethnicized too, as were the dozens of sitcoms that were to follow in the next fifteen years, only accentuating and enlarging the racist polarization that fragments our nation, ten times worse now, in my belief, than in the early seventies when "All in the Family" first spewed forth those side-splitting words, Hebe and coon and spic and yenta and all the lovable rest.

Not through those fifteen years did I ever catch one ethnic sitcom that didn't strike me as being a descendant of that first essay at bigotry-for-laughs. Not until 1985, with the advent of "The Cosby Show," with its dignity, its decency and its lack of ethnicity, did the Nielsen millions have a chance to go for a comedy about a black family where color doesn't count, where you forget it, because the show itself is color-blind and thus lets the adoring audience be color-blind too.

Another few weeks had to elapse before I could really put the whole Archie furor behind me. But of course right through all of it, during the interviewing and the writing and then the turmoil of the aftermath, I was never fully free of that difficult novel I had already committed myself to try, constantly harking back to its obvious problems, its challenges. And then, suddenly, my log noted the very moment when the line to actual writing was crossed.

5 A.M.
wrote page 1 of
possible novel
Zeke

That is the entry for Oct. 11, 1971. Below it is a line added by me years later.

(1985 note—this became *Consenting Adult*)

Why the *Zeke* I do not know. Names for my characters are always simple ones, usually the first one that occurs to me. Zeke was to be the adolescent son of my main family; perhaps the Z sprang from something in me about my own Z (Zeke was to become Jeff).

By now I had arrived at some vital decisions: I'd given up my first idea of two "opposing" families, seeing that it would mean too many major characters, too much diversity, too little of the good old Greek unities. I had come to see that I could put the two opposing forces right into the same family, an intelligent decent family, free of prejudice, concerned with most of the world's real concerns, suddenly faced with a wholly new one.

This did not mean that each member of my family would handle difficulty or pain in the same way or at the same tempo. There would be no carbon copies; instead there would be contrast and, inevitably, conflict.

That page one was a letter from young Jeff, away at school, to tell his mother that he was homosexual. The real letter, the "lost letter" of five narrow pages from Chris, was still securely hidden away in my safe-deposit box at the bank, not to be discovered and recovered by me for another decade, but I wrote this short letter on page one in a sweep of sureness about what it should say.

For by then I had learned that the vast majority of sons and daughters who had carried the burden of "How do I tell them?" had finally ended not by a confrontation, but by a letter. I had read many such letters, reprinted in medical journals or in the growing crop of gay liberation newspapers, and there was a kinship in all the letters, a kind of universality of emotion: I love you, I hate to hurt you or shock you, but I can't go on living this lie any longer, so there is nothing for it except for me to tell you . . .

Making up Jeff's letter to his mother, as dawn approached on that October morning in 1971, I wept once more as if I were that fictional mother Tessa, stooping down to pick up her mail at the front door of her apartment, and I wept for all the other mothers and fathers who had ever read just such a letter, or who one day in the future might still have to read such a letter.

At the end of that particular page one I was too drained to go on, but I knew I had at last found the way to start my novel. In the weeks that followed, I wrote four pages of "Notes on a Possible Novel," a private technique I had long ago established as if to create a sounding-board to myself for my general attitudes and hopes for what would occupy the next years of my life.

> If it is true that there are between 20 million and 30 million homosexuals in the United States alone, then it must be true that there are between 40 million and 60 million parents of homosexuals—and it is for them, primarily, that I would write this novel.

282

It would be a novel, at the beginning, of traditional grief and horror, but it would go slowly on to a re-education of two parents, to changing attitudes of those parents, who first learn the devastating truth from their brilliant 17-year-old son, who admire at once his courage in telling them, and begin at once on a long effort to "help him" through psychoanalysis, as he has asked them to do.

It would try to show the grief or shame or fear that the boy himself feels at the beginning, though it would in no way try to compete with the novels written by homosexuals themselves . . .

It would end in a new understanding in the lives of the parents, reached at last by themselves through years of effort, and finally clinched by the homosexual revolution that their son and others have been developing for years, finally emerged into "Gay Liberation."

I do not want this book to be in any sense a clinical book, a psychiatrist's book, a moralist's book . . .

My notes went on to the dilemmas that would face these parents, the changing professional attitudes that would create a rift in psychiatry itself, with growing suspicions that the usual help once sought from the usual analytic treatment might in itself only damage the young homosexual.

All through these early stages I found myself in my own dilemmas, about how Chris would feel about this book. When I began *The Tenth Month,* I wrote him at once, in effect asking his permission to put into fictional form a part of my life that was a part of his life as well. Now I could find no way to write him about this new intention of mine; never had we been able to talk easily about homosexuality, even in the most general and impersonal terms. Or even to talk at all about it.

Today, as I read once more those first draft notes, with the problems and dilemmas I could foresee for my characters, I see revelations of the inner anxieties, not only of my fictional Tessa and Ken, but anxieties of my own, that were to hold me in their grip for so long a time, far into the future:

There is not any lovely loving rapport between the young homosexual of the novel and his parents—he will for years reject every effort they make to reach him; he will show a savage cruelty, particularly to his mother . . .

But slowly, inevitably, as he matures, as his parents mature

. . . there will be the first signs of some new peacefulness in the relationship between the parents themselves in this part of their lives, and in the relationship between them and their son. . . .

The resolution of the book . . . might give, perhaps, some new point of view for other parents to consider . . . one dares to hope that those parents who read may find, somehow, an easing of their own Puritan pain and grief, an understanding that among the other changing attitudes (so slowly changing) in the world, about people of different races, different colors, different sexes, different religions, different political principles, there must surely arise a greater freedom, an equality in employment, in status, in political position for those who are homosexual.

One day I telephoned my editor about these pages of notes on my "secret novel" and he came up to my house to read them and talk about the handful of pages of manuscript that was all I had thus far managed to write. Again the entry in my log brings that day to instant life.

Jonathan Dolger—4 PM
"Zeke" or "Jeff"
"Dynamite"—his first word. Then 2 hrs. of talk—all good, all responsive on some deep level. In other words, first came the "publisher's reaction," then admiration for the idea of writing such a novel.

By another of those coincidences that can spice life so unexpectedly, I went, a couple of weeks later and a bit reluctantly, to a meeting at Goethe House on upper Fifth Avenue, where Dr. Richard Sterba was to be the principal speaker.

The reluctance came only from my general distaste for lectures— I'd had it at college and had never grown out of it. I was always eager to see the Sterbas, who still lived and practiced analysis in Grosse Pointe, though most frequently it was Richard alone whom I saw, for he, a gifted amateur violinist who had once studied with the great Adolf Busch, was still coming to New York at regular intervals for lessons. By now he had published many papers in psychoanalytic journals and several books, *Beethoven and His Nephew* (written in collaboration with his wife Editha) being my favorite, as it would be to anybody who cared both for music and analysis.

On this evening Richard was speaking about Freud, whom he had known in Vienna, and like everybody in the audience, I listened with a kind of venerating intensity to every word.

But suddenly my own intensity deepened. Richard was reading aloud a letter Freud had received from an unknown American woman whose son was homosexual. In my own research I had come across references to such a letter, but though I had consulted various library indexes, I had never been able to locate the letter itself. Now as Richard began reading it, saying first that Freud had written it in English and in longhand, it was as if every cell of my body had leaped alive.

Dear Mrs. ———,

I gather from your letter that your son is a homosexual. I am impressed by the fact that you do not mention this term yourself in your information about him. May I question you, why do you avoid it? Homosexuality is assuredly no advantage but it is nothing to be ashamed of, no vice, no degradation, it cannot be classified as an illness; we consider it to be a variation of the sexual function. . . .

The letter went on to the familiar litany of immortal names, Plato, Michelangelo, Leonardo, and to some discussion about the then-prevailing theories about homosexuality's causes and treatment.

By asking me if I can help you, you mean, I suppose, if I can abolish homosexuality and make normal heterosexuality take its place. The answer is, in a general way, we cannot promise to achieve it. . . .
What analysis can do for your son runs in a different line. If he is unhappy, neurotic, torn by conflicts, inhibited in his social life, analysis may bring him harmony, peace of mind, full efficiency . . .

I can still remember how I felt as Richard, in his soft voice, read that letter, can still remember my gratitude for the humanity, the simple kindness with which Freud had written this unknown woman who had appealed to him in her despair.

I asked Richard for a copy of his lecture and so became the possessor of Freud's letter. Only later did I learn that nearly forty years had passed since the unnamed American mother had written Freud, back in the early thirties before the Nazis had taken over Austria, forcing Freud to leave. For fifteen years she had kept his answer secret, but after the Kinsey report she had sent it to Kinsey, saying, "Here is a letter

285

from a great and good man." Then Kinsey published it in the American Journal of Psychiatry.

A great and good man. I wondered why it was that none of the highly regarded analysts Chris was seeing, right through his years at Harvard and beyond, why not one of them had ever shown me any of that simple kindness when I had approached any of them with any request for some time. Once when Chris was to appear in a students' play in Cambridge, I had written his analyst to suggest that while I was up there, perhaps I might be permitted a visit. In a two-line note the analyst had declined: it was not in the best interest of the patient.

The patient, the patient—parents didn't count. Perhaps it was right then that my unconscious had risen up in its first rebellion about the way parents were so often set aside in these matters. That night at Goethe House, hearing Freud's letter, I had reached only page ten or twelve in my novel—I went home more certain than ever that parents would read what I was trying to say to them. By the time Chris came home for Christmas, I was at page 50.

Not that I had any intention of showing him my manuscript. Except for that one time I'd asked Mike to read the pages Random House had turned down, it hadn't been in me to show unfinished work to my friends or my family.

But one night just before Chris was to return to Detroit, I did speak of the book I was starting, and offered him my four pages of notes.

"I'll go upstairs for a bit," I said. "When you're finished, call me and we can talk."

All the wait I had expected was ten minutes or so. Ten minutes passed and there was no sound from downstairs. Another ten; still no word. Half an hour—this time I knew. My body seemed to constrict at its core, gathered together to hold the cold rocky mass that had somehow formed during that protracted silence. I knew what that rocklike thing was—it was fear, fear of conflict and quarrels, fear of my son's opposition.

I went down to a silent room. Chris had set the four sheets aside; he was sitting motionless, staring at the carpet. I can still remember thinking, He is rigid with rejection.

SIXTEEN

I HAD NOT IMAGINED the rejection, nor was it a momentary thing; the conflict was real, the quarrels were real. The three years that it took me to write *Consenting Adult*—all the while reading the new literature on the subject, interviewing psychiatrists of every school of thought—those years were so mixed of grief and achievement that there was no dissolving one from the other. Nor was there any success for me in trying to ascribe reasons or apportion blame.

Perhaps now I can name some of my own mistakes, as I have come to see them. For example, I know that on too many separate occasions I asked Chris if he were "really out," not just in Detroit, asked it so often that once he shouted that for God's sake he had told me a million times that he was out, out everywhere, out with everybody, out with the whole goddamn world.

More grievous mistakes sprang from the overwhelming longing in me to try to persuade him that it was "right" for me to attempt this book, a longing to "get him on my side," to feel his acceptance, however reluctant, of what I felt I had to write.

But most importantly, I can now wish that I had just gone ahead, writing this novel as I had written all my novels—never before had I made Mike or Chris part of the process of my thinking about a book or writing it.

Yet in the very moment of wishing it, I see that saying nothing to Chris about this particular book until it was published, springing it on him, as it were, would have been the most grievous mistake of all.

Of what may have been his mistakes across the years, or his reasons for the way he felt about my book, I find it unseemly to write, for try as I might, I would still be seeing them through my own mindset, my own needs, my own neuroses.

I was never able to feel certain of myself anyway during most of the writing of *Consenting Adult*. I could no longer turn to Dr. Gosselin for the help that always came to me through an unhampered, uninhibited discussion with a professional, for he had retired from practice after serious illness and had moved away from the city.

At the very beginning, about two months after that night of the four pages, I did turn once to Richard Sterba on one of his visits to New York. My log for March 3, 1972, is succinct with my need for reassurance.

R. Sterba here
4:30 to 6:45
re book and Chris

After those two hours I felt sure again; he urged me to go on, helped me, for a while at least, to regain some of my own ability to think, to be independent of disagreement or disapproval. Later on that spring I talked it out with Mike, now the father of a second daughter, Kate. Mike, too, heartened me and gave me new support, respite from worry.

But by midsummer I was only at page 75, when the long-dreaded cataract operation on my right eye took place. For the time, everything else was set aside in my small family except the wait for the final outcome. Chris drove all the way from Detroit in his secondhand car to get me home from the hospital and then live at home for the first week of my bandaged eye and my existence with no depth perception at all. Neither of us even mentioned my book.

It was a long time before my log changed its mood.

Back to work! First time since surgery. Dr. N. ordered only 1 hr. 1 p. new

The next day has another happy entry:

Dr. Newton—all O.K. that #10 lens—the room swam into view!

But it was late fall before a different kind of note appeared:

Rode my bike!! 6,441 m. First time since Aug. 14 & hospital for cataract.

And by the start of 1973, with contact lenses in both eyes, I could again write things like, "Worked hard—6 hrs." Another six hours every night through the rest of that year and well into 1974 went into watching public television's nightly broadcasts of the entire day's proceedings in the Watergate hearings, the impeachment scandal, the whole horrifying mess.

How often I found myself wishing that Eric were still alive so that we could talk about the missing tapes and the laundered checks and the smoking gun. Going further back I longed again for Carroll Whedon—she would have been at my house every other night watching with me, or me at hers, watching there. But one of the inevitables, if you are in your seventies, is the loss of some of your dearest friends —Bernardine Scherman's death gave me my most recent sense of loss; Harry Scherman had died a few years earlier.

So I spent many evenings alone at my television set, my days at the typewriter, learning again the absence of any real social life that I had purposely sought out almost a decade before in that year when I wrote half of *First Papers*.

And I did at last come to that tremendous day when I could write, "Final, final, final edit & revise of *Con. Ad.*" As with all my books, this one had ended in a burst of compulsive concentration and long intense stretches of work. My publishers, Doubleday, accepted it—not Simon & Schuster, whose top management did not share my editor's belief in it—and in London it was taken by Heinemann. In some ways I felt full of that enviable sense of accomplishment that means you are happy.

But the doubts kept recurring, and the hurt and uncertainty about Chris and what he would feel when at last he came to read it. The emptiness that always came to me after finishing a long hard bout of writing again invaded my soul or spirit or whatever it is that becomes a burden during a spell of idleness.

And once again my body betrayed me, landing me at New York

Hospital on Christmas Day for a stay of a full month, with a puzzling skin ailment, a severe feverish one, that was diagnosed variously as a drug allergy, a food allergy, a tactile allergy, until in a moment of insight I said to Dr. Benjamin, "Bry, it's not any kind of allergy, it's something psychological, I ought to be seeing an analyst again."

The next morning I had an appointment with Dr. Irving Robbins; he would make a hospital visit and see me that very day. He was a longtime colleague of Dr. Benjamin's, not a psychoanalyst but a psychotherapist of repute. Dr. Benjamin had briefed him very fully about me; he had read some of my books and soon enough I was talking about my new one, and revealing God knows what of all my thousand anguishes about the writing of it.

Before he left, at his request I telephoned Doubleday to ask if they could send a special messenger that very day with a copy of my manuscript to Dr. Robbins' office; he proposed to read it overnight and see me once more in the morning.

When he did he talked about it at some length; he was clearly responsive to its purpose and to it as a novel, though he refrained from any estimate about how the critics or the public would receive it. Then he asked me a question I was completely unprepared for.

"What are you afraid of?"

"Afraid of?"

I fumbled for answers. I told him I felt sure it would get no major reviews, that it would rate only one of those two-inch notices collected under the headline "Books in Brief," that it would not earn its advance, that it would be turned down by all paperback houses, that it would sink out of sight in a month.

I went on to tell him of some fantasies I kept having about the newly formed National Gay Task Force setting up a picket line in front of my apartment house, marching up and down for days to protest a false, meretricious, rotten book. I told him of the letter I fancied would appear in the newspapers some day by that one psychiatrist I had interviewed who had proudly labeled himself to me as "Enemy Number One of the Gay Movement."

And then at last in a storming finish I told him the real reasons, the ones I couldn't shake off, the ones I had lived with for over three years, the ones that were still tearing me apart.

Much later he was to tell me that as I did so, I was, in fact, clawing at my myself, tearing at my ruptured skin. But I was at last talking without inhibition to a professional, to somebody I could trust.

And so began a new experience for me, not the old classic Freudian analysis but a modern development based on it yet newly developed, therapy where you do not try to interpret your dreams, where you do not search back to your early childhood, to your mother, your father, your first traumas, but where you are lodged in your life as you are living it, able to ask for and get some answers, some suggestions, reactions, even, though rarely, a directive about handling some specific crisis facing you then and there.

After a few intensive months my new therapy sessions settled into visits twice a week, and then only once a week. And when my book finally came out it proved fortunate that, for the second time in my life, I had recourse to the support and help offered by a compassionate doctor.

For nothing changed between me and Chris after he did read *Consenting Adult*. And indeed the strain between us about it and our life in general soon deepened to a point where Chris, now living in New York again, stopped seeing me or calling me, in a complete estrangement that was to last for three more years.

He did not see Mike either. He was absent for Christmas, for Thanksgiving, for his birthday, for mine, for everything, absent and silent. How happily I would have had him back, quarrels and all.

Consenting Adult appeared in June of 1975 to the best and most widespread reviews I had had on any book since *Gentleman's Agreement*. The lengthy piece in the Sunday *Times,* by Professor of History Martin Duberman, called it "a milestone in the history of social attitudes," and said, "most of the novel's success hinges on the complexities of her two main characters . . . mother and son, and also on her decision—unique in the literature about homosexuality—to tell the story from the parents' point of view."

It received various special awards, both in this country and in London when it was published there, won a sizable paperback deal and drew almost at once assorted queries about options for motion picture and television rights.

But unlike anything I had ever had with any of my books was the quality—the passion—of the letters that poured in with every mail, sometimes as many as eight or ten in a single day. Most of them were from young people who were gay; many of them were from their parents. It is hard to select samples or to excerpt any of them.

One of the earliest was from a father in Illinois, obviously a professional man, to judge from his letterhead and stationery.

I finished *Consenting Adult* sometime in the middle of last night
. . . a fine novel . . . an important human document . . .

As the fifty-two-year-old father of two sons and a daughter,
it was not too difficult to identify with Ken and Tessa and
Jeff . . .

I was inundated with tears, tears of the bitterest sadness for the
pain of a youth like Jeff, one without even the freedom to write
a letter . . .

Most of the letters were from people still in school or college, but
one of the first arrivals was from a young man in his middle thirties
in California.

1:34 A.M. Thank you for writing *CA*. I'm not even through
reading it, but it affected me so much . . . that I just now sat down
and wrote a 3-page letter to my mother telling her I was gay,
something I really never thought I would do, something I had
fooled myself into thinking I should not do . . . Her reaction,
though important, very important to me, is less important than
the burden I lost when I did it. . . .

But the majority of the letters were from the young, in their middle
or late teens, like this one from Texas.

I recently received *Consenting Adult* . . . and I would like to thank
you for such a beautiful, real story.

I am currently in my sophomore years of college and find
myself facing the same decisions Jeff faced at seventeen. Though
I am very unsure about everything, I feel I need to give everything an equal "college try." I am now looking for a psychoanalyst to talk to. I found it interesting that religion did not play
an important part in your book. In my experiences I have found
it of little use.

Your insight and understanding touched me very much.
Happy endings are always wonderful, I just hope that somewhere
along the way there will be one for me.

The letters never failed to move me, with pleasure, with pity, with
curiosity, with a deep sorrow that society still was being so punitive
so much of the time. I answered each letter for more than half a year,
but at last I did something I had never done before. With the rush of

292

mail after *Gentleman's Agreement* I had finally turned over the answering to my publishers, but these letters were too intimate, too secret in many cases, to be turned over to anybody.

So I wrote a brief reply, had it printed up on blue postcards with my name and address right at the top. After the printed "Dear" of the salutation, I always turned to pen and ink to write the name of the person who had been moved to reach out to me.

> Thanks for writing as you did about *Consenting Adult,* and let me tell you why I'm turning to this form of reply. For the first seven months I answered each letter myself, me at the typewriter, not dictating to any third person—I seemed to feel some real need to do just that. (I still do.) But now the paperback is out, and I simply have to squelch that impulse or never write another book. I'm still reading every letter word for word, of course, as I read yours, so this is no perfunctory reply to "fan mail" but the only feasible way I can find to thank you for it myself. Yours,

I left enough blank space across the bottom of the card to allow for my signature and a handwritten sentence aimed at some specific point in the letter I had received, to assure those writers out there, in big cities and small towns, that I really had read what they wrote.

In a very few instances there would be a follow-up response, written to me not at my publishers but at my own address, which I had purposely put in. By far the greatest number of people understood from my own words that I simply had to curtail further correspondence.

But even with the help of the postcards my days were still filled with distractions, offers to consider, decisions to make, people to see. I often wonder how other authors who have a successful book—many far more successful than *Consenting Adult*—how they manage to go on to the next book. Most of them, of course, have husbands, wives, secretaries, assistants to lift some of the daily load, but I have none of the above. Since my days at Time Inc. I have never had a secretary, though in the past I did turn over batches of manuscript to a typist. I don't even do that anymore, for I find that I keep on editing and rewriting even while I am typing the final, final, final, and that sometimes those last-minute changes or additions strike me as being better than what I had thought was final, final, final.

The offers and the decisions spanned television and Hollywood. The first was easy—long ago I had decided that I would not go on anybody's talk show to tout my own wares, no matter how many public relations experts said that was the only way to sell books. But my agent kept reporting the requests, perhaps hoping I would change my mind. Our conversations were always the same: "Barbara Walters would like you on her show." "I can just imagine her digging at me with the cruel questions she specializes in."

And the letters came asking about options for motion-picture rights. I accepted one from a Raymond Aghayan of Los Angeles, a man I had never heard of, a man my agent had never heard of, whom the Hollywood office of my agent could identify only as "a partner of Bob Mackie," the designer of women's evening clothes. His offer was $2,500 for a year, with an extension clause for another six months at the same rate to give him leeway if it should be needed.

For a whole year after we signed I didn't even talk to Mr. Aghayan by telephone; but when at last I did meet him, I at once felt an earnestness in him. He had underlined hundreds of lines in his copy of *Consenting Adult,* lines he felt *had* to be intact in the film. I sensed the same earnestness in his questions to me about what I thought would be right or wrong for the film. We spent eight hours together that afternoon and evening—part of it was typical Hollywood, the limo, the expensive restaurant—but growing in me all through was the conviction that this unknown Ray Aghayan would never knuckle under to the front office, never whittle down or eviscerate *Consenting Adult.*

But it never occurred to me that this was the beginning of a relationship that was to last for many years. Ray was in his middle forties then, a nice-looking man with dark eyes, shorter than I, soft-spoken, unemphatic. When the option and its extension expired, he asked for a further extension, this time for a year. My agent doubled the option fee and he agreed, but still nothing happened. One day he sent me a card.

> There really has been no news; that is why you have not heard from me. Three months ago all network TV had turned it down, but . . . there suddenly seems to be new interest . . . Please do not lose heart; I am *not.*

I did lose heart, though, and when he suggested yet another year's option, my agent, my attorney, my other advisers all agreed that it would be better to have the book on the open market once more. My

agent (no longer Phyllis Jackson; she died of a heart attack that spring)
wrote one of those impersonal agent letters some agents always manage
to write—"We think it imprudent to extend . . . when so little has
happened to get the project moving . . ." I felt the letter as an affront,
and wrote Ray myself, as one who had known disappointment. Then,
on the day his option formally expired, he astonished me by sending
the most lavish arrangement of flowers I had seen in many years. I
wrote back at once:

> I think it's the most gracious and loving gesture . . . It filled me
> . . . with longing for a year or two ago, when you and I both
> had such high hopes of seeing *Consenting Adult* made into a fine
> film by you. I'd be only too delighted if through some magic
> they could suddenly be ours again. . . .
>
> I'm giving my full energy to my next novel—now at page
> 310, and thus in the home stretch . . . but I had to drop everything
> to send you this real thank-you on End-of-Option day, and my
> love too.

It was now nearly three years since I had seen Chris. What brought
him back was the news of another operation, a major one, for cancer.
A friend of mine had told my sister Alice; she thought he ought to
know. He telephoned me at the hospital. I remember the jump of my
pulse when he said, "Hi, it's Chris" . . .

Some years after that, following what now seems to have been our
final quarrel, it was Chris himself who led me to some new understanding about them all.

"Go to your bookshelf with all the Trollopes," he said one night
at the end of a call in which we "made up" after a silence of ten days.
"Get *The Last Chronicle of Barset,* and read the start of chapter forty-
nine."

"*The Last Chronicle of*—?"

"But don't call me back after you've read it," he said. "I mean, not
tonight. Just read it."

I had read all the Barsetshire novels years before, but I could not
imagine what he was selecting for me to reread now. I went to the
one shelf in my bookcase that held over a dozen of the small blue-
bound volumes of the Oxford edition, and with some kind of tense
eagerness found *The Last Chronicle* and chapter forty-nine.

I wonder [wrote Trollope] whether any one will read these pages who has never known anything of the bitterness of a family quarrel? If so, I shall have a reader very fortunate, or else very cold-blooded. It would be wrong to say that love produces quarrels; but love does produce those intimate relations of which quarreling is too often one of the consequences—one of the consequences which frequently seem to be so natural and sometimes seem to be unavoidable.

One brother rebukes the other—and what brothers ever lived together between whom there is no such rebuking?—then some warm word is misunderstood and hotter words follow and there is a quarrel. The husband tyrannizes, knowing that it is his duty to direct, and the wife disobeys, or only partially obeys, thinking that a little independence will become her—and so there is a quarrel. The father, anxious only for his son's good, looks into that son's future with other eyes than those of his son himself—and so there is a quarrel.

They come very easily, these quarrels, but the quittance from them is sometimes terribly difficult. Much of thought is necessary before the angry man can remember that he too in part may have been wrong; and any attempt at such thinking is almost beyond the power of him who is carefully nursing his wrath, lest it cool!

But the nursing of such quarreling kills all happiness. The very man who is nursing his wrath lest it cool—his wrath against one whom he loves perhaps the best of all whom it has been given to him to love—is himself wretched as long as it lasts. He is sullen at his meals, and cannot understand his book as he turns its pages. His work, let it be what it may, is ill done. He is full of his quarrel —nursing it.

He is telling himself how much he has loved that wicked one, how many have been his sacrifices for that wicked one, and that now that wicked one is repaying him simply with wickedness! And yet the wicked one is at that very moment dearer to him than ever. If that wicked one could only be forgiven, how sweet would the world be again! And yet he nurses his wrath.

I read those sentences ten times over before I could think of sleep. At some time during the night I found myself thinking, I will quote it somewhere in my autobiography, when I get to the part I so dread writing, about me and Chris and the book, quote it just as Trollope wrote it over a century ago, and if the reader doesn't get from it a total picture of what it reveals about my life with Chris, and about what

Chris is telling me about his life with me, then the hell with the reader and his insensitivity.

Just seeing that I could do that sent a high flood of relief rolling over me and through me. And a surge of love for Chris.

I never asked him directly what he had felt when he first came upon chapter forty-nine in *The Last Chronicle,* but it is true that since that night when he told me about it, though we have had disagreements about various matters, we have not had even one more fierce quarrel.

Laura Hobson's Proposed
"Final Page of Volume Two"

Long ago, my editor and I agreed to call my autobiography *Laura Z: A Life*. Having now reached the end of this second volume, I find myself remembering that maternal grandmother of mine, whom I never saw, who, at the age of ninety-four, was still marching through the gates of Russian prisons, past the guards, carrying messages in invisible ink on snippets of cloth tucked into peaches, plums and apples —still carrying baskets of fruits inside to the political prisoners of Russia.

Presumably I will never be using invisible ink on snippets of cloth, but I do know that for whatever time there may be left for me, I will, in one form or another, go right on "writing it down."

AFTERWORD

BY

Christopher Z. Hobson

ON THE TITLE PAGE of my mother's manuscript for this volume, in her usual precise way, she noted the dates when she sent successive installments to her editor, Donald Fine:

> L.Z.H. copy
> To Don 6/3/84—p. 102
> To Don 9/4/84—p. 204
> To Don 1/5/85—p. 300
> To Don 8/26/85—p. 402

The dates offer a kind of tabulation of her last two years. At first, rapid progress—a hundred pages every few months up through page 300. (Manuscript page 300 corresponds to the start of chapter eleven.) Then came her first severe illness: she needed nearly eight months for the next hundred pages. Then illness again, and when she died, on February 28, 1986, she had completed only another fifty manuscript pages, through chapter sixteen.

Back in 1984 she had also written a brief "Final Page of Volume Two," which she meant to place at the end. It is printed here after chapter sixteen; the two or three chapters that would have intervened were never written.

She had cared desperately about finding the right approach to chapters fifteen and sixteen—the material about *Consenting Adult* and our estrangement. She wrote them carefully and revised painstakingly, choosing at every crucial point to understate, to withhold detail. In New York Hospital, the night before her last operation, my mother told me she had revised and retyped the "Trollope" pages ending chapter sixteen, and added, "If it has to be, that could be the end of the book." And when I tried to be "reassuring," she said impatiently, "I have to think about these things—people do die, you know."

But if this suggests she had said all she had to say, and was ready to face death, that would be both trite and misleading. Her idea was a forced makeshift; she meant to continue the story. Indeed, in the same conversation she directed that several first-draft pages dealing with Ray Aghayan, the producer, should be inserted between the description of readers' responses to *Consenting Adult* and the account of our reconciliation, which originally followed directly. Always the professional, she was thinking in terms of timing and pacing, not having this final section of the chapter follow too abruptly.

Those first-draft pages that my mother mentioned in the hospital also began a discussion of her eighth novel, *Over and Above,* which she had mentioned in her thank-you to Ray Aghayan. She had long considered writing about the differing attitudes of three generations of women in one family. Originally she had meant to focus on attitudes to McCarthyism and the Communist issue in the fifties. Eventually, she shaped the novel around a different issue, conflicting feelings about being Jewish and her own sense of what it meant to be Jewish—themes foreshadowed in the 1964 notes on assimilated and nonassimilated Jews which she reproduces here in chapter twelve. Finally and most topically, she used the novel to express her attitudes toward Israel, Palestine, and terrorism—with time, she had become pro-Israel, though with specific criticisms. In *Over and Above,* the "middle" generation of the mother, Amy, has views paralleling my mother's: pro-Israel, antiterrorist, and in the novel at least, dismissive of the idea of a Palestinian nationality. The oldest generation, represented by the grandmother, Eugenie, embodies the problems of aging and continued creativity; Eugenie's experiences of a cataract operation, the recovery of sight and the return to her work as a painter draw directly on the author's life. The young generation is shown through the daughter, Julie, who is drawn to and later repelled by a pro-Palestinian, pro-terrorist New Left "collective." As presented in the novel, Julie's attitudes express an inability to come to grips with her identity as a Jew; the novel ends with an exchange between her and her mother:

> "Mom, there's one thing I'd like to ask you. How long do you stay Jewish anyway? . . . Do I have to keep saying I'm a Jew forever?"
> "You don't, Julie. But I do."

Though my mother regarded *Over and Above* as an important statement on a major theme—and though she had put much research into it—the book did poorly. Published in the fall of 1979, it was not reviewed either in the daily New York *Times* or in the *Times Book Review,* and sold badly. Doubleday, the publisher, did little to promote it, and my mother's dissatisfaction with Doubleday led her to seek both another publisher and another agent.

She found the agent in Robert (Robbie) Lantz, whose office handled both literary and entertainment artists. After the failure of *Over and Above,* and on the eve of her eightieth birthday, my mother needed a major infusion of confidence: she had begun another novel, but doubted whether it would find a publisher. Lantz assured her it would, with exactly the right combination of shrewd professional judgment and Viennese charm. Before long the new novel had a publisher, Harper and Row, and an editor my mother respected and liked, Lawrence P. Ashmead.

Untold Millions was the title for her ninth and last novel. The title was meant to evoke multiple associations—the ambitions of youth, the coercive power of money and, finally, the inner richness that comes with maturity. The storyline was a fictionalization of her own twenties —the beginning of her career in advertising, her long affair with Tom Mount. Rick, the character based on Tom Mount, aspires to be a writer but never makes progress on his projected novel; Jossie, the protagonist, like my mother in her youth, supports Rick by working in advertising, pays his debts and pretends too long that her sacrifices will indeed make it possible for him to become an artist. Eventually she finds the strength to break off the affair. My mother laid the action in the 1920s, rather than transposing to the present, and, with her usual attention to detail, hired a young researcher, Bill Holliday, to chase down such matters as the exact cost of a red canoe in 1923. (Rick gives the canoe to Jossie as a present; only later does she discover that it is her own money that paid for it.) But some of the most successful detail in the book is invented—Jossie's ads, like this one for "Stuyvesant of New York":

> It's spring
> and you're young
> (or not so young)
> If you are young you know the longing for one special suit
> or dress to greet the new season.
> And if you are not so young, you know the impulse toward
> renewal, and want at least one important dress to satisfy it.

My mother's love affair with advertising lasted her whole life.

All the time she was working on *Over and Above* and *Untold Millions,* my mother never stopped hoping for a film or stage deal for *Consenting Adult.* In 1977, while the novel was still under option to Ray Aghayan, she received an inquiry about a possible stage production from a young producer, Robert Callely. Since the book was under option, she had to turn him down. Callely kept trying, eventually took an option, but was no more successful than Aghayan had been in getting an adaptation produced. But my mother gained a new friend. Callely knew how to poke gentle fun at her in a way that was not threatening. He sometimes turned to her for advice, and she turned to him for advice as well. Among her notes for this volume is one dated 9/2/85:

> Bob Callely.
> Untold Millions last 2 or 3 chapters
> "It kind of helps me"
> "don't tell anybody"

She had begun reading him her work—at first insisting that he keep this secret—and went on doing so through volume one of the autobiography and this volume as well.

Not that these sessions were always peaceful; though my mother requested criticisms, she could bridle when she got them. Once, Callely remembered later, he had criticized some aspect of the pages she read before assuring her that he liked them overall. "She practically threw me out of the house," he said. When he phoned the next day she bawled him out all over again. My mother, after all, was a writer above and beyond, and writers, including those who ask for criticism, really want praise.

She made other new friends, most of them twenty or thirty years younger than herself. And she had new interests as well. One was baseball—as she turned away from social life, and went out less in the evening, she watched more television, and became first a Yankees and later a Mets partisan. Another interest was bridge. She had belonged to New York's Regency Whist Club for years, but as she entered her eighties she began to work on her game seriously, finally enrolling in a weekly master class to learn and practice the latest conventions. (Typically, after winning first place in the class twice in a row, she stayed away the third week to avoid a possible embarrassing third win.) Bridge helped her through fallow periods; when she was writing well she played little. But bridge was also a source of pride in her ability to continue learning when she was in her eighties.

Puzzles had a similar function. She had always relished the day or so a month she spent editing the Saturday Review's double crostics; she loved the far more difficult London *Times* crosswords. But in her seventies and eighties, her continued skill at puzzles was reassurance that her mental functioning was unimpaired. Much later, home after cancer surgery, still feeling the effects of weeks of painkillers, she was worried for days by her slowness in solving a difficult Sunday double crostic. The following Sunday she called before noon to tell me she had done the new one in her usual twenty minutes.

Despite the new friends and interests, her old friends remained the best ones. In 1981 she spent a happy week with her beloved Richard and Editha Sterba at their summer home in Vermont, reading and criticizing the manuscript of Richard's *Memoirs of a Viennese Psychoanalyst,* published the following year. She grew closer to Bay Meynell, whose husband Francis had died in 1975. These friends would ultimately outlive her. But others—John Wharton, Harry and Bernardine Scherman—were dead now. And in May of 1980, her sister Alice died too.

Among my mother's notes for this volume is one headed "Alice," clearly jotted down for possible use later:

> It was Chris who effected this "reconciliation," asking if I would like to see her in the hospital. He went with me the first time, it was all I could do to conceal my emotions when I saw her; death was written into her shrunken face.

She had not heard from Alice since 1968, but I had kept on seeing my aunt. Always afflicted by dangerously high blood pressure, Alice suffered a bad stroke in early 1979. In one of the less common stroke patterns, it left her able to speak quite clearly, but—at first—unable to understand other people's speech at all or to read. Later Alice told me of a moment of triumph: "In the hospital I kept wondering and wondering—why everyone was speaking absolute nonsense? And then I suddenly realized—*I* must be the one who wasn't making sense." With the same ironic detachment she described her reading therapy: "It's very interesting to watch how you learn to tell one word from another. The first time I wasn't aware of what was going on."

By summer Alice was able to take walks in Central Park, and these were some of her happiest times. But early in 1980 she had a series of seizures, or perhaps minor strokes. Near death at one point, she recovered slightly, and it was at this time that my mother began to come see her—first at Roosevelt Hospital, then at her home, since eventually Alice insisted on discharging herself. During these visits, few enough as it turned out, they talked about their childhood and younger years and did not touch on the quarrels that had kept them apart for nearly a third of their lives. But it was important to my mother that they were together at the end—which came only a few weeks after Alice returned home.

When her sister died—a few weeks short of their common eightieth birthday—my mother was in the middle of work on *Untold Millions*. By the next summer the book had been delivered to her publisher. It was to be published in February, 1982—my mother herself wanted the delay, to publish on the same date as *Gentleman's Agreement* thirty-five years earlier. It would do somewhat better than *Over and Above*—getting a favorable review, though only a brief one, in the New York *Times Book Review*, and selling moderately.

But meanwhile she was in her usual period of depression between books, wondering what to do next. Still nothing had materialized on a *Consenting Adult* adaptation. There were no good ideas for a novel. Then, as she recounted in the first volume of this work, came a letter from Donald I. Fine. At lunch with Mike Hobson—they were old friends—Fine had asked about her work, and Mike had asked what Fine thought of the idea of her doing an autobiography.

> Of course [Fine wrote] I thought it was a wonderful idea.
> . . . He said, "Well, why don't you write her and say so?" So
> that's what I'm doing.

My mother hesitated before accepting the offer. She had always dismissed the idea of an autobiography. All she wanted to tell about her life, she liked to say, was already in her novels. And this was true in perhaps an unusually direct way. She had written about the Sterbas and Ralph Ingersoll in *The Trespassers,* her childhood and parents in *First Papers,* my own birth and her feelings about my sexuality in *The Tenth Month* and *Consenting Adult,* and her own twenties in her most recent book. But she had always had to shape the material according to the requirements of fiction, and she had also had the veil of fiction to conceal her. Now, if she went ahead, she would be free from the constraints, but she would also have to go through trauma in reliving the past, and in revealing herself. But in some deep way the proposal was now right for her. Certainly it appealed to her vanity, but on another level, she felt her life was emblematic of larger issues—the struggles of professional women to compete in a world of men, the problems and responsibilities of single women providing for children, and the continuing relevance of the liberal ideals she believed in. "I don't think I want to write more novels," she was to say later. "Writing about my life is much more interesting."

Accepting Fine's offer meant changing publishers; my mother was deeply grateful for the graciousness with which Larry Ashmead of Harper and Row—to whom she was contractually obligated for her next novel, though not, strictly speaking, for an autobiography— urged her to go ahead. Soon she was putting in days of four, six, eight hours at the typewriter. And all too soon it began to be clear that the one volume originally envisaged would not be enough. Unwilling to propose a change, perhaps afraid that Fine would say no, for weeks my mother kept struggling to compress each new episode, only to give way at last to the urge to tell her story fully. Finally she made her decision. As she later told the story, dressing it up just a little, in an interview with Publishers Weekly:

> I said to him [Fine], "Listen, the best book of the year is *Growing Up,* by Russell Baker; it only took *him* to age 21. Why do I have to do it in one massive volume?" And I could see he was excited; his eyes just flamed. He said he'd think about it over the weekend, and he called on Monday and said, "The book is in production."

Laura Z: A Life (Fine avoided calling it volume one, which would suggest only half a life) came out in October 1983, to the kind of

305

notices that had evaded my mother on her two previous books. Commenting both on the book and on its author, Anatole Broyard wrote in the New York *Times:*

> On the evidence of *Laura Z,* she was, and is, what used to be called "a good person," an expression we now tend to give an ironical inflection, as if it were equivalent to belonging to a mildly fanatical religious sect. . . . While *Gentleman's Agreement* was an important story for its time, *Laura Z* is a better one.

And in Saturday Review, Anne Roiphe concluded:

> Laura Hobson has lived an honorable life and has written a fascinating memoir. We can look forward to the second volume.

There were interviews in Jewish Book World—in which she tried to make amends for her long-ago refusal of the National Jewish Book Award—and in the English-language supplement of the *Jewish Daily Forward,* now a weekly. And much more.

She was touched in a more personal way by letters from two of her readers—each of whom wrote briefly about himself and about his father. One was Eric Hodgins's son Roderic, who followed his letter with a visit. She gave Roderic the edition of Mahler's symphonies she had received from Eric so many years before. Later, a letter came from Timothy Hobson, Thayer Hobson's son by an earlier marriage, whom she had last known in the thirties as "Timmy"—and who signed himself that way, in quotation marks. With these letters, and a few others like them, her late work seemed to be bringing closure to earlier parts of her life.

These were years of serenity for my mother. Aside from her satisfaction with her work, and with a life spent fighting not just one but many "good fights," another reason was that she and I were finally at peace. In a phrase she used about her own mother in volume one of this work, she was "pure mother." She could never be happy while we were at odds, and though she was tough enough to go on with her life and work even so, our fights took an enormous toll on her self-confidence, even her health. She chose—undoubtedly so as not to risk offending me further—to avoid detail about the most important of these fights, the one over *Consenting Adult.* But I think that without

306

violating her right to tell her story as she chose, and taking the risk of speaking when she can no longer reply, I can fill in some of the pages she left blank.

Like those family quarrels that Trollope wrote so movingly about, ours grow up naturally, virtually inevitably. Our disagreement was very deep. She felt that her experience of coming to terms with her son's sexuality, transmuted into fiction, would help countless parents and their children who were in a similar situation. More than that, she saw her book as a plea for enlightenment and tolerance, as all her important work was. I could sympathize with her aims, but I felt she should not write the book at all. I was disturbed by the amount of detail the mauscript drew from my own life—as I suppose many authors' relatives have been. More fundamentally, I felt, rightly or wrongly, that to focus as the book did on the parents' reactions and conflicts inevitably gave some ground to the idea that homosexuality itself was a problem, that it was undesirable, even if accepted in the end. And reading the finished book, I felt that the idea of gay *liberation* —of gay people themselves transforming their own lives through changed consciousness and polictical struggle, the idea that gayness is not just to be accepted, but is good and beautiful in itself—I felt this was absent. Yet that idea was at the core of my own life and work in the early 1970s, and today.

Only very slowly did I accept that my mother's "angle" of focusing on the parents could be a valid one, that millions of parents facing the situation *do* feel the homosexuality of their child is a tragedy, and that the story of Tessa Lynn may help them transcend that feeling. But rereading the book today, I still balk at the limitedness of its view of gay liberation.

We never resolved our disagreement over the book. Our attempts to compromise and "respect our differences" went overboard in quarrel after quarrel. My letters (I find rereading them now) grew cold and hard, "implacable" as my mother frequently said—regardless of their arguments. Eventually, as she has told, we went nearly three years without speaking at all. It was a silence more bitter than a mere "I love you" could bridge. I can only guess how often she must have tried to think of how to break it. I know that as it stretched, I looked for a way to end it, aware that she would soon be seventy-eight. But I found none either, until cancer—of the womb, the organ that bears children —provided the way, and Alice's hesitant "Don't you think it's time?" provided the impetus.

Then we did agree to disagree—we had no other choice. We argued or fought over other issues. We shared her disappointment over the continuing lack of a *Consenting Adult* adaptation. But we never discussed the book itself, for we each knew that though we might have reconsidered specifics, neither of us had changed our fundamental views. And this time we were determined to hurt each other no more —not in those deep, fundamental ways that tear families apart, and too often find no healing before death.

The news she had waited for so long came in the summer of 1984, when she was already at work on this present volume. Ray Aghayan had never given up on *Consenting Adult;* now he told her he had succeeded in putting together a deal for a made-for-television film. After so many years without forward motion, things had fallen together with a rush. A script was in preparation; ABC was to do the film; Marlo Thomas and Martin Sheen would play the parents, Tessa and Ken, with a young, not well-known actor named Barry Tubb as Jeff. For various reasons, the time of the story was updated to the present and the locale shifted from New York to Seattle; shooting would take place in September in Vancouver—which looks much like its sister city across Puget Sound and is much cheaper to make films in. The movie would show in November. The deal would bring $40,000, with lesser amounts for reruns.

Just before the shooting began, Aghayan invited her to fly to Vancouver, all expenses paid, to watch production. There followed a strenuous, deeply satisfying week—meeting the cast, the director, the staff; viewing key scenes as they unfolded before the camera; sometimes commenting on the script. (She had had nothing to do with the scriptwriting, trusting Aghayan's taste completely; now she suggested only a few changes.) When she took an afternoon off from the set she made her way to the Vancouver public library, where—to her immense pleasure—she found all three shelf copies of *Laura Z: A Life* checked out.

Back in New York, exhausted, bothered by a skin allergy reminiscent of similar flare-ups going back for years, she worked forward on this present volume and waited for the film to show. When it did— delayed until February 4 because ABC wanted it to show during the "sweeps" when ratings are determined—John J. O'Connor in the New York *Times* called it a "small movie that is likely to have enormous reverberations," and which delivered its message "with an admirable combination of emotional clout and dignity." While a few reviewers suggested that the film was not as daring as it might have been ten years earlier, or that its focus on exemplary middle-class characters was too narrow, O'Connor's review set the general tone. Later, the film was to win the Alliance of Lesbian and Gay Artists' Media Award for "the responsible portrayal of gay and lesbian characters and issues in the entertainment media."

More satisfying than the reviews and awards, though, as with the novel a decade earlier, were the letters that arrived, many from young gays in, or just coming out of, the closet. And most gratifying of all, perhaps, was a benefit showing a few days before the actual broadcast, arranged by the Ms. Foundation for Women and chaired by Gloria Steinem.

My mother was guest of honor. Ray Aghayan, Marlo Thomas, and Barry Tubb were there, of course, as well as Don Fine, Paul Sherman (my mother's lawyer), my brother Mike, and Ann, his wife. I watched the film later on television: I was apprehensive enough about my own reaction to want to see it at home. (Afterward, I told her I liked it, but with criticisms—and we set that discussion to one side, as we had so many others.) But though she was certainly disappointed that I wasn't there, in every other way it was a triumphant night.

Then, two weeks after *Consenting Adult* showed on ABC, my mother's skin allergy blew up out of control. She was never to be fully healthy again.

When working on a book my mother seldom said much about what she planned to write. But in the case of this volume I know she meant to include a chapter on old age. It was to begin with a quotation from Bette Davis: "Old age ain't no place for sissies."

In her eighties my mother remained active and energetic. She biked regularly, her normal stint seven miles, her target a thousand miles a year. In her apartment, a four-room duplex with her custom-built kidney-shaped red-topped desk in one corner of the large living room, she would go up and down the stairs twenty times a day, stride from her desk to her work closet to hunt some entry in an old log or to consult a check stub from forty years before. There was no exaggeration when an interviewer wrote in 1983, "Hobson in no way looks or acts her 83 years. Exuding energy and joie de vivre, a tall, slim, very attractive woman with a commanding presence, Hobson exhibits the animated drive that fueled several careers. . . ." Her self-image was similar. Though she hated euphemisms like "senior citizen," and bluntly called herself "old," she was also capable of remarking to her therapist Dr. Robbins that a lucrative option deal was important because "I have to put something by for my old age."

But there was another side to all this: over the years she had known a great deal of illness. Some, but by no means all, she has mentioned in this volume: cystitis and tachycardia in 1958, two major operations in the single year 1962, pneumonia in 1968, the terrible skin problems brought on by anxiety in 1974–75, a hysterectomy for uterine cancer in 1978. There was more, even during those same years, and around 1976 the first of several polyps in the bladder, which had to be removed surgically. In 1984, after one of these polyp operations, she was hospitalized for a slowed heartbeat and atrial fibrillation—spasmodic, irregular contractions of the right atrial chamber of the heart. This was a continuation of problems she had had at least since 1958; her cardiologist assured her that her heart was basically sound.

Many of her earlier illnesses may have been "stress-related," as my mother herself put it. She had spent much of her sixties and seventies in almost continuous stress, and was aware of the toll it took on her health. Stress threw her into tears, set her heartbeat racing, inflamed the nerve endings of her skin. And it made her, at times, a burden to everyone around her. Only in her last years did she seem to gain some inner peace, did she learn to laugh at herself—a little uneasily, it is true. And the "stress-related" illnesses seemed to recede into the past. The years after her cancer operation in 1978 were more free of illness than the preceding fifteen.

But while my mother would sometimes speak of the need to accept "the deficits of age," all her illnesses had been episodic, not chronic. She had never had a stroke, like Eric or Alice; after her two cataract operations (the left eye was done in 1979) she had near-perfect eyesight. Her only chronic problem was a difficulty in walking. Though her biking wasn't affected, beginning around 1981 she had found it increasingly difficult to walk any distance. Her ankles tended to sag inward (to "pronate," in runners' jargon) and her breathing grew labored after a block or two. Doggedly, she set herself a regimen of walking ten blocks a day.

Now, on February 22, 1985, her log noted: "Allergy worse." Again, on March 2, "Itch much worse," with notes on a consultation with a dermatologist. Then, for the five days March 4–8, a single-word entry each day:

ill
ill
ill
ill
ill

The "allergy" or "itch" had become an inflammation of the skin of her whole body—stomach, back, legs, arms were red, leathery, and cracked. She grew weak and at one point—probably those five days —simply lay upstairs without eating. After this she took care of herself, but the illness grew worse. A new dermatologist prescribed massive cortisone, with no improvement. Early in May, after two and a half months of illness, she was so weak that she couldn't come home from the dermatologist on her own. The log notes: "Dr. Hill—scabies? *Chris took me home.* The lowest point yet."

It was, in fact, the lowest point—her dermatologist now suspected the "allergy" was scabies, a skin infestation caused by a parasite, and treated by a lotion sold in any drugstore. (Scabies is usually found in crowded, unclean conditions, which is why no one had thought of it before.) Though the diagnosis was never confirmed in the laboratory, the treatment worked: very slowly, but continuously, the inflammation cleared up. On May 22, her log notes, "Bike—half mile—first time in about 3 months."

On her 85th birthday, June 19, we took her to Shea Stadium. Ray Aghayan had pried box seats loose at the last minute; Doubleday, part-owners of the Mets, apparently still considering her a Doubleday author, arranged for the big screen in left field to flash "Happy Birthday Laura Hobson." She could barely hobble across the parking lot, but she wrote in the log: "85 years old!! I don't believe it. . . . An original and wonderful evening!" (The Mets beat Chicago, 1–0, behind Dwight Gooden's pitching.)

Through the summer the log kept noting work days of two, four, five hours. By August she was biking five to six miles a day for the first time since February. At the beginning of September she was in New York Hospital for removal of yet another bladder polyp—"A little tougher than last year," she noted the day after the surgery. She was home in three days.

Then, a week later, a note on a conversation with her urologist: "Biopsy shows some low-grade cancer, but a bit *into* the muscle. Another op. Dec. 1—to remove affected part. (Very depressed at news.)"

She was, in fact, filled with terror and foreboding; though the urologist assured her that the cancer would grow slowly, she insisted on advancing the date for the second operation to October 28. It was to be a simple procedure, done through the urethra without an incision; but in the operating room, the surgeon found that not all the cancer could be removed this way. My mother was sent home and a third hospitalization scheduled for ten days later. This time it was general anesthesia and an abdominal incision; days later, when she had recovered a little, she wrote under the date of the surgery: "Cancer of the bladder—half my bladder removed. Horrible operation."

She was in the hospital for three weeks, and under a nurse's care for her first days at home. Once again the prognosis was optimistic: extensive biopsies all around the affected area were "clean." My mother was only partly reassured: writing to Bay Meynell on December 9, a month after surgery—the first letter she was able to write—she reported the doctors' views and added, "You know and I know that only time will tell . . ." She was, in fact, to be home for only about two months. They were months of slow, uneven recovery—hardly surprising at her age: several good days, then an episode of fibrillation, frightening and exhausting; good days again, flu for a week, and so on. They were months of renewed work on this volume—first rereading and making notes for revisions, then working forward. And they were months of fear: she was not gaining weight, there were continuing bladder spasms, and fluid swelling her ankles and legs—all explained by her doctors as part of the process of adjustment following surgery. Again and again she returned to the idea of a recurrence of the cancer.

But she was not thinking "cancer" when she was taken back to New York Hospital on February 9 after two days of sudden, agonizing abdominal pain. She was only afraid, terrified, of more surgery. She had developed an intestinal blockage, and for a week the doctors tried to let it resolve itself, feeding her intravenously and then trying slowly to introduce liquids by mouth. When it became clear that they would have to operate, my mother—who had been in tears, querulous, complaining about her nurses for most of the week—grew calm. She wanted only to get it over.

That was the night when she spoke about how the book might end "if it has to be." We agreed that this was premature, but her own inner sense was more accurate. Surgery repaired the intestinal blockage but revealed that it had been caused by the presence of inoperable cancer in the peritoneum, presumably a spread from the original site. Dr. Benjamin postponed giving her the diagnosis until she would be alert enough to take it in. But day by day there was more fever and more pain, controlled only by morphine. One of the last things she did— fitting enough for someone who had spent her whole life worrying about financial security—was to sign a bank document letting us write checks for the nurses on her account. She managed "Laura" in very nearly her normal bold hand; the rest of the signature was a shapeless streak. On February 28, after a day when her blood pressure hovered all day at thirty over zero, she died at ten o'clock at night.

The next day I had to go to my brother's to begin making the arrangements that follow a death. It was the first of March, a clear, cloudless, warm day—the kind of day when my mother would have loved to be on her bike. I found myself thinking of how much pleasure she had taken in her rides and in Central Park, how much she loved the world.

But she never was satisfied with the world as it was. I remembered now that a few years ago (it was in 1982) she had been asked for a short piece on the theme of "civil rights" for the twenty-fifth anniversary issue of Perspectives, a magazine published by the United States Commission on Civil Rights. She chose to write about what she would, and would not, have to change if she were writing *Gentleman's Agreement* in 1982.

> . . . I would not be writing about a young student worrying about whether he could get into a good medical school because he's Jewish; I would not be writing about a landlord or real estate broker asking a direct question like, "Are you of the Hebrew persuasion?" . . .
>
> No, I couldn't write those scenes now in 1982. But what if Phil [in *Gentleman's Agreement*] were black or Puerto Rican or Mexican-American and trying to rent or buy a house in certain neighborhoods? What about his getting into those good medical schools or renting an apartment or finding a job if he was known to be gay, and refusing to remain a closet gay?
>
> Alas, if I were writing that book this very minute, and merely changed the word Jew to black or Puerto Rican or gay or Mexican-American, I could leave most of its scenes intact, marked for the printer, *stet except for corrections.*
>
> And . . . what about the discrimination and prejudice—denied

and unacknowledged, of course, as most prejudice is—what about it if you're a woman? . . . It is hard for me to believe that there exist today men and women warped enough in their conception of justice to make them fight against having our constitution guarantee equal rights to women, not just voting rights, but equal rights in all areas of working and living.

But equal rights for everybody cannot be forever denied, even by the warped. They will eventually come for all people whose skin is different from the majority's, or whose sex life is different from the majority's, or whose political beliefs are different from the majority's.

Yes, I still hope. Despite all the recent setbacks we talk about so glumly—and so realistically—I still am a believer in decency and change. Like the ebb and flow of the tides, every setback seems to engender a new surge forward. But I confess I am impatient for that return tide of strength in the wide-sweeping ocean of civil rights.

It was good to remember that now. My mother and I frequently disagreed about politics—as she did with Alice, as she did with others. Over the years we argued many times, often violently and woundingly. But what mattered now, on this clear calm March day, was that all through her long life she had worked to make the world a better place, and that she never felt her work was finished. That was what gave her writing its meaning and purpose.

What I remember about my mother's last year isn't the illnesses and the decline, but her effort to go on: to return to normal health and vigor, and particularly to write, for writing was life to her—it was her greatest pleasure, and in some sense she only felt truly alive when she was writing. As I look over the logs, which have been so central to her telling of her life, entry after entry shows what those months were like:

August 31: 5½ m. on bike—first time since illness in Feb!!
November 5: Worked hard—end of chapter XV p. 432

This was two days before she went to the hospital for the operation on her bladder.

December 27: Dr. Bry Benjamin here—very reassuring.

(Dr. Benjamin was trying to quiet her fear of a recurrence of cancer. On separate memo sheets she made meticulous notes on the conversation: "No immediate dangers; made very fine strides. . . . Me: Couple of yrs? Bry: 'Why not?' . . . 'If by remote chance there *is* a local recurrence of tumor, it would be treated transurethrally.' ")

> **January 6:** Wrote a whole page! "my own mistakes." To Sterba's visit here.
> **January 28:** Shuttle exploded in mid-air— . . . *New* 1½ pp. —re TV, options, etc.—R. Aghayan.
> **January 30:** Chris 6 P.M.—dinner and concert! My first evening out since Nov. 5, '85!!!
> **February 6:** Running shoes "Inhibits pronation." ½ p.

They were Saucony running shoes, purchased on recommendation of an orthopedist in an effort to overcome her continuing walking problem. Three days before her last hospitalization, terrified of a return of cancer, my mother was struggling for life and health.

TAPE-RECORDED PASSAGE
FROM FILM OF
GENTLEMAN'S AGREEMENT

Dave: Hello.

Kathy: Oh Dave, hello. Thank you for coming; it was good of you. You know about Phil and me.

Dave: Yes.

Kathy: I want to ask you something and I want you to answer me honestly.

Dave: Go ahead.

Kathy: Do you think I'm anti-Semitic?

Dave: No, Kathy, I don't.

Kathy: Phil does.

Dave: Does he?

Kathy: You know I'm not anti-Semitic; you're a Jew and you know it. Why can I make it clear to everyone but Phil? Why, I was the one who suggested the series, did you know that?

Dave: No, I didn't.

Kathy: I hate this thing just as much as he does. Why can't he see it? Why, tonight at dinner a man told a vicious little story and I was ill. I was sick with rage and shame, but Phil actually made me . . .

Dave: What kind of story, Kathy?

Kathy: Oh, it was just a story. It had nothing to do . . .

Dave: Well, suppose you tell me.

Kathy: It was just a vulgar little joke a man told at dinner. It had nothing to do with . . .

Dave: Well, take it easy, Kathy, maybe it has. What kind of joke? I can take naughty words, you know.

Kathy: But *why?* Oh, all right. It was a man named Lockhardt Jones and he tried to get laughs with words like "kike" and "coon" and I despised him and everybody else at the table . . .

Dave: What did you do, Kathy, when he told the joke?

Kathy: What do you mean?

Dave: I mean, what did you say when he finished?

Kathy: I wanted to yell at him, I wanted to get up and leave. I wanted to say to every one at that table, "Why do we sit here and take it, when he's attacking everything we believe in? Why don't we call him on it?"

Dave: What did you do?

Kathy: I just sat there. I felt ashamed. We all just sat there.

Dave: Yeah. And then you left, and got me on the phone.

Kathy: Later, after dinner was over, I said I was ill. And I am, sick through.

Dave: I wonder if you'd feel so sick now, Kathy, if you had nailed him. There's a funny kind of elation about socking back. I learned that a long time ago. Phil's learned it.

Kathy: And I haven't?

Dave: Lots of things are pretty rough, Kathy. This is just a different kind of war.

Kathy: And anybody who crawls away is a quitter just as much . . .

Dave: I didn't say that; you did. Somebody told a story. Sure, a man at a dinner table told a story and the nice people didn't laugh. They even despised him for it, sure. And behind that joke is Flume Inn and Darien and Tommy and those kids . . .

Kathy: If you don't start with that joke, where do you start? Is that what you mean?

Dave: That's right.

Kathy: Where do you call a halt? I've been getting mad at Phil because he expected me to fight this, instead of getting mad at the people who help it along, like Lockhardt.

Dave: Not just old Lockhardt. At least he's out in the open, but what about the rest of the dinner guests? They're supposed to be on your side and they didn't help you.

Kathy: No, they didn't and I didn't and that's the trouble—we never do. . . . except Phil. Phil will fight. He can fight. He always will fight. And if I just sit by and feel sick, then I'm not a fit wife for him. It was always on those deeper issues that we had our quarrels. Always. And I never knew it until now.

Dave: Sure. A man wants his wife to be more than just a companion, Kathy. More than his beloved girl. More even than the mother of his children. He wants a sidekick, a buddy, to go through the rough spots with him. And she has to feel that the same things *are* the rough spots, or they're always out of line with each other. . . . You're not cast in bronze, sweetie; you're nice and soft and pliable, and you can do anything you have to do, or want to do, with yourself.

Kathy: Can I? But it's got to be more than talk—

INDEX

322